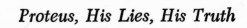

Proteus, His Lies, His Truth

ROBERT M. ADAMS

Proteus, His Lies, His Truth

discussions of
literary translation

W · W · NORTON & COMPANY · INC ·

NEW YORK

Copyright © 1973 by W. W. Norton & Company, Inc.

FIRST EDITION

Library of Congress Cataloging in Publication Data
Adams, Robert Martin, 1915–
 Proteus, his lies, his truth.

 Bibliography: p. 183
 1. Translating and interpreting. I. Title.
PN241.A32   418'.02   70-139372
ISBN 0-393-04353-3

1 2 3 4 5 6 7 8 9 0

Pray Mr. *Lintott* (said I) now you talk of Translators, what is your method of managing them? "Sir (reply'd he) those are the saddest pack of rogues in the world: In a hungry fit, they'll swear they understand all the languages in the universe: I have known one of them take down a *Greek* book upon my counter and cry, Ay this is *Hebrew*, I must read it from the latter end. By G-d I can never be sure in these fellows, for I neither understand *Greek*, *Latin*, *French*, nor *Italian* myself. But this is my way: I agree with them for ten shillings per sheet, with a proviso, that I will have their doings corrected by whom I please; so by one or other they are led at last to the true sense of an author; my judgement giving the negative to all my Translators." But how are you secure that these correctors may not impose upon you? "Why I get any civil gentleman, (especially any *Scotchman*) that comes into my shop, to read the original to me in *English;* by this I know whether my first Translator be deficient, and whether my Corrector merits his money or no."

Alexander Pope to the Earl of Burlington,
November, 1716

Contents

Preface

A book about translations is bound to be tentative and exploratory because nobody can know all the languages or can be aware of all the disparate concepts and values that are involved in getting even a single work of literature from one language to another. To try to discuss many works of art as they pass in different directions through and across language barriers is to invite mental distraction. Still, impossible subjects may be well worth discussing; and one way to do it is to talk about what one in fact knows, whether or not it's all there is to be known. However far it falls short of the genuinely "adequate," such a discussion may aspire to widen a few horizons and organize a few standing prejudices.

For we don't, any of us, decline to form opinions about translation simply because we haven't read all the translations. We think about those translations we're familiar with—generally about those which seem to us very bad; and we recall, not as translations, but as old, cherished originals, those versions that we became familiar with and admired long ago. Thus, though we don't have any opinions about translation in general, we know what we don't like, and are prepared to defend to the death what we do. An effort to rationalize so chaotic a subject, if only by a degree or two, can hardly be amiss.

Whatever falsehood a translator may be forced to put on his title page— Homer's *Iliad,* Flaubert's *Madame Bovary,* the Bible—what he gives is not the original, but a proposed equivalent. Here, at the onset of our topic, questions start to proliferate. What elements of the original does the translator seek to provide an equivalent for? What elements are available to him in the new language and the new cultural situation into which he is translating? What is his working definition of equivalence itself? As we become aware of the many possible answers to these questions, it's possible that we'll be able to formulate (each of us for himself) a partially systematic set of ideas on this highly unsystematic subject.

Perfunctory, superficial, and incoherent judgments about translation we all have—in the course of meditating this book, I have worked through a good many of them, though perhaps not enough. It's particularly hard to avoid making these casual judgments because we don't generally think of translation as a literary category—as the focus of our attention, as a process in itself. If for some reason we are interested in Aeschylus, we read Aeschylus (as we think) without worrying too much whose translation we are using. We are reading for Aeschylus, not for the consciousness of translation. In one potent sense, when we are aware of reading a translation, it is a clear sign that the translation has failed, in its task of making us feel the presence of the original. Thus the chief contribution of a book *about* translation may be to make its readers conscious of the many ways in which a translation can succeed or fail, alert to the many different levels of equivalence. That must be my excuse for proliferating examples in this book, perhaps at the expense of generalizations. It is a subject that has to be looked at by twisting and turning it from side to side. I have taken units of the subject as they seemed manageable, talking now about specific books as a way to get at principles, now about principles as an approach to specific books. The elusiveness of the topic lies entirely in that single equivocal concept, equivalence. It implies similarity in difference, difference in similarity: and of such paradoxes there is no quick end or easy resolution.

It isn't a particularly agreeable metaphor, but a reader sometimes has to confront a translator with very much the same distrustful attitude as an attractive heiress brings to an oily-tongued flatterer. It's inherent in the situation that the fellow is going to con you as much as he safely and profitably can. The whole point of the translational act is to evoke a response from the reader. Unless he's completely unscrupulous, the translator doesn't aim to do this at any price; but unless he's wholly indifferent to the fate of his original author, he is bound to bend, adjust, and modify through the spectrum of equivalencies, to make the original more accessible (and what does that include if not the notion of "more agreeable"?) to his reader. And the reader, for his part, can hardly fail to be gratified when he finds that Aeschylus and Apuleius, Isaiah and Ovid, can all be made to sound so "fresh" and "modern." I don't think he will necessarily be any happier when he sees that this sort of flattery has been performed, again and again, for people in wholly different situations. But he may well develop some practical skepticism about the faith that should be granted to translators, when he sees how many originals have served, so to speak, as noses of wax, to be twisted this way and that as fashion invites. Not that translators are therefore to be dismissed to outer darkness. Like our heiress with her flatterer, the reader can have all sorts of fun with translators, as long as he doesn't write any blank checks. And that kind of wariness (not to call it cynicism) may be one of the rewards of seeing, in the degree to which this is possible, the main sorts of duplicity and ingenuity which translators have brought to their calling.

Because it has grown under the hand, and can pretend to no inexorable logic, either of its own formulation or of its chosen subject, the book may profit from a preview in the shape of a brief outline. It consists of the following elements:

> Two chapters laying out in a general way the shape of the problems and arguing their immediacy;
> A chapter on the two gigantic, many-times-translated, central books of our culture, Homer and the Bible—books which challenge the full energy and intent of the translators;
> A chapter by way of contrast on allusive-translations, translations inserted parenthetically into the texture of a work otherwise original;
> A chapter on levels of diction in translation, with special reference to grandiloquence, obscenity, and the contemporary-colloquial;
> A chapter on imitations, which point up superficial difference in order to emphasize underlying similarity;
> A chapter on the special problems of rendering rough texture and high polish, with primary reference to Milton and Racine;
> A chapter on some original authors, particularly Joyce, who took special interest in the translation of their own works;
> Two concluding chapters, on the limits of the possible and a conceivable definition of the desirable in translation.

In order to facilitate checking on my citations while cutting down on apparatus, I have whenever feasible identified passages by their position in the work (*Le rouge et le noir,* Book II, Chap. 13) rather than by edition and page number: they can thus be located conveniently in whatever edition lies to hand. But this has not always been possible (*The Sound and the Fury* has only four long units), so the specific books that I have used are identified in a "List of Books" at the back of the volume, and sometimes referred to by page number. Unless otherwise specified, a reference to Dryden or Johnson in the text is to the book in the list. Thus any reader who's interested in doing so should be able to follow my footsteps through the library stacks without trouble; others won't be pestered with irrelevant erudition.

In the matter of citations and examples, I have tried to steer a civilized middle course, feeling that a person wholly without literary information really has no business to transact with a book of this nature, but that an author owes his reader a modest amount of guidance, if not explanation, when he strays from the fenced and beaten path of allusion. Where I've quoted non-English originals (or translations), I've tried to have English translations (or originals) of some sort nearby, even when the point of the comparison is to express disapproval of the version. Being semilanguaged myself in some five different tongues (Latin, French, Italian, German, and Spanish), I have written for my fellows in the community of the semi-languaged (that linguistic *Club des Sans-Club*), supposing that for an imaginative reader a well-formed argument may have its own suggestive interest, even though now and then it takes a detail for granted. And in fact, outside the imaginative, semilanguaged reader, I can think of nobody for whom a book about translation has any potential value at all. The monocular fellow who reads only English is like a man obliged to buy from a used-car dealer: the best thing you can tell him is that they're all cheats, but it's sometimes possible to use one to check on another. The polyglot who speaks all languages needn't lower himself to consider trans-lation one way or the other. It is we, the company of the semilanguaged, who can and must worry about the ungraspable problem—must grapple with Proteus on the shifting sands by the treacherous sea, and try to learn what we can from his inevitable lies, his distant, problematic, and (perhaps) lucky truth.

Los Angeles, 1972

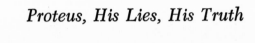

Proteus, His Lies, His Truth

CHAPTER I

Carte du Jour

About literary translation in the abstract there probably is not a great deal to say beyond the two trite observations that it is inevitable and inevitably inadequate. But both these observations call for some expansion and explanation; and both then bring us up against the complexity of specific for-instances; and to roam this broken terrain, flushing whatever game the copses conceal and pursuing it as far as the trail remains hot, is the present recreation.

Translation is inevitable, in the first place, because of the curse of Babel; even those with the gift of tongues cannot learn enough languages, and learn them thoroughly enough, to read in the original all the literary works that have impinged on our culture. And relatively few of us have the gift of tongues, to any impressive degree. Doubtless it is very desirable to read the Bible in Hebrew, Dante in Italian, Homer in Greek, and *The Tale of Genji* in Japanese; but one doesn't go far in compiling such a list without becoming absurd. Any man who knows more than four or five languages is pretty sure to know some of them badly, perhaps all—in effect, he will be a versatile, not very accurate, translator, converting some of his languages into others. Since the power of acquiring new languages fades with age, the languages most of us learn (in the intimate sense of "learning to speak and think in this tongue as a native") are largely a matter of accident, of influences quite beyond our control. The "dead" languages cannot really be experienced as living languages, regardless of the amount of energy we invest in them, and there are primitive languages, based on primitive thought patterns, which we could make our own only by putting off our entire stock of mental categories and processes. "Knowing a language" as we use the term in common speech is knowing how to read, write, and speak it; but

1

knowing it in a literary sense generally involves a good deal more. A man who can read an article in the daily paper and discuss it literately is not necessarily equipped to read Milton. Even taking the polyglot at his very best, speaking each of the five languages he knows "like a native," it is arguable that he brings to it from the other four overtones, implications, and awareness of possibilities that may enrich, but may also clog and impede, his acceptance of the present idiom.* But that is only an incidental difficulty; the main thing is that one cannot possibly know enough languages, and know them well enough, to be altogether independent of translation. If it is rare to have full command of several different languages, impossible to have full command of some, and if the culture increasingly presumes acquaintance with books written in many different tongues, the case for translation as an inevitable cultural activity seems made. And the annual U.N. bibliography of translations, as it lines up on a shelf, shows at a glance a fatter volume every year.

As a matter of fact, though we rarely focus on the notion, a distinction between translation and original creation is often rather hard to make, and much that we consider firsthand is really second. The *Chanson de Roland* exists in only a single manuscript, which is an Anglo-French translation of an unknown original; Chaucer's *Troilus and Criseyde* claims to be a translation of Lollius, and is actually in good part a translation of Boccaccio, with some Petrarch thrown in for good measure. Spenser thought nothing of translating into his *Faerie Queene* swatches of Tasso and Ariosto (who had not infrequently themselves translated from Vergil, Ovid, or Catullus, who had in turn adapted Homer, Hesiod, or Sappho); and one of the most admired speeches in Shakespeare's *Antony and Cleopatra* is a translation into blank verse of North's translation of Amyot's translation of Plutarch's "Life of Antony." The collected poetical works of Doctor Johnson and Ezra Pound—strange bedfellows—would be a good deal shorter and less interesting, were their free translations, or imitations, removed from the canon. The same thing could be said of Stefan Georg, Dante Gabriel Rossetti, Pierre Ronsard, and Thomas Wyatt as well—to draw four names, more or less at random, out of a hat containing thousands.

Translation is inevitable, therefore, on a second score—not only as a practical matter, because we can't know all the tongues, but historically: because translation has been a part of our literary culture from the beginning, and translations are woven into the warp and woof of our language and literature. The great exemplar in this, as in so many other matters involving translation, is the Bible. Over the centuries, it has become so much

---

* Anatole France, we are told, refused to learn any foreign living language (he excepted the classic tongues) lest his French style suffer from the contamination. At least, Hilaire Belloc declares, that was the excuse he gave for his ignorance: *On Translation* (Oxford, Clarendon, 1931), p. 14.

a part of the language and the culture that we scarcely feel it is a translation at all. When we speak of "the parable of the talents" or "a good Samaritan," only occasionally do we remember what a Roman talent was, or where Samaria was. A translation, like a metaphor, may be so successful that its original source is altogether buried under the acquired meaning; "Samaritan" now has practically no other meaning than the one it has acquired from the fable.* There is not one of us who does not live some part of his life in unconscious paraphrase from another culture.

Translation is an enormous but indistinct part of a large and continuing process of communication. We translate automatically in speaking our own language—into the idiom or dialect appropriate to the audience and circumstances at hand. Paul Valéry, in the preface to his translation of Vergil's eclogues, makes a point of the many different languages involved in what we call "everyday speech." We have a dialect for friends, for public occasions, for law courts, for love affairs, for all the occasions of life.** Even in ordinary speech, we accompany our spoken words with a set of other symbols—shakes of the head, nods, gestures, smiles, frowns, menaces —which supplement and modify our meaning, into which we translate our intent, and from which the understander instantly decodes them. Only the other day I was trying to park a car in a crowded and noisy square supervised by a harassed Italian official, who had filled it to overflowing. I caught his eye, lifted my chin, widened my eyes, and asked in effect, "Non c'è posto?" He in return shrugged his shoulders, threw out his hands, dropped his jaw, and answered in unmistakable idiom, "It beats me. I can't do anything more. It's your problem now." And throughout the course of this eloquent, wordless exchange (much like Panurge's scholastic debate with the speechless doctor), translation was busily at work. We usually mean by the word a transformation into one verbal idiom of a message which has taken distinct form in another; but that process may be absorbed in others, or replaced by them. When I am driving a car, and see a certain sort of

---

* The fact is that, apart from Saint Luke, the Samaritans have never had a very good press, being obnoxious to practically everyone as Jews, and to the Jews as Samaritans, i.e., heretics. They have not even had the good taste to get themselves exterminated and sentimentalized; there are apparently still a few hundred surviving Samaritans in Israel. Saint Luke, when he told the story of the Good Samaritan, may have been incorporating an additional moral, largely lost on readers today: even among the Samaritans, there's one good one.

** A suit at law and a suit at love offer an interesting contrast in dialects; John Donne, who had studied them both, exploited the joke to good effect in his Second Satire, where a man named Coscus is described as soliciting a girl in law-language:

> A motion, Lady; Speak, Coscus; I have been
> In love, ever since *tricesimo* of the Queen,
> Continual claims I have made, injunctions got
> To stay my rival's suit, that he should not
> Proceed; spare me; in Hilary term I went,
> You said, If I return'd next size in Lent
> I should be in remitter of your grace.

red light in a certain position, a kind of direct translation of signal to action takes place without any intervening words at all. We translate certain gestures as threats or endearments, and respond to them all the better because they have not taken articulate form. When I am in foreign countries, I translate usage and customs into their equivalents. Rubbing noses *here* is about equal to shaking hands *there;* a piercing whistle in an American stadium means "Yea, team!", the same sound in an Italian stadium or a Spanish bullring conveys intense disapproval; "Yours sincerely" in America is more or less equivalent to "Veuillez avoir la bonté, Monsieur, d'agréer l'expression de mes sentiments les plus respecteux." Both these latter expressions can be translated literally into the other tongue, but in that form they *mean* something entirely different. This carrying back and forth of cultural equivalents, this adjustment of what we "mean" to our expectations of what we will be understood as saying, is cultural translation as we perform it, instinctively and every day, within a single language as well as between languages. What under one set of circumstances would be a gross insult, to which the only reply was a blow, might under different circumstances be understood as a gesture of intimate friendship, an endearment. In some circles, "You bastard!" is such a versatile expression, which, depending on the tone and feeling surrounding it, can convey either admiration or loathing or affection or some other sentiment richly compounded of these elements, but like all of them very remote from dictionary definitions of the word. Ethnic groups sometimes make private jokes which involve using the prejudice terminology of an outside group in a favorable, inside sense, or at least with a favorable inside feeling. Holland won its freedom from Spain under the leadership of a group proudly calling themselves "Gueux"—"Beggars," a name given them in contempt by the Duchess of Parma. And translation may be called upon to help render the levels of meaning and feeling implicit in any one of these terminological layer cakes. We sometimes get a feeling of how little translation of mere words counts for when we watch dubbed movies, in which the words of one culture are accompanied by gestures and intonations appropriate to another—with effects that are often ludicrous.

When considering translators and their hardships, we naturally think first of all the disadvantages of the host language, all the rigidities and inadequacies which prevent the original from reflowering in its full beauty, as if the original language necessarily expressed the last nuance of the original writer's thought. But that isn't necessarily the case at all; no man's language fits his thoughts like a glove. We read of an enchanting African tongue called Kaka, which possesses two words for fruit, one meaning bananas and pineapples, the other meaning all other sorts of fruit, plus testicles, glands, hearts, kidneys, eyeballs, soccer balls, pills, and the seed of any fruit or plant. One can imagine a Kaka poet bursting with sentiments he was eager to express on the subject of oranges or cherries, but reluctantly dismissing these themes as involving extravagant circumlocution or else grotesque *double-entendres*—but who, when he was made free of the resources of another language, would become aware of all sorts of new things to say about his cherished topic, and all sorts of welcome ways to say them. Or, if this seems like too primitive an example, we may note that German students of Kant regularly find it useful to read the philosopher in English translation*—the exact contours of the master's thought being more successfully profiled when they can be studied through the distorting glasses of two distinct and mutually correcting idioms, than when seen through either one by itself. Be it noted here that the problem doesn't arise exclusively when German is inadequate to express the Kantian concept, but also in special cases like the following: the language may express a concept completely, but with a limitation that may or may not be understood; or through a word containing a buried metaphor the force of which may or may not be felt; or through an idiom which may or may not color the concept outside the particular context of its use. And under all these circumstances a translation may make one aware of ways in which a language, like even the best fitting of shoes, leaves a man's thought a little extra room here, and squeezes, pushes, compresses it out of its "natural" shape there.

We should be particularly aware of the power of our native tongue to impose on our thoughts because of the common experience of everyday speech. How often do we frame our thoughts into the associative connections of the word we have just used, exploring its moribund or buried metaphors perhaps in direct cross-purposes to the thread of our overt discourse. If we were speaking some other language, even one we knew less well than our own, we would be likely to define our intent more purely, or at any rate more narrowly. Translating artistic discourse into a language where the particular cross-purposes indigenous to it (whether fruitful or distracting) have no play, or a different sort of play, may well result in an inferior literary artifact; but the very differences of the translation may help us see what the original is, and how much of its shape (concave as well as convex) is owing to the graining of its original tongue.

Doubtless, to preserve a little precision in the terminology, it is desirable to limit the word "translation" to conversion of literary texts from one language to another. Even so, there remains a variety of translation, within a single language, for which we shall have no proper term. Chaucer's language is partially inaccessible to the modern reader, so that to read it one needs either copious marginal notes (which are themselves partial

---

* Both these instances are from Reuben Brower's useful anthology of essays *On Translation* (Cambridge, Harvard, 1959)—the first from Eugene Nida's essay, the second from John Hollander's.

translations) or a wholly new version; and what is true of Chaucer is even
more true of "Sir Gawain and the Green Knight." Shall we call this re-
furbishing of a dialect which time has rendered obsolete "re-Englishing"
or "Englishing anew"? Old French is sometimes unfamiliar enough to need
"re-Frenching" or "Frenching anew," and so with German—so that if our
vocabulary is not to get out of hand altogether, we might stretch the word
"translation" a bit to include intra- as well as inter-lingual translations.

The reader has doubtless noticed an itchy tendency on the part of the
word "translation" to expand, or even explode, into an equivalent of the
word "communication." It is a tendency to be resisted, and as a rule I shall
resist it; but to indulge it, just for a moment, may reward us with an extra
sense of the fragility and intricacy of the process which concerns us. The
word "translation" itself lends some color to our impulse, since "carrying
across" or "carrying over" is in fact what a good deal of communication
amounts to. And ordinary language, in its everyday use, acts very frequently as a code into which one translates various feelings or ideas, so
that they may be decoded by the recipient or hearer. Crossing a gap, send-
ing a message across a distance, is the essential process;* if we so define
it, we may be somewhat calmer in the face of the fact that no reader (except, perhaps, by accident) ever gets out of a translation, or a communication of any sort, exactly what the original speaker put in. "Traduttore,
traditore," says the trite and timeless Italian proverb, "A translator is a
traitor." It is true. But it is true of any man who opens his mouth, or puts
pencil to paper, with the implication (tacit or overt) that he is going to "say
what he means." He isn't going to, because he can't. Language is a system
of common counters only crudely and provisionally defined by those who
use them; the fact that they are "common" in one sense (the possession of
all) works against their being "common" in the other sense (of equivalent
significance).** All we can say is that they have an accepted value and im-
port, a certain lowest-common-denominator meaning, in the marketplace.

Perhaps some day we shall have, as Mallarmé thought, a purely literary
language. But that day is not yet, and words must be rattled about in the
bag of common usage, picking up nicks and marks and grease and dirt,
losing one metaphorical extremity and growing another, undergoing universal accident. Even though used with the greatest conceivable sublety

---

* A pleasant illustration of primitive symbol-language, in which all the connectives are to be
provided by the recipient of the message, occurs in Stevenson's *Kidnapped,* where Alan Breck
sends an intricate message to his illiterate cousin by means of a silver button and a few plant
sprigs tied up in a little cross.
** A reader of Ben Jonson's "Discoveries" is struck by his use of "translation" as a synonym
for "metaphor"; it is philologically exact, "transfer" and "translate" stemming from the identical Latin root. But it also suggests the practical reality that metaphorical language requires a
double translation, into and then out of the metaphor, with inevitable loss and perhaps the
adventitious gain of a little static at each stage of transition.

and precision, they can be only imperfectly controlled, because each hearer or reader not only may but must bring to the basic word a different set of connotations. Indeed, much "modernist" writing expects him to construct, precisely from these overtones and connotations, the structural pattern of "the work as he sees it." Thus the creation of the work of literary art is the first half, and its interpretation is the second half, of a process which in its entirety may be described as an act of translation which is both inevitably necessary and inevitably imperfect. Its ordained images are a cast of the dice and a shipwreck.

Probably it is not very important that when the word "tree" is used, a Norwegian thinks automatically of a pine, while a Polynesian thinks of a palm; but it is a more serious problem when the word is set before an Eskimo who has never laid eyes on a tree of any sort.* Translation then is faced with a double leap, to explain the word and then to explain the experience—by giving, one supposes, the tree-experience itself, either through the original vegetable or through whatever rough equivalents one can develop, and then synthesizing thousands, perhaps millions, of these remarkable, enormous, various creatures into the general concept "tree." An instance like this makes us aware that in all writing, and particularly in translation, one has to know what a man is talking about *before* one can understand what he's saying. The visitor to Venice is offered by an enthusiastic waiter one of the great regional specialties—"coda di rospo," translated on the menu "tail of sea-toad"; quite naturally, he rejects it in horror. If, on the other hand, a reassuring friend tells him it's "something like halibut," he may also reject it, this time as too ordinary and dull. Why should he come to Venice just to eat halibut? This comedy-in-a-menu confirms that one has to have in advance most of the information words "convey" (but which in reality their appearance evokes from one's memory or imagination) before he can have any understanding of the specific statement being made. The rule holds in everyday conversation, as in international diplomacy—we must be in basic agreement and understanding before we can even attempt the discussions which are supposed to lead to agreement and understanding.

---

* Translators of the Bible into Eskimo tell us with understandable pleasure that, in casting about for an equivalent to "Lamb of God," they find a very successful rendering in the phrase "Seal of God." It is a triumph, no doubt about it. But how then does one translate "The Lord is my shepherd"?

Some years ago, while trying to teach Freshman English to a class containing a Nigerian student, I ran unexpectedly into an equivalent problem. The student's English was excellent, and he wrote beautiful descriptions of his native village, set deep amid rubber plantations at the edge of a tropical jungle, where the hum of the mosquito was heard day and night. I tried to tell him that the mosquito struck a discordant note here: everything else in the scene was idyllic, the mosquito might cause his reader some misgivings. He looked at me with liquid eyes, showed all his filed teeth, and said softly, "But we *like* the mosquito, it kept the white man away so long." Our mosquito-experiences had been so different that the same word or concept carried diametrically different connotations for us, which couldn't be translated without major circumlocution.

Translation, then, is simply a special instance of the general, but terribly fragile, power of language to cross gaps, to communicate. It leads across a somewhat wider and more precisely defined gap than everyday speech tries to cross, but attempts to connect one mind with another in much the same way.* And since everyday speech—where we have the inestimable advantages of intonation, gesture, and often of clearly defined context as well—is so slovenly a process, can it be doubted that translation from one idiom to another, from one cultural context to another, will be even more precarious? It is, it must be; and yet the comparison with everyday speech (with its implication that "if *this* is hard to understand, what troubles must be experienced with more elaborate prose?") is partly misleading. Imprecise or multiple equivalence is the great problem of all translation. When the original language is doing several different things at once, the translator is likely to have difficulty in imitating all of them. But when the original language is doing only one main thing (conveying information, for example), the complexity of that single project is not likely to present insuperable difficulties. Technical vocabulary, for example, grows up in a language or can be imported into it, fairly readily; if a technical term is lacking, one can compound an elaborate concept by joining simple ones. The only objective of a technical translation is clarity, as measured by a simple manipulative standard (can one repeat the process being described and get the same results?), and whatever devices lead to that end are justified. Thus technical translations are, or can be, perfectly correct in terms of their chosen objectives; one can assemble the chair or prepare the soup just as well, whether one reads the instructions in Spanish, German, or Greek. (This isn't always saying a great deal; do-it-yourself instructions seem to have built-in confusions, beyond the power of any language to surmount: that, however, is a tune from another opera.)

But everyday conversational speech, like literature though in a different mode, is often enough concerned with several different things at once. It expresses a fact and an attitude toward the fact, as well as a set of relations to antecedent or subsequent facts; with an inflection or an abrupt, wordless transition (means of the utmost economy), it implies contexts of extravagant complexity. And what conversation does with its characteristic methods of allusion, irony, innuendo, gesture, inflection, and tonal variation, literature also does with its equivalent devices. It is multivalent speech, just like common conversation—the full complexity of which we don't

---

* More than most problems, perhaps, those involving communication can be represented as either wholly insoluble or perfectly simple, depending on the attitude with which one approaches them. A sentence like "The cat is on the mat" bristles with semantic difficulties, if one wants to become aware of them; on the other hand, it's an everyday matter to communicate complex notions about completely hypothetical constructs ("genes," for example) without any particular difficulties of verbal transfer.

often appreciate, because it's so common; besides which, literature is involved in more or less formal arrangements, using such patterns as rhyme, rhythm, stanza, high and low styles, comic and tragic modes, structures of imaginative reality, and so forth and so on. It is the multiplication of these various objects of imitation, and the restrictions imposed upon the translator's freedom to build up a single knotted complexity out of multiplicity of particulars (one word with twelve important overtones just isn't the equivalent of twelve words) that thin prematurely the translator's sparse gray hackle.

Take for instance the title of Stendhal's great novel, *La chartreuse de Parme;* it is traditionally translated in English as *The Charterhouse of Parma.* There are only latent problems with Parma; it is the same city in either language. But "chartreuse" carries all sorts of rich overtones in French which not only don't carry over into English, but are directly antipathetic to the English "charterhouse." What, after all, *is* a charterhouse? A boy's school, primarily, redolent of Lamb and DeQuincey, with perhaps a few medieval recollections of a charitable institution operating under a charter, perhaps for royal pensioners or decayed military men. Remotely, and only at third hand, it refers back to the Carthusian order, by a semantic mistake primarily.* Whereas in French, and especially for Stendhal who was born in nearby Grenoble, the word immediately implies La Grande Chartreuse, an immense austere monastery high in the French Alps, where one would find Carthusian monks, vowed to asceticism, penitence, and eternal silence. At some indefinite distance behind the word stands a still more sinister concept—Latin "carcer," prison, which survives in modern Italian as "carceri," prisons. Setting aside these dark overtones, we find the grand Chartreuse is famous also for the production of two richly aromatic and fragrant liqueurs, one green, the other yellow. Parma stands in a plain, not amid mountains, but is also famous for the production of an aromatic fragrance, the perfume known as "violette de Parme," which may, not inconceivably, have a relation to the violet stockings worn by our hero Fabrizio (or Fabrice—are we more authentic in calling him by the name he would have had in Italy where he is supposed to live, or by the French form of the name which Stendhal actually used in writing the novel?)—in his quasi-ecclesiastical capacity. There are of course Carthusian monasteries in Italy, and *La certosa di Parma* is a natural form of the title in Italian, but there is (and was) no operative Certosa near Parma,** and the word

---

* "Charterhouse" is evidently an English back-formation from a mispronounced French original; it's the same principle on which the Colorado river which French explorers baptised "Purgatoire" was transformed to American "Picketwire."

** My colleague Herbert Morris, in an interesting monograph on Stendhal's title (*The Masked Citadel,* Berkeley and Los Angeles, U. of California, 1968), describes an actual Certosa di Parma, about a mile southeast of Parma, i.e., just about where Stendhal locates the citadel, but a considerable distance from the place where he locates (ambiguously enough, in all con-does not bear in Italian anything like the special resonance of "Chartreuse" in French. In fact, "Chartreuse" has a special meaning outside French; Matthew Arnold's mournful poem is not about "The Great Charterhouse," under which title nobody in the world would recognize a reference to the monastery at Grenoble, but about the "Grande Chartreuse." Therefore locating the Chartreuse at Parma (as the French title does) includes just a bit of a shock—an exaggeration of this effect in English would be something like "The Great Basilica at Tuscaloosa." In any case, the English translation must forego this effect, since a charterhouse (whatever it may be) is just as likely to be found at Parma as anywhere else. The color chartreuse (which combines the two colors of the liqueur, green and yellow) may have some special significance through contrast with Stendhal's previous novel, *Le rouge et le noir;* instead of colors which flatly oppose one another, the later novel is drawn in colors which can, and do, combine. It is to be a novel, as it were, of rapprochement. And indeed, we find that our hero is not, like Julien Sorel, at war to the knife with society; that he lives both in the world and against it. But a charterhouse has no color associations of any sort.

Now it's no great problem to write a paragraph explaining, more or less after this fashion, the implications of "Chartreuse de Parme," but to find three or four English words which will, in combination, produce something like this effect, is the literary translator's overwhelming dilemma—and all the choices open to him are in various ways and for various reasons impossible. The choice is simply between different ways of murdering the original; and there is evidently a good deal to be said, in the present instance, for the classic compromise—a translation as bald and literal as possible, giving the basic sense of the words, standing on a veritable mountain of circumstantial footnotes. Such a proceeding has in its favor the circumstance that it helps one to approach the text more or less in a proper order. Not even a thoroughly prepared French reader, looking at the title of Stendhal's novel, gets all its implications in a single charge; if one thinks of reading a book as a progress not only horizontally from beginning to end, but vertically from the surface to the subtler implications of the text, it seems arguable that one might want to withhold some of one's overflowing insights into the title till such later passages in the novel as might be expected to reinforce them. The observation reminds us that a proper literary translation does not simply convey to us the elements of the original, in such fullness as may be, but conveys them to us in something of the same order and structure of relatedness as the original. One

science) the Chartreuse. But the Certosa di Parma had not been active as a monastery since 1778—so that the odds are at least 5 to 1 that a perceptive reader of Beyle's first edition would have sensed the title as an incongruity, rather than as a "natural" property or an enigma capable of solution.

might as well have puzzles which begin with the answer or jokes which begin with the punch line, as translations—or for that matter editions—which diffuse explanations long before the problems to which they represent triumphant solutions have made themselves felt. For a translator this may become a problem, when he is obliged to translate awkwardly a passage on page 23 in order to sustain a parallel or set up a special effect that will become apparent only on page 156. (Lest the example seem extreme, let us note that Joyce used the deliberately incorrect word "crosstrees" in the third unit of *Ulysses* in order to set up a second use of the word, in a wholly different context, in the ninth.) In short, there is often an artistic question whether a translation or edition is being prepared for a first reader or a rereader—and, the translator being generally the latter, it is an extra act of the imagination for him to put himself in the position of the former.

The art of original composition is the art of choosing the exactly right word, and includes the option of changing what one is "saying" if the exact right word ("right" means not only right in itself, but in all its overtones and interconnections with adjacent words) cannot be found to express it. The art of the translator is the art of choosing among a set of possible compromises; it does not allow that important option. (Some literary works are harder to read than they were to write; all literary works are harder to translate than they were to compose.) We may summarize the situation in

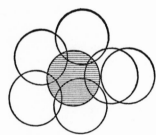

a diagram, the dark circle representing the original meaning of a word of text, along with its connotations, the various intersecting, incongruent (and sometimes incongruous) circles representing possible "equivalents" in the language into which the original is being rendered. (With a grateful bow to Professor Nabokov—from whose contribution to Professor Brower's anthology we coöpt it—let us henceforth simplify this distinction into the rubric "From-language," "To-language.") Each possible "equivalent" word intersects some part of the original, but includes a considerable range of meaning which is not in the original at all. We have only to look at various versions of a much-translated work to see how translators, selecting among the various tonalities that they find implicit in the original, find different equivalents for the same passage. Pope's decorous and dignified *Iliad* emphasizes values wholly different from Rouse's humorous and rowdy one—for example, Hera's answer to Zeus's mockery at the opening of Book IV:

"O you dreadful creature, what a thing to say! How can you wish me to waste Shall then, O Tyrant of th'Aethereal Reign!

all my trouble for nothing! How I
sweated and sweated! All my drudgery
thrown away, the horses tired out with
collecting people to destroy Priam and
his sons! Go on, do as you like, but let
me tell you, we do not all agree!"

> *The Iliad,* tr. W. H. D. Rouse
> (Mentor Books).

My Schemes, my Labours, and my
  Hopes be vain?
Have I, for this, shook Ilion with
  Alarms,
Assembled Nations, set two Worlds in
  Arms?
To spread the War, I flew from Shore
  to Shore;
Th'Immortal Coursers scarce the La-
  bour bore.
At length, ripe Vengeance o'er their
  Heads impends,
But Jove himself the faithless race de-
  fends:
Loth as thou art to punish lawless
  Lust,
Not all the Gods are partial and unjust.

IV, 35–44

Indeed the very question of what one does and doesn't translate is involved
in the matter of giving one's translation a particular tone. The names of
Greek heroes, and the epithets applied to them, often contain buried puns:
Eurynome as Milton noted (*Paradise Lost,* X, 581), means "wide-encroach-
ing," Prometheus means "foresighted," Epimetheus "after-sighted," and so
forth. When one translates these names out of their familiar forms in such
a way as to emphasize their components, is one gaining greater authenticity?
Or is it as odd an exercise as if one were to call Napoleon Mr. Goodbody
(Buonaparte), and a well known Midwestern town Monks, Iowa? Even
common English names retain meanings which we don't, in everyday usage,
raise to consciousness. If one were translating an English novel into Italian,
under what circumstances would one feel obligated to rebaptize Mr. Porter
as Signor Facchino? If for some special symbolic purpose one was obligated
to play this trick on Mr. Porter (the stories and novels of Henry James, for
example, swarm with names like Christopher Newman, Isabel Archer, Madame Merle, Hyacinth Robinson, John Marcher, and so forth, which carry
overt meanings sometimes calling for translation), how could one keep
Signor Facchino from standing out in a society of Smiths and Joneses as
wholly alien to their culture?

   The line between an actual verbal equivalent and a cross-cultural perver-
sity is a delicate and difficult one to draw; perhaps no more precise recom-
mendation for handling it can be drawn up than to use extreme tact.
Suppose we are doing a novel out of French into English. Paris cannot be
London or New York, it must be Paris; our hero must be Pierre, not Peter;
he must drink an aperitif, not a cocktail; smoke Gauloises, not Kents; and
walk down the rue du Bac, not Back Street. On the other hand, when he is
introduced to a lady, he'll sound silly if he says, "I am enchanted, Madame,

to make your acquaintance." So it's a matter of coloring, of flavoring; one •
translates into equivalents when a word-translation would be ungainly or •
misleading; one translates literally when the available equivalents would •
be intrusive or off key; when one can't get the best of one's alternatives, •
one settles for the least of one's evils. A story in an Italian newspaper the
other day carried the account of a shoot-out between Chicago policemen
and activists of the Black Panther movement; according to the story,
violence began when some police cars drew up in front of the "palazzo" in
which the Panthers had their headquarters. The newspapermen know well
enough, no doubt, that there aren't very many "palaces" in Chicago, and
that Black Panthers aren't likely to have their headquarters in reproduc-
tions of Versailles or El Escorial. There is indeed a colloquial use of
"palazzo" to mean "tenement" or "slum dwelling"; but there is also a
general, and not at all sarcastic use of the word, according to which any
multiple dwelling is a "palazzo"—it is a historical phenomenon, going back
to the fact that a lot of big buildings in Italy, originally intended for just one
grand family, have been subdivided into flats, offices, and stores. So Italian
really doesn't have any word which will convey, much better than "palazzo,"
the idea of a large multipurpose building, such as might serve (among other
things) to house the headquarters of the Black Panthers. Still, there is an
incongruity about "palaces" on the South Side of Chicago which nothing
will remove.

When we translate from classical languages, do we translate for the togas
or for the human relationships? Togas are, for us, an exotic dress; for the
Roman of Cicero's day, they were something like a business suit. But if
we dress our stage Romans in business suits, they aren't Roman any more;
if we dress them in togas, the manipulation of those exotic garments will take
up so much of their attention that they will scarcely be able to act like
human beings. Between these awful alternatives, there is a temptation
sometimes to opt for an eclectic, never-never style made up for the occasion.
I recall a rather cheerful *As You Like It* in which the characters wore more
or less Ruritanian uniforms flavored with Arcadia, and Touchstone had the
distinct flavor of a gay cocktail lounge. More hideous and tasteless instances
than this doubtless lurk among the repressed memories of every theater-
goer. These productions of barbecued Shakespeare, Ibsen, Sophocles, or
Congreve are getting more and more frequent nowadays; they range from
serious efforts to bring out a value which the original actually contained,
and which needs only a little emphasis in the production, to ruthless
travesties, designed primarily to show off the perverse ingenuity of the
"adapter." There are no hard-and-fast rules for judging what liberties can
be taken with a classic—which is not by any means to suggest that disasters
of pretentious bad taste are hard to distinguish from resourceful and imaginative adaptations.

The ailments and dilemmas of translators are long and elaborate enough to make a veritable Job's-chronicle of complaints. A familiar, even obvious, difficulty arises when the From-language contains grammatical distinctions of which the To-language is innocent. A classic instance is French "tu." When lovers across the Channel modulate from "vous" to "tu," they have made a notable advance in intimacy, which it would be altogether ridiculous to render in English by having them change to "thee" and "thou." At a climactic moment in Stendhal's *Le rouge and le noir* (Book II, chap. 19), Julien Sorel, after weeks of solitary suffering, has finally climbed back into Mathilde de la Mole's good graces, and so undertakes once more the perilous ascent, via a ladder, to her midnight bedroom. She receives him with ecstatic, unbounded delight, crying, "C'est donc toi!" And just here C. K. Scott-Moncrieff—for whose extraordinary gifts as a translator I have, as a general rule, only the highest respect—slips on the insidious banana peel, and translates, "So it is thou!" What girl of high social rank and free social manners ever greeted a lover that way? In North Country working-class speech (as rendered, for example, by D. H. Lawrence), an indeterminate "tha" still seems to survive as part of a dialect used only between intimates, and Edwin Muir tells us that in his youth it was common among the Orkney Islanders; but everywhere else, English appears to have lost the distinction entirely. "Thee" and "thou" belong, for most people, to obsolete or ecclesiastical language; intimacy is the feeling these terms preeminently *don't* express. So here again the translator must search for roundabouts and alternatives—endearments of another character, which though they cannot possibly imply the *commitment* implicit in the decision to *tutoyer*, may nonetheless convey some sense of intimacy and tenderness.* And it's still more difficult to imagine what one does with languages which are even more complexly inflected than those of contemporary Europe—with those Indonesian dialects, for instance, which are said to have six or eight different forms for every verbal inflection, to express six or eight different possible social relationships between speaker and hearer. No doubt what one language does with declensions and enclitics, the other must do with adverbs; but one can't repeat the adverbs with that automatic persistence which one can achieve with accepted and established verbal forms. In a word, if one concentrates attention on the insoluble problems of translation, it is not hard to convince oneself that the whole job is madness.

---

* Conversely, the single English form sometimes involves a translator in a set of explanations which are wholly unnecessary. When Alexey Karenin sits down to write a letter to his faithless wife, we are told he faces a complex problem of tone which he solves with a deftly modulated middle course: "He wrote without using any form of address to her, in French, making use of the plural "you" which has not the same note of coldness as the corresponding Russian form" (*Anna Karenin,* tr. Rosemary Edmonds, Book III. Chap. 14). But what comes out in English, ungainly as it is, could not be simpler and more inevitable as far as the second-person pronoun is concerned: "At our last conversation, I notified you of my intention to communicate to you my decision in regard to the subject of that conversation." The coldness here lies elsewhere than in the pronouns, and there is nothing in the English usage which would give either the husband or his lady a minute's uneasiness.

Yet the problems have a way of looking less tragic in practice; the impossible has been attempted again and again, and not just by poor devils desperate for a sordid sixpence, but by artists, and simply for the fun of it. Why should Spenser, after bringing Sir Guyon a long and painful pilgrimage into the Bower of Bliss, imagine an undescribed figure there, and have him or it carol a song translated direct from Tasso? Why should Chaucer, when he wanted Troilus to express his love for Criseyde in song, have fallen back on a sonnet of Petrarch's, which he duly translated? It seems idle to think that such poets as these could not have composed original poems for the occasion, had they been so minded; it seems apparent also that, whatever difficulties they faced in the translation process, the results are in no way inferior to the surrounding "original" material—quite the contrary, if anything.

Poets find a fascination in the art of translation, and recognize no bar to attempting a poem again in the fact that it may have been translated many times before. Sir Ronald Storrs and his friends, who made a hobby of this particular versicle, collected no fewer than 451 versions of Horace's little ode to Pyrrha (I, v), of which 181 were in English; since his book was published, in 1959, there have been many more. Milton tried his hand, early on, with Horace's stylish redhead (or she may have been a blonde); he is traditionally a hard man to follow, but his performance hasn't intimidated professors, journalists, civil servants, and at least one prime minister from having a go on their own. Quite apart from the pleasures of competing with one's betters, too, there is the excuse for retranslation, that translations age as rapidly as originals. Chapman's is a fine poem, but we should be disastrously handicapped if we relied on it exclusively for an understanding of Homer. Poor old Ibsen has survived many years in those extraordinary Archer versions, and is only now starting to come out from behind the Victorian woodwork, and to reveal himself for what he really was all along. Perhaps because they fall with the years into that fabulous kingdom known as "the public domain," old translations tend to attain, like Struldbrugs, immortality of years without immortal youth. They are reprinted, generation after generation, and acquire a kind of immunity to criticism, partly because the original is known to be great, and partly because translations all too often aren't expected to have any particular style or idiom, other than "translatorese." Stilted and artificial translations thus pass down the years, relatively unchallenged—until a new translator comes along, with a bit of insight and freshness, to cut through the guff.

For many years the figure of Father Ocean was something of a problem for translators of *Prometheus Bound*. Father Ocean enters relatively late in the play; he is "father" to the sea nymphs who constitute the chorus, and he represents one of the elemental forces in whose presence the clash of divine dynasties is to be enacted. On the other hand, he arrives aboard a four-footed bird which is not very easy to visualize onstage; and what he has to contribute to the drama is pretty rigmarole stuff, a Polonius-like set of unctuous common places masking a senile cowardice not much more attractive than the brash opportunism of Hermes. Let Mr. T. A. Buckley represent the old school of translators, and Miss Edith Hamilton the new:

I am arrived at the end of a long journey, having passed over [it] to thee, Prometheus, guiding this winged steed of mine, swift of pinion, by my will, without a bit; and, rest assured, I sorrow with thy misfortunes. For both the tie of kindred thus constrains me, and, relationship apart, there is no one on whom I would bestow a larger share [of my regard] than to [sic] thyself.

tr. T. A. Buckley (1893)

Well, here at last, an end to a long journey.
I've made my way to you, Prometheus.
This bird of mine is swift of wing
but I can guide him by my will,
without a bridle.
Now you must know, I'm grieved at your misfortunes,
Of course I must be, I'm your kinsman.
And that apart, there's no one I think more of.

tr. Edith Hamilton,
in *Three Greek Plays* (1937)

Miss Hamilton was, I think, the first translator to see that Father Ocean had to be translated with a sense of his grotesque humor. He does no harm to the dignity of Aeschylus' play if seen in this fashion; and it's probably a fair rule that almost anything in a translation is better than a false front, a pompous façade. At least that is the modern taste, and that taste evidently helped Miss Hamilton to do Father Ocean, with his wise twaddle and his four-footed bird, in another way. And so it seems likely each age will be impelled by its own developing standards of taste and distaste, as well as its own scholarship, to make adjustments here and there in its picture of what are, for all ages alike, the classics.

. We change the classics as we live with them, adapting them to our needs
• and defining our needs precisely by what we see reflected in them. Transla-
• tion, because it cannot be accurate in all ways at once, offers us space to
• work changes and adjustments in our relations with these permanent yet
• always relevant books. We need our twentieth-century versions of the *Iliad* and *The Divine Comedy* even if, and perhaps just because, our own original literature is alien to the very ideal of an *Iliad* or a *Divine Comedy*. More or less as criticism keeps interpreting and reinterpreting the classics of our own tongue—not just to understand them more fully in themselves, but to bring them into a living dialectic with our inescapable contemporary values and existence—so successive translations mediate between the parochialisms of past and present. There is no reason to think that inevitable progress or even a norm of progress results from the interactions; a glance at recent versions of the Bible is enough to dispel the illusion that just because they are more accessible than King James, they must have other literary merits as well. Still, language does grow obsolete, as do certain styles of feeling

and ways of expressing things, and if the sacred books are to be more than sacred fetishes and formulas, there may be value in having them retranslated from time to time.

Of course translation has a history, like any other art, however humble—a history and an interest quite independent of the literary merit of the translations actually produced at any particular moment. What sort of standards men worked to, what sort of values they prized in translation, what conceptions they had of cultures and values far removed from them by time or space—these are matters to agitate and delight the historian of translation in all its many forms. Moralized Ovid turns out, against all expectation, to be remarkably useful as a guide to the conduct of monks in a monastery or nuns in a nunnery; and Homer, under the ministration of the exegetes, is sometimes elaborately translated into the language of experimental chemistry. Shakespeare's Romans wear trunk hose and listen to the tolling of clocks; the great Talma created riots in the public streets by enacting a Roman play while wearing a Roman sandal instead of a red velvet "cothurne." Because translations consist so largely of proposed equivalents, they tell us, in striking detail, how men saw themselves by showing us how they saw, or refused to see, others. The Reverend Bowdler's versions of Shakespeare tell us far more about the nineteenth century than about the sixteenth; it's not beyond thought that the Brecht-Weil musical of *The Beggar's Opera* and Signor Fellini's movie translation of Petronius' *Satyricon* will someday have an equivalent "period" interest.

Until the last paragraph of this discussion, it was quietly assumed that fidelity is an automatic virtue of translations; and no doubt under many, perhaps most, circumstances, it is. On occasion, it is the only virtue; there are no others. But fidelity may be more of a virtue than a translator dare aspire to, and infidelity, conscious or otherwise, may have a value beyond the symptomatic. The faithful translator doubtless deserves all the rewards he is bound to get; but infidelity is so widespread and often so deliberate that doubtless it has its rewards too. At least, it might well be investigated on the assumption that there may be something which motivates it beyond original sin. And in fact, it takes no great ingenuity to discover many different varieties of deliberately unfaithful translations, as well as many different motives for the infidelity. A translator may feel he best serves his author, or his reader, by abridging the original text; inspired by emulation, or mere generous enthusiasm for a good idea, he may go beyond it. It is the point of Sancho Panza's repetition of rural adages that he throws into the pot any piece of proverbial wisdom that comes to hand—can one suppose that early translators like Shelton and Motteux offended very deeply against the shade of Cervantes when they added a few chestnuts from their own local store? Sir Thomas Urquhart was put on this earth to translate Rabelais; could he have had the zesty, exuberant, vociferous spirit to appreciate his author without exercising it in attempts, now and then, to go beyond him? If the existence of loose translations in any way precluded the production of accurate ones, there might be more reason to complain of them. But the very ideal of painful accuracy in translation is of recent growth.* The Middle Ages, with their casual concern over "original composition," often allowed their literary compositions to grow, like their cathedrals, out of materials contributed by undistinguished hands. When he plundered Petrarch (or was it Boccaccio?) for the story of faithful Griselda, Chaucer had no notion at all of remaining "faithful" to his original. Nor did Dryden (to skip a few hundred years), when he translated Chaucer, hesitate to diverge from the trodden path in order to cast a few poisoned darts at his local enemies. George Chapman thought much of the value of an epic poem resided in its *sententiae,* its illustrated maxims for the conduct of human life—where he found embryo maxims in Homer, he developed them; where he found no maxims at all, he sometimes created them. We may hold up our hands in holy horror at these transgressions; yet it's hard to escape the sense that we too bring characteristic values to the works of the past and express them (no doubt more subtly) in our choices among the various options that the text places before us.

The eighteenth century was particularly fond of systematic mistranslation, which it quickly came to call "imitation"—that is, the reproduction of an original text with contemporary overtones in such a way as to amplify the overtones without altogether abandoning the text. Dr. Johnson's *The Vanity of Human Wishes* is replete with allusions to seventeenth and eighteenth-century events and personalities, but a reader familiar with Juvenal's Tenth Satire will continually get the sense of a historical diphthong being sounded, a reverberation of cognate chords which creates a special timeless perspective by joining Hannibal with Charles VIII in a single focus as recurrent, transitory examples of the same unchanging phenomenon. Pope deals in much the same way with Horace, though there is a subtle point at which the application of the classical parallel turns from a universalizing to a collusive device: we, who are members of the private club, are asked to understand the special point which is being made via learned allusion— Clods Kindly Keep Out. From imitation with respect it is but a step to imitation with derision, and not a very long step at that. Between translator and original there always lies that admirable free space, that open possi-

---

* Andrew Marvell, a puritan on this as well as on other scores, was an early and severe spokesman for accuracy and restraint:

> He is Translation's thief that addeth more,
> As much as he that taketh from the Store
> Of the first author. Here he maketh blots
> That mends; and added beauties are but spots.
>   "To his Worthy Friend Doctor Witty"

bility for fresh growth to take root. A travesty may be a tribute, as some tributes have turned (alas!) to travesty. What Scarron did to Vergil makes us appreciate all the more how skillful Vergil must have been not to Scarronize himself—and sometimes how close he came to doing just that. The great poem is improved by the test of a loving, malicious parody; the abominable poem finds in the same process its passport to eternity. Who would remember Southey's awful poem on George the Third if it weren't for Byron's *Vision of Judgment,* or those inane little letters of Philostratus if it weren't for Ben Jonson's generosity in plagiarizing them into an immortal lyric? Finally, while imitation and travesty keep the "original" in constant view, they are to be distinguished from a more evanescent sort of imitation, where only the first hint comes from outside, but the whole later development is independent. We see this formula often enough in the other arts, where, for example, Van Gogh painted a great many pictures "after Millet," which resemble Millet only peripherally, and where Picasso, taking off from Delacroix, plays extreme variations on the thematic components of his "original" picture. It is hard to think that Beethoven didn't get a special sort of Diabellic pleasure out of overwhelming the naïve little theme he was given with all those thunderous, intricate variations. And so in literature—though doubtless here we move beyond the bounds of anything that's legitimately called "translation." The standard stories, of Don Juan, Antony and Cleopatra, Odysseus, Helen of Troy, Tristan, and Oedipus challenge adaptation to a new age, a new set of values; when we cannot take them seriously any more, it is a relief to take them out of the mothballed cupboards of our minds, and set them to dancing jigs—translating them, in this manner, from one context to another.

Through all these various instances of translation, we may trace the idea of equivalence in the different forms of which it is capable. There is, at one extreme, a sort of parodic parallel which maintains just the least shred of trivial equivalence in one minimal respect, so that it may violate equivalence the more outrageously in all other respects. There is, at an opposite extreme, the technique of exact literal translation, which renders the meaning of the original word for word, without respect for the violence done to the idiom of the new tongue—which is, so to speak, *abjectly* faithful. Between these two rapes—one of the From-language, the other of the To-language—all sorts of more agreeable and equable arrangements are possible. They can very well be conceived of as bargains, in which one sort of equivalence is accomplished at the expense of others. The gains and losses that are possible in these different transactions may not be either dismissed or summarized in a sentence; they are our subject.

CHAPTER II

Sample Perspectives

Looking at translations and originals with a critical eye makes us immediately aware of differences, and then of the differences between differences;
and there's the crucial point. We have to discriminate between a translation
that creates, deliberately or otherwise, wholly different effects than its original; and a translation that makes use of different means toward a similar
"ultimate" effect. That involves distinguishing means from ends in a way
that, within the frame of a literary work, is certainly not automatic or easy,
and may not necessarily be possible. We can sometimes discriminate a peripheral, parodic likeness from a central parallel, a passing from a permanent bond, a detour which avoids a washout and shortly puts us back on
the main highway from a cross-country ramble without point or terminus.
Still, at best, it's not a simple problem when we get out of the metaphors
into the actual work of literary analysis.

The primary business of translators is of course to bury, far from the
reader's consciousness, the whole difficult range of problems that students
of translation are actively at work exhuming. Whenever a translation is
thoroughly successful, like Mrs. Lowe-Porter's *Magic Mountain* or Mr.
Scott-Moncrieff's *Remembrance of Things Past* (and by "successful" in this
context I don't mean "beyond criticism" or "unimprovable" but simply that
the version has held the field, critically as well as practically, for a period
of time), one doesn't see around it any more, it is accepted as a global
presence in itself. Where the translator couldn't do the same thing as his
original author, he cleverly did something equivalent, something of the same
order, so that one feels no unexplained gap, nothing strained or strange. The
translation thus builds itself into our confidence, as every proper literary

work aspires to do, establishes itself in our minds as the way in which certain thoughts and feelings must inevitably be patterned.* Every translator raises before the reader, in lieu of the original work, a façade; the more substantial and coherent it seems, the better it entertains our inquisitive eye, the more secure we feel in its presence, and the less we are inclined to look behind it. Our security cannot possibly be justified, as it is when we rest in the bosom of an original, not only because translators may be less than good, but because it is the natural function of a translator to exercise the prestidigitator's art, to distract us with a bit of flimflam business over *here,* to prevent our noticing a crucial little substitution of handkerchief for rabbit *there.* Even when they do not set out, with malice aforethought, to pull wool over our eyes, the fact that they are trying to work in one not necessarily-pliable medium effects already achieved in another, often imposes on them a necessity for verbal legerdemain. And sometimes, when they would seem to be absolutely trustworthy—without need to alter the original, without motive to do so, without visible advantage to be gained, without the possibility of careless error—they cross us up, with a most perfidious duplicity.

An absolutely ideal circumstance for accurate, precise translation is provided by Samuel Beckett's plays. They are in prose of the utmost simplicity —stripped, stark, incisive. The sentences are short, the syntax primitive, the metaphors few, idioms sparse, local color nonexistent. The author, who is wholly bilingual, translates his own scripts; as he presumably knows his own intent better than anyone else, he must render it about as well as anyone can. And yet a play like *Endgame–Fin de partie,* as it adapts itself to two very different idioms, assumes quite different colorings and characteristics. Some of the differences are so considerable that it's apparent Beckett was not trying to get an exact or even an approximate equivalent.

In its concluding sections, *Fin de partie* has some extra business, a bit of extra dialogue, that *Endgame* simply omits. For instance, Clov sings for Hamm's benefit a small, sour song:

---

* With regard to Scott-Moncrieff's rendering of Proust's very title, *A la recherche du temps perdu,* we note how shrewdly he has taken advantage of the connotations and overtones of Shakespeare's Sonnet 30:

> When to the sessions of sweet silent thought
> I summon up rememberance of things past.

Even though he has not tried to translate the first half of Proust's title (*A la recherche*), recollections of "summoning" and "sessions" still linger to provide an equivalent for it. And the echo from Shakespeare, of whom (needless to say) Proust never thought, provides a grave, deep sense of reflective antiquity. So that it is as if Scott-Moncrieff's literary sense had calculated that the reminiscence of Shakespeare would just serve to provide a kind of depth and motion that would atone for the absence of any equivalent at all for *A la recherche.* Our difference here, between original and translation, is thus felt to be at work in the service of similarity.

Joli oiseau, quitte ta cage
Vole vers ma bien-aimée,
Niche-toi dans son corsage,
Dis-lui combien je suis emmerdé.

There is no such song in *Endgame;* Clov hums a bit, but raising his voice in song, even sardonic song, seems too light-hearted a gesture for his despair. The French original devotes a good deal of dialogue to the description of a personage that Clov thinks he has seen. In the English version all we learn is that he looks like a small boy, that Clov's instinct is to exterminate him (lest life, through the agency of this potential procreator, have to drag through still another weary, anguished cycle), but that Hamm withholds decisive action. In the French, Clov is rather more ambiguous: "On dirait un môme" ("You'd think it was a brat"), there is no answer to the question about the creature's sex, and Clov adds a detail of his behavior: "Il a l'air assis par terre, adossé à quelque chose"—upon which Hamm comments, "La pierre levée."These look like small details but they could be important. Always in the background of this play, which seems to deny us social, ma- terial realities as a way of becoming transparent to metaphysical meanings, there is a possibility of religious myth. Hamm's words, present in the French but dropped from the English, suggest at once the angel of the Lord who "descended from Heaven, and came and rolled back the stone from the door and sat upon it" (Matthew xxviii, 2). As a youthful figure of dubious sex, the person seen by Clov could well be a heavenly messenger, an angel; and "la pierre levée" has no conceivable meaning except in terms of the story of the Resurrection. Yet Beckett left it out of the English version en- tirely. One doesn't have to take the innuendo as Gospel truth to see that its presence could alter strongly the play's delicate, indecisive balance. On the other hand, the English version makes several references (profane, to be sure, but no less potent for that) to Christ and the Christian scene; the French version seems carefully to avoid them. "Putain! Elle est sous l'eau!" became in English, "Christ, she's under water!" and "What for Christ's sake does it matter?" derived from "Qu'est-ce que ça peut foutre?" There is little difference in time between the two versions; it is not a matter of a youthful French play being transformed toward a later and differently con- ceived English one. Quite possibly Beckett varied his texts to adjust to the peculiarities of the two cultures. He may well have thought that an English- speaking audience would be all too eager to find a Christ figure in the play or to impute a religious dimension to the action; thus, suggesting the angel sitting on the stone would be too heavy-handed. Precisely for that reason, the equivalent blasphemy for French "putain" and "foutre" (literal transla- tions of which, at least in 1958, would have been off key in *Endgame*) might well have been considered the simple expletive, "Christ!" I do not put forward this explanation with unlimited confidence, or for that matter with any confidence at all. The only man who can pull the rabbit out of this particular hat is M. Beckett, and he's too smart. "Maybe-this-and-maybe-that" answers to literary problems aren't really answers at all, just flexings of the original India-rubber problems. Either our author had two meanings, or one meaning with a number of ways to get at it, or. . . . The possibilities are too many, we cannot be sure of any of them. And if we uncover interpretive problems of this complexity when we compare two versions of the same play by a single author, what sorts of confusion will we find when the translator stands at a distance from the author, when he is a wholly different mind, with special preoccupations and problems of his own, as well as (perhaps) a different set of cultural categories, values, and equivalents?

The answer to that question is, of course, sublimely simple: we get major variations, from howlers through pallid correctness to sublime but intrusive ingenuities. We get gross mistranslation, where an idiom or an allusion is altogether lost on the translator; we get something which looks very much the same, but is absolutely different—the inspired mistranslation, where a statement is deliberately altered from misleading literal correctness to something which produces an exactly corresponding impression. We find translations which obliterate completely one whole dimension of a book's existence, translations which add felicities quite beyond the capacity of the original author. Once we peep behind the façade of translation, we become aware of a spectrum of literary happenings; and, by good fortune, they are not always as frustrating as those involving Samuel Beckett. Crude errors and major improvements often explain themselves; the puzzles sometimes have answers. And there is one major consideration going for us: what a translator is doing with his text, whether for good or for evil, generally becomes clearer as we look at more of it. One felicity, one disaster, one imperception or insight seems to comment on and help explain another. Without more ado, then, let us go behind the façade to see what happens to a novel well known in English when it is converted to French.

William Faulkner's *The Sound and the Fury* was translated into French (out of the "américain") by Maurice E. Coindreau as long ago as 1937, and in this form the book has provided a cornerstone for Faulkner's very considerable French reputation.* It isn't on the whole a bad translation, and appears here as representative rather than as a horrible example. Yet, every so often, where Faulkner's syntax gets loose and his allusions casual, one finds an idiom slipping past M. Coindreau unrecognized and unren-

---

* *The Sound and the Fury* (N.Y., Modern Library, 1946), hereafter M.L.; *Le bruit et la fureur* (Paris, Gallimard, Livre de Poche, 1949), hereafter *Le bruit.*

dered. For instance, in the course of Quentin's monologue, he has occasion to reflect on the social attitudes of Gerald Bland's mother, and says: "She approved of Gerald's associating with me because I at least revealed a blundering sense of noblesse oblige by getting myself born below Mason and Dixon, and a few others whose geography met the requirements . . ." (M.L., p. 110). The problem with Faulkner's syntax has to do with "a few others"—is it controlled by "below" or "with"? ("Below Mason and Dixon and a few others," or alternatively, "associating with me and a few others"?) Naturally, it helps a lot to know who or what Mason and Dixon actually are. M. Coindreau translates. "Elle ne voyait pas d'inconvénient à ce que Gerald me fréquentât parce que moi, au moins, je faisais preuve d'une espèce de sens de noblesse oblige, étant né au sud de Mason, Dixon, et autres villes dont la géographie remplissait les conditions . . ." (Le bruit, p. 136). Apart from not recognizing what the Mason-and-Dixon line is in American history, M. Coindreau was misled here by a peculiarity of French idiom, which isn't happy without concrete nouns. Faulkner often slurs, blurs, or omits nouns to indicate an act of mental censorship. Sometimes French cannot do in this respect what English can; sometimes M. Coindreau just does not try to follow the Faulknerian distortion. "We have sold Benjy's" (M.L., p. 113) is an entire sentence as it forms in Quentin's mind; he is thinking of Benjy's meadow, which was sold to become a golf course, and which represented such an important part of the dwindling Compson patrimony. French simply cannot follow this abruptness; "Nous avons vendu le pré de Benjy," (Le bruit, p. 140), is M. Coindreau's rendering. He has the meaning right, of course, but the tone, the jagged cutoff, the guilty suppression, has changed completely. Again, and with less reason, the translation alters a sentence uttered by Mrs. Compson in the course of her whimperings over Quentin's suicide and his father's death: " 'It's so terrible to me,' she says, 'having the two of them like this, in less than two years' " (M.L., p. 215). The euphemism "like this" is the essence of the woman's character; whenever there's a hard fact to be faced, she manages to duck or conceal it. So that having the sentence read in the French translation, "les voir disparaître ainsi tous les deux" (Le bruit, p. 275) is doing real violence to Faulkner's latent representation of her cold, selfish, and cowardly mind, even as it fills out and renders more explicit the surface of his statement. "Disparaître" is not even as marked a euphemism in French as "pass away" is in English; "like this" is a major nuance in the original, which drops out of the French, for all that the tongue would perfectly well accommodate it as "ainsi."

But the larger and more pervasive problem with M. Coindreau's translation is the matter of dialect. Faulkner's novel represents a particular challenge to translation because, though deeply committed to its own basic

idiom, it imposes on the Mississippi brand of "American" four sharply contrasting articulations. Benjy's section, being semi-incoherent most of the
time, is curiously less colloquial than Jason's (Benjy simply isn't up to slang
or sarcasm or indirection). Quentin's is more deeply fragmented and remotely allusive than Dilsey's—a good deal of which is in standard, third-
person-observer diction. Thus the novel imposes on the translator an obligation to diversify as well as to unify, to discriminate speech patterns as
well as to convey the familiar Faulknerian atmosphere of Southern Gothic.
The first thing to say about M. Coindreau's solutions is that they're partial;
before solving any problems he has radically diminished them. Thus, he declares that he has had to forego any effort at rendering Southern dialect,
particularly Negro dialect. The statement is exaggerated, but it's a fact
that the French version leaves out a good deal of the book's characteristic
flavor, while the new idiom forces it into a good deal more syntactical precision than the English requires. A good sample of these proceedings is
the passage in which Faulkner describes a lazy, snide little squabble between
Jason Compson and old man Job, his fellow employee in Earl's hardware
store; Job has just returned from an extended, unexplained absence:

> "Well," I says, "Was it a good show?"
> "I ain't been yit," he says. "But I kin be arrested in dat tent tonight,
> dough."
> "Like hell you haven't," I says. "You've been away from here since three
> o'clock. Mr Earl was just back here looking for you."
> "I been tendin to my business," he says. "Mr Earl knows whar I been."
> "You may can fool him," I says. "I won't tell on you."
> "Den he's de onliest man here I'd try to fool," he says. "Whut I want to
> waste my time foolin a man whut I dont keer whether I sees him Sat'day
> night er not? I wont try to fool you," he says. "You too smart fer me. Yes,
> suh," he says, looking busy as hell, putting five or six little packages into
> the wagon, "You's too smart fer me. Aint a man in dis town kin keep up
> wid you fer smartness. You fools a man whut so smart he can't even keep
> up wid hisself," he says. . . .
>
> (M. L., p. 266)

—Alors, dis-je, la représentation était belle?
—J'y ai point été, dit-il. Mais, dame, ce soir, on pourrait bien m'arrêter
  sous cette tente.
—Avec ça que tu n'y as pas été! dis-je. Trois heures sonnaient quand tu es
  parti. Mr. Earl te cherchait par ici il n'y a qu'un instant.
—J'ai été à mes affaires, dit-il. Mr. Earl sait où que j'ai été.
—Tu peux essayer de le tromper, dis-je. Je ne te dénoncerai pas.
—Ben, il est ben l'seul ici que j'essaierais de tromper, dit-il. Pourquoi que
  je perdrais mon temps à essayer de tromper un homme si ça m'fait rien

de le voir ou non le samedi soir. Vous, j'essaierai pas de vous tromper.
Vous êtes trop malin pou' moi, bien sûr, dit-il en affectant de travailler
comme quatre pour charger quatre ou cinq petits paquets sur la charrette.
Vous êtes trop malin pou' moi. Y en a pas un dans la ville qui pourrait
vous battre pour ce qui est d'être malin. Vous roulez un homme qu'est
si malin qu'il ne peut même pas se suiv' lui-même, dit-il. . . .

(*Le bruit*, p. 344)

The big difference here is in tone. "La représentation était belle?" is much
more formal and literary than "Was it a good show?" Simply to put it as
"Joli spectacle?" might get some of the concision and brutal innuendo of
Jason's question. Again, Jason twice uses mild profanity ("like hell" and
"busy as hell") for which French certainly has plenty of equivalents; they
are dropped out of the translation, and so is the back-country locution,
"You may can fool him." That phrase doesn't mean "You can try to fool
him"; it means, "You might be able to fool him." And "malin" is also a
shade inexact as a translation of "smart," because it gives away Job's animus too soon and too overtly; Jason is not *malin*/malicious, he is smart/
clever (Italian, *furbo*), so much so that he outwits himself. As for the
dialect, M. Coindreau tried to make Uncle Job Southern and Negro by
making him talk *méridionale* and talk it sloppily. "Ben" for "bien," "pou' "
for "pour," and an occasional bit of slurred grammar represent the garbled
speech of Uncle Job, and it is only a gesture in the direction of the dialect.
A proper French equivalent could very well be Creole or Cajun. It might
strain the translator's resources a bit—and yet, why not?

For if Job, Dilsey, and their like spoke low Creole or Cajun, there might
then be room to give the educated or semi-educated Southerner a flavoring
of dialect—as M. Coindreau has generally failed to do. A case in point is
provided by a locution that Faulkner uses very frequently to give his characters a flavor of country—"I reckon." Jason Compson is particularly fond
of this phrase, which he generally uses under stress of sardonic or satiric
feeling; "I reckon" often carries the connotation, "this is just the kind of
thing that *would* happen." M. Coindreau's French renders the locution
variously as "j'imagine" (255), "je pense" (123), "je crois" (284), "je
suppose" (286), and "probablement" (256). The point is not that it's wrong
to translate a single English phrase in five different ways (it could perfectly
well have five different connotations), but that "I reckon" has a different
and quite distinctive flavor that sets it apart from all these renderings. If
there were no French alternative, one might make do with an uncouth ad-
verbial; but in fact there is a whole spectrum of rural idioms, ranging from
"peut-être que" to " 't-être ben que," or "ça se peut que" or "des fois que."
At all events, there is an earthy, country quality to the locution, without
which the French translation is notably impoverished. One last nuance con-

nected with this matter of dialect: Quentin, riding a tram through Cambridge, Mass., sits down (and is very conscious of doing what he would never do down South) beside a Negro. After a while the Negro rises to get off the tram, and brushes past Quentin, saying "Pardon me"; and the comedy of the scene lies precisely in a Southerner's expectation of uncouth dialect and rural manners, which is frustrated by the Northern Negro's perfectly "correct" speech. Yet precisely here the French version, so sparing of dialect, attempts it: "Pa'don."

Other problems come up in connection with the metaphorical exuberance and subtlety of Southern speech on the tongue of a spiteful, inventive man like Jason Compson; talking of his Uncle Maury's fondness for the liquor cabinet, he says, "We'd all been a damn sight better off if he'd sold that sideboard and bought himself a one-armed strait jacket with part of the money" (M. L., p. 215). The translation has it: "il aurait bougrement mieux valu pour tous qu'il vendit le buffet, et employât une partie de l'argent à s'acheter une camisole de force" (Le bruit, p. 276). The power of the English joke lies in the concision with which it jostles together incongruous ideas. A one-armed strait jacket is a glorious idiocy just suited to Uncle Maury's weakness, which is limited to his drinking hand. German might render the phrase acceptably ("ein-armige Zwangsjacke") but French has to draw it out into something like "une camisole de force à un bras," or "pour la main droite," and most of the joke evaporates under the strain of expressing the idea. "I'm not running a bucket-shop" the telegraph operator tells Jason (M. L. p. 235); "J'dirige pas un office clandestin," (Le bruit, p. 302) is M. Coindreau's almost dictionary version, and it raises too many questions about a "clandestin" operation which is clearly the social center of a small town. Or, finally, Jason recalls the occasion when his mother caught Candace kissing a boy and so went round the house mourning for her lost daughter in a black dress and veil: ". . . only in three years she'd been wearing haircloth or probably sandpaper at that rate" (M. L. p. 247). It's the metaphorical excess that's funny here; the mourning, escalated in proportion to the occasion, becomes ludicrous. "Du train dont elle y allait," translates M. Coindreau, "c'est le grand deuil qu'elle aurait dû porter trois ans plus tard crêpe et le reste" (Le bruit, p. 318). The translation irons out those levels of exaggeration which are the humor of the original; from a black dress and veil to "le grand deuil" it's no great step; "haire ou papier sablé probablement" lie ready to hand, and would give the passage that snide, grotesque, funny quality that is characteristic of Jason.

Finally, as one might expect when a translation's prevailing quality is meagerness, M. Coindreau often disappoints us when there is something just a bit below the surface of Faulkner's prose that might be an addition or an alternative to the rendering. For example, Quentin Compson, as he rides in a streetcar by the Charles River in Massachusetts, remembers the experience of going to sleep in Mississippi, and associates it with a particular phrase:

> The draft in the door smelled of water, a damp steady breath. Sometimes I could put myself to sleep saying that over and over until the honeysuckle got all mixed up in it the whole thing came to symbolise night and unrest. . . . (M. L., p. 188)

"Damp steady breath" does not seem, in itself, like a particularly meaningful or memorable phrase; why should Quentin choose those particular words to repeat over and over? M. Coindreau doesn't question them, he translates dictionary-meaning for dictionary-meaning: "un souffle humide, continu" (*Le bruit,* p. 238). An unsuspicious French reader couldn't possible guess from the translation what the point of the passage is in English. The potent word, lurking behind the movement of Quentin's mind, rhyming and alliterating, and teasing consciousness just under the surface of his monologue, is simply "death." Death is his obsession as a character, death is what makes the smell of water fascinating to him, death (so Faulkner tells us in the foreword that he prefixed to the novel for *The Portable Faulkner*) is his only infatuation, far deeper than his infatuation for Caddy or Caddy's virgin state. Even if a translator had to neglect the surface meaning of Faulkner's words, it would seem that he ought to reach after the subsurface meaning that controls their use. But with adjectives like "moite" and "forte" one needn't even forego the semblance of Faulkner's duplicity.

There's reason to conclude, therefore, that M. Coindreau's low-voltage version transmits to its readers a good deal less than the full energy of Faulkner's novel. It was not selected, by any means, as a horrible example, indeed there's a good deal to be said in its favor. The problems of the original were formidable, and the translator obviously brought to his task genuine care and respect. Yet, perhaps for that very reason, his translation tends to level, to soften, to iron out the asperities and tangles of Faulkner's text. What Freud called "dream-work," which is the energy devoted by the mind to softening and transforming the raw materials of psychic trauma into endurable dream-equivalents, has its counterpart in "translation-work." In the case of *Le bruit et la fureur,* this translation-work takes its simplest, most ordinary, and most depressing form—it is prevailingly inertia, friction, and occasionally static. But to define translation-work only in terms of negatives, passives, and deficiencies is far too limiting; we will get a much broader idea of the spectrum of possibilities by inspecting a single novel in several different versions created by several different hands. When we read *Madame Bovary* in English translation, for instance, a great deal of what we get depends on the particular version we happen to have picked up. Flaubert's is one of the most frequently translated novels in the world— and an incidental pleasure of comparing the translations is the way in which each claims to correct the errors of its predecessors, and each is promptly dismissed by its successors as the continuer if not the perpetrator of ancient error. For the sake of brief allusion, we can line up half a dozen of the many versions of Flaubert's novel, in numerical and chronological order, referring to them thereafter by number.

1. Eleanor Marx-Aveling (1886)	4. G. Hopkins (1949)
2. W. Blaydes (1902)	5. F. Steegmuller (1957)
3. J. L. May (1940)	6. P. deMan (1965), based on (1)

The chief scene to be considered is the ball at Vaubyessard (Section I, Part 8).

As she enters the chateau where the dance is to be held, Mme. Bovary is greeted by the marquise, an aristocratic lady of middle years, who wears in her auburn hair a beguiling bit of drapery which the translators describe in a variety of different ways. Version 5 calls it a simple bit of lace, version 4 makes it a simple lace shawl, version 3 gives us a plain lace fichu, version 2 a simple fichu of guipure lace, while versions 1 and 6 content themselves with a simple guipure fichu. What is the article of clothing which these various versions are trying to put before us? Flaubert's original calls it "un simple fichu de guipure"; from which we can at least decipher, however little French we know, that "fichu" is a noun and "guipure" probably the substance of which the "fichu" is made. But in the version offered by 1 and 6, "a simple guipure fichu" we don't even know that— "guipure" could perfectly well be the main noun, and "fichu" a participle modifying it—a pinned-up or fastened guipure: it gives rise to dizzying prospects. But even when they make some effort to get Flaubert out of French and into English, our translators vary considerably in the sartorial effects they produce. A lady who walks around with a simple bit of lace draped over her head (5) may be wearing anything between a mantilla and a handkerchief; but one who wears a shawl (4) is not far from resembling grandmother in her babushka. What the lady is really wearing is something close to a coif; and the lace of which it is made, rather than "guipure," would be much better understood by an English reader if it were called simply "needlepoint," or "point lace."

Costumes produce difficulties. When the translators are faced with the problem of describing the dress Emma will wear to the ball, 1 and 6 describe it simply as a "barège" dress, leaving the English reader to decide for himself whether "barège" is a color, a style, or a material. Version 5 gives us a little more information by calling it a gauzy "barège" gown (but we still

don't know if "barège" is color, style, or material), version 2 calls it a
gown of "barège," while version 4 describes it as a filmy dress, and 3 char-
acterizes it as a delicate muslin frock. (One imagines something that a Kate
Greenaway child might wear.) The main point is that the material of the dress
is thin; but three of the six versions do not even tell us that. Another source
of difficulty is the straps that worry Charles because they might interfere
with his dancing:

> Charles's trousers were too tight around the waist. "These straps will get
> in my way when I dance," he said.

So runs translation 4—with the clear implication that it's the bellyband of
Charles's pants that will get in his way. (We are likely to wonder: Is he
strapped in? What kind of cumbersome contraption does he have around
his middle?) Versions 1, 2, and 6 all suggest the same thing; but 3 and 5
distinguish sharply, and illuminate the passage thereby. It is the shoe-straps
(5) or foot-straps (3) that will interfere with his dancing. What is in question is a little strap passing under the instep, serving to keep the trousers
sleek, but also rendering bowing precarious—Charles is perhaps worried
about split seams. Nowadays, the only "strap" a man is likely to wear is
a belt around his waist, so the modern translation had better be decisive
on this point. The French text is explicit: "sous-pieds."

In a number of different passages, translation 5 by Mr. Steegmuller stands
quite alone against the other five; as Mr. Steegmuller was a shrewd and
considering man, his idiosyncrasies are likely to be a result of principles,
not accident. And indeed they illustrate a specially interesting conception of
translation-work, with its own list of successes and failures. At one point
Flaubert is introducing Emma (and through Emma's eyes, his reader) to
the group of aristocratic young "bloods" who stand out in the crowded
ballroom by virtue of their special complexions and manners. "Quelques
hommes (une quinzaine)" is Flaubert's offhand, introductory phrase for
them. All the other translators duly render the number as "fifteen"; but
Mr. Steegmuller gives it as "a dozen or so." He does this, not because he
doesn't know that *quinze* is "fifteen," but because we don't, in English,
make a rough estimate of "about eleven" or "about fifteen." Anything in
that neighborhood is "about a dozen," especially for a somewhat flustered
young lady sweeping a crowded room with her eye. To translate "quinzaine"
by the word "fifteen" would give Emma's observation, and the French
expression itself, more precision than they should have. As between
"douzaine" (twelve) and "quinzaine" (about fifteen), Flaubert chose the
vaguer figure; if English has no such vague alternative to "a dozen," we
can blur the edges of that figure with a modifier, and get what a hasty impression on a hazy mind would naturally amount to.

Another success of this nature lies in the rendering of a conversation which Emma overhears at the ball, but does not fully understand. This conversation, as Mr. Steegmuller renders the passage, "was coming from a circle that had formed around a very young man who only the week before had 'beaten Miss Arabella and Romulus' and seemed to have won two thousand louis d'or by jumping a certain ditch in England." In this passage, the interior quotation marks are Mr. Steegmuller's own addition, the "seemed to have won" construction is without warrant in the original (Flaubert says simply "avait gagné"), and there is nothing in the original to correspond with the adjective "certain" as applied to "ditch." But the tone which all this vigorous translation-work produces is exactly right. Each of the alterations emphasizes Emma's process of hearing strange words without understanding them. "Miss Arabella and Romulus"—she does not know if they are people or boats or horses or what they are. When one treats them typographically correctly, as they would appear in a studbook (*Miss Arabella* and *Romulus*), one emphasizes an exact understanding of what the names are and what they represent; but that is just what poor Emma does *not* have. She hears the two strangely assorted names as a unit; she does not know what a steeplechase is, and winning all that money for jumping a special ditch in England (obviously quite unlike any other ditch, but she can't imagine how) is what bemuses her mind. At the cost of perhaps out-Flauberting Flaubert, that is Mr. Steegmuller's achievement, his special definition of translation-work, his chosen equivalence.

Is out-Flauberting Flaubert a legitimate undertaking? Perhaps the most we can say is that it carries its own perils. After her whirl with the viscount, Emma watches him waltz with a more experienced and perhaps better-conditioned partner, and she thinks (in the various versions):

(1,6) That woman knew how to waltz!
(2) She knew how to waltz, that woman!
(3) Ah, she could waltz, she could!
(4) She certainly knew how to waltz!
(5) This time he had a partner worthy of him!

Mr. Steegmuller (5) has translated here for the overtone and not for the sense or meaning. Under Emma's admiration for the other woman there lies inevitably an invidious comparison with herself; it is strongly felt in Flaubert's "Elle savait valser, celle-là!" But it is veiled and indirect; for Emma, under these circumstances, it's a vanity-thing, not a sex-thing. Her focus is not on the viscount, but on the dream of being herself the best waltzer at the ball (and so of having her pick among viscounts). So here it would seem that the conventional translation is better, even though the bolder one has its truth.

Hard-and-fast rules in translation tend not to be very useful; there are times, as we have seen, when deliberate infidelity is the best form of truth, and other times when we must simply suspend judgment between alternative translations—each is possible, each has advantages, there is literally no knowing which Flaubert would prefer. In the course of the ball, Emma overhears a pale young lady discussing Italy with a knowing gentleman; among other things, they discuss a place which Flaubert calls "Cassines," and which the translators render variously as Cassini (3), Cassines (1), the Cascine (4,5), or the Cascines (6). What's involved is no doubt the Cascine Gardens in Florence, but Flaubert might have wanted to represent the blurred sound picked up by Emma's untrained ear; so that the original error would be nearer to truth than the knowing translator's correction of it. This isn't to defend absolute fluffs, like that of translation 4 when it takes Charles in his student days, singing "couplets aux bienvenues" (i.e., songs at student gatherings) and makes him chant "snatches of song with which he entertained the women who were always welcome visitors there." That flagrant error is to be avoided goes without saying. But translations may be literally accurate without being good or even true, and may deliberately depart from a plain statement of numerical fact without being bad, or even inaccurate. After the miserable couple have returned to the routine of Tostes from the excitement of the ball, Flaubert specifies in a single dry, technical little paragraph a symptom of Emma's deteriorating moral and physical condition:

> Le printemps reparut. Elle eut des étouffements aux premières chaleurs, quand les poiriers fleurirent.

The translations blossom into full bouquet of medical symptoms:

> Spring came round. With the first warm weather, when the pear-trees began to blossom, she suffered from dyspnea (1).

> Spring returned. At the first summer heats, when the pear-trees were in blossom, she had moments of half suffocation (2).

> The springtime came again. With the first touch of heat, when the pear-trees were in blossom, she began to have attacks of breathlessness (3).

> Spring returned. With the first of the hot weather, when the blossom showed upon the pear trees, she had spasms of breathlessness (4).

> Spring came again. She found it hard to breathe, the first warm days, when the pear trees were bursting into bloom (5).

> Spring came round. With the first warm weather, when the pear-trees began to blossom, she had fainting-spells (6).

There is a significant difference between "finding it hard to breathe" and "fainting spells" (the latter could stem from many causes besides shortness of breath). "Dyspnea" is a perfectly respectable word for shortness of breath, as "erythema" is for "redness of the skin"—but how many readers will understand it, how many will get a vague impression of kidney poisoning? Another translator speaks of "a tendency to asthma"; this isn't bad in itself, but in context it raises the specter of hay fever. Dramatically, Flaubert seems to be aiming at the impression that Emma is gasping for breath like a fish out of water; but this metaphor can easily be pushed to the ludicrous. Yet in fact, none of the translations is wholly indefensible. Without really betraying his original to the extent of a suit for breach of promise, a translator can simply, by the choice and positioning of his equivalent for Flaubert's "étouffements," give the impression that Emma is whimpering over a trifle, or that she is genuinely and seriously ill.

To summarize into the inevitable platitude, there appears to be a broad band of free choice for the exercise of literary judgment in translation. How much and what sort of work a translator chooses to perform upon his original is altogether up to him. He must decide how much to translate, what a cross-cultural equivalent amounts to, what weight should be given to words and what weight to the dramatic situation in which the words are spoken. As he chooses among these options, a translator influences decisively the experience that his reader is likely to have; he recasts the original in his own style, or, if he is subtler than that, in one of the styles which can by direction or indirection be attributed to the original author. There is no such thing as a single "right" path for a translator to follow; his decisions are all relative, involving so much loss and so much gain. The price of a felicity is sometimes a folly; the price of a safe translation is sometimes a neutral and imperceptive one.

The more deeply the original is entwined with specific social circumstances, with the mores of a particular time and place, the less consistently one can hope to translate. Even though the equivalents are there, Monsieur Homais should not, need not, cannot be Mr. Homais. The gain is nil, the loss in distraction and in tonality is immense. But "M. le Maire" might well become "Mr. Mayor" without difficulty or awkwardness. "M. le Prefet," on the other hand, is a stumbling block, no matter what we do; he will probably be least obtrusive if we call him "the Prefect," and footnote to explain that he has certain functions in a *département,* which is in turn halfway between an English county and an American state—obviously we are in serious trouble with that word "Prefet." Basic to all these decisions is the recognition that *Madame Bovary,* however translated, must be a novel of nineteenth-century Normandy, as *The Sound and the Fury* is a novel of twentieth-century Mississippi. The one can no more be itself without prefects, Calvados, and a flavor of French manners than the other can do without sheriffs, whiskey, and some sort of souf' in the mouf'. On the other hand, the vehicle in which Charles and Emma go to the ball, though Flaubert deviates into Norman patois to describe it as a "boc," cannot be so precisely named in a translation that the English reader doesn't know what's involved. It has to be some sort of cart or shay or buggy—and the flavor of the actual French milieu is immediately drowned in New England. Again, when in Faulkner's novel, that showman in the red tie picks up a little box on the lawn outside Quentin Compson's window, and finds it labeled "Agnes, Mabel, Becky," a translator into whatever language can't simply follow the words on the printed page. Somehow he has to communicate, not too clearly, not too blatantly (for Faulkner has been allusive about it himself) what "Merry Widows" were, and what was printed on the box containing three of them. (My colleague, Professor Leon Howard, helped me at this stile.)

In a word, there's no easy formula for translating specifics or leaving them in the original; one has to balance the demand for comprehension against the need to be authentic and specific. The footnote may be, as I've heard it called, the translator's white flag of surrender; it's also a way of taking care of comprehension, for those who need help, at the foot of the page, while freeing the translator in his text to translate for a word's contours and overtones, its full linguistic dimensions. Still, there's no burking the fact that it is a device of desperation.

Lyric poetry is proverbially more difficult to translate than prose; but this particular difficulty, of a complex social milieu to be rendered in its details through a language which accommodates none of those details, poetry often escapes. It atones with its own special varieties of difficulty, having to do, not simply with rhyme and meter, but with the allusive richness of verse, the fullness and complexity of poetic metaphor. As the poise of verse is more precarious, the chances of falling on one's prat are multiplied; and the balances of rendering one formula into another are impossible when every phrase has to have a distinctive poise and resonance of its own. Let us set up a couple of pages in which a pair of poems by Rainer Maria Rilke stand at the head of the page with three versions by the better-known translators into English at east, southeast, and south. These are all translators into rhyme and meter—that is, they take the translational task at its hardest; while the poems are small, taut, and delicately balanced. In short, the task of rendering lyric poetry is seen here at its most naked and challenging:

Da neigt sich die Stunde und rührt
    mich an
mit klaren, metallenem Schlag:
mir zittern die Sinne. Ich fühle ich
    kann—
und ich fasse den plastischen Tag.

Nichts war noch vollendet, eh ich es
    erschaut,
ein jedes Werden stand still.
Meine Blicke sind reif, und wie eine
    Braut
kommt jedem das Ding, das er will.

Nichts ist mir zu klein, und ich lieb es
    trotzdem
und mal'es auf Goldgrund und gross
und halte es hoch, und ich weiss nicht
    wem
löst es die Seele los . . .

Das Stundenbuch (Leipzig, 1913)

With stroke that rings clear and me-
    tallic, the hour
to touch me bends down on its way;
my senses are quivering. I feel I have
    power—
and seize hold on the pliable day.

Nothing came to completion till I it
    espied;
all becoming delayed its advance.
Now my vision is ripe; there comes
    like a bride,
the thing that it wills, to each glance.

None's too small to be loved; large I
    paint it, and choose
pure gold its whole background to be,
and hold it most precious, and know
    not whose
soul it alone sets free. . . .

                        —J. B. Leishman
            tr. Rilke, *Poems* (London,
                        Hogarth, 1934)

How the hour bows down, it touches
    me, throbs
metallic and lucid and bold:
my senses are trembling. I feel my own
    power—
on the plastic day I lay hold.

Until I perceived it, no thing was
    complete
but waited, hushed, unfulfilled.
My vision is ripe, to each glance like a
    bride
comes softly the thing that was willed.

There is nothing too small, but my
    tenderness paints
it large on a background of gold,
and I prize it, not knowing whose soul
    at the sight,
released, may unfold . . .
                        —Babette Deutsch
            Poems from the Book of Hours
            (Norfolk, Conn., New Directions,
                        1941)

With strokes that ring clear and me-
    tallic, the hour
to touch me bends down on its way:
my senses are quivering. I feel I've the
    power—
and I seize on the pliable day.

Not a thing was complete till by me it
    was eyed,
every kind of becoming stood still.
Now my glances are ripe and there
    comes like a bride
to each of them just what it will.

There's nothing so small but I love it
    and choose
to paint it gold-groundly and great
and hold it most precious and know
    not whose
soul it may liberate . . .

                        —A. L. Peck
            tr. Rilke, *The Book of Hours*
            (London, Hogarth, 1961)

Alles wird wieder gross sein und ge-
waltig,
die Lande einfach und die Wasser fal-
tig,
die Bäume riesig und sehr klein die
Mauern;
und in den Tälern, stark und vielge-
staltig,
ein Volk von Hirten und von Acker-
bauern.

Und keine Kirchen, welche Gott um-
klammern
wie einen Flüchtling und ihn dann be-
jammern
wie ein gefangenes und wundes
Tier,—
die Häuser gastlich allen Einlassklop-
fern
und ein Gefühl von unbegrenztem
Opfern
in allem Handeln und in dir und mir.

Kein Jenseitswarten und kein Schaun
nach drüben,
nur Sehnsucht, auch den Tod nicht zu
entweihn
und dienend sich am Irdischen zu
üben,
um seinen Händen nicht mehr neu zu
sein.

Grandeur in all things shall be rein-
stated,
the lands outsmoothed, the waters corrugated,
walls inconspicuous and trees tremendous;
and in the valleys, strong and varie-
gated,
a race of shepherds and of crop-attenders.

No churches, which first capture God
and gaol him
like some absconder, and which then
bewail him
like some trapped creature panting
woundedly,—
houses to every knocker hospitable
and sense of sacrifice immeasurable
in all transactions and in you and me.

No waiting for, no gaze at, things cel-
estial,
just longing to give even Death his due
and humbly train ourselves on the ter-
restrial
so that his hands shan't find us wholly
new.

—J. B. Leishman

All will grow great and powerful again:
the seas be wrinkled and the land be
    plain,
the trees gigantic and the walls be low;
and in the valleys, strong and multi-
    form,
a race of herdsmen and of farmers
    grow.

No churches to encircle God as though
he were a fugitive, and then bewail him
as if he were a captured wounded crea-
    ture,—
all houses will prove friendly, there will
    be
a sense of boundless sacrifice prevailing
in dealings between men, in you, in me.

No waiting the beyond, no peering to-
    ward it,
but longing to degrade not even death;
we shall learn earthliness, and serve its
    ends,
To feel its hands about us like a friend's.

—Babette Deutsch

All shall be great again and filled with
    power,
walls shall be tiny and the trees shall
    tower,
continents smooth and seas and lakes
    uneven;
and strong and multiform a race shall
    flower,
herdsmen and farmers, in the vales deep-
    riven.

No churches, then, that hem God in and
    jail him
just like a fugitive, and then bewail him
like wounded beast deprived of lib-
    erty—
houses thrown open when the door-
    bell's sounded,
and a great sense of sacrifice unbounded
in all men's dealings and in you and me.

No seeking the hereafter; only yearning
to keep even death itself yet unpro-
    faned,
and, earthliness's ways and service learn-
    ing,
to be no longer strange beneath his
    hand.

—A. L. Peck

We can scarcely avoid noticing the way in which, translating the first poem (it's the first lyric of *The Book of Hours*), Mr. Peck (1961) and Mr. Leishman (1967) find almost identical words for stanza one. There's nothing against this, obviously; translating from the same text, two men are bound to follow the same path every now and then, conceivably because it's the best path. On the other hand, Mr. Peck's second stanza starts swinging like a nursery rhyme—it's *The Hunting of the Snark* all over again:

> There was silence supreme, not a shriek, not a scream,
> Scarcely even a howl or a moan,
> As the man they called "Ho" told his story of woe,
> In an antediluvian tone.

Galloping dactyls alternating tetrameter and trimeter represent a major sand trap guarding the approach to Rilke's poem; one can't allow them to absorb one's sense of an individual rhythm in the original. Mr. Leishman escapes this fate partially by making his lines difficult through inversions—"till I it espied" and "there comes like a bride, / the thing that it wills, to each glance" do something to keep the translation from swinging, no doubt; they also do something to make it seem stiff and artificial. But Mr. Leishman's triumph in this direction is his line "all becoming delayed its advance"—which requires a good deal of help from the other versions and the original before explaining itself as "each developing thing stopped short." In the unhappy matter of the "plastischen Tag," technology has been unkind to Rilke; set against the "metallenem Schlag" of the hour, a "plastic" day inevitably sounds like one that you would pick up at the five-and-ten. No fault of Miss Deutsch if she fell into this trap, as it closed behind her; but the other translators are tasked for an equivalent which will imply the limitless possibilities of the advancing day. The verb ("erschaut") at the end of the first line of the second stanza provides a nice crux—Mr. Peck clearly uses "eyed" as an equivalent for "used one's eyes on," i.e., "saw"; Mr. Leishman prefers "espied," which is less unnatural as English, but carries almost as many overtones of voyeuristic suspicion. "Perceived" by Miss Deutsch is clearly the best alternative here. We get a confirmation of this judgment if we consider the problem of the gold background presented in stanza three; Mr. Peck's "gold-groundly" is really ludicrous; Mr. Leishman's making "pure gold its background to be" is considerably better (despite the dislocated and therefore intrusive infinitive), but perhaps gives too much weight and solidity to the gold by making it "pure" (Rilke evidently had in mind the sort of gold background (i.e., gilt) painting traditional in the early Italian Renaissance, for example in a monkish painter like Fra Angelico), and adds an odd emphasis with the word "whole"—as if it were somehow possible to have a half-gold background. These little emphases of Mr. Leishman's, apparently intended as fillers, do funny things to Rilke's verse. There is no textual warrant for the "alone" he introduces into the last line of his poem, and the restrictive effect of the imported word seems very alien to the free, indiscriminate, and undirected liberating impulse of the poet-painter-monk.

If Miss Deutsch is the winner of this four-way competition (and so far she seems like it), what are the strong and weak points of her rendering? Though this could be valued either way, I think her idea of beginning with an exclamation (no warrant for this in Rilke) is a fortunate stroke; it gives the opening sentence needed impetus, and interferes with nothing else in the poem. "Throbs" and "bold" aren't in Rilke's text; they are further efforts to give energy and immediacy to the first stanza. "Bold" strikes my ear as quite right—one might even say it was implicit in "Schlag"; but "throbs" may well be excessive. Like a bell, the hour may clang, strike, or resound; but "throb," with its overtones of idling motorcars, is perhaps too busy a word for a monastic scene. If we look at the three concluding lines of her stanzas, the three lines where she was most constrained by the need to rhyme, we shall be likely to feel that they are the three lines where she's fallen most short of Rilke's simple inevitability; and, incidentally, making the comparison is an admirable way of getting to feel, to see the importance of that simple inevitability to Rilke's poem. Finally, in controlling the difficult first two lines of the second stanza, Miss Deutsch has evidently opted for smoothness rather than fullness of rendering; "ein jenes Werden," every developing thing, or rather every development taking place within things, is a concept that won't fit comfortably in the limited accommodations available for it in an English version—there seems to be a little more natural animism in Rilke's world than in Miss Deutsch's rendition of it, but this again is a marginal observation. A small element but an important one in the last stanza is the presence and placing of two "ich's." In a strict economy, the second one ("ich weiss night wem") is redundant—the active presence of the first one would be understood, even if the second weren't expressed. And so Mr. Peck and Mr. Leishman have left it out. But it's really needed, to set the last statement apart, as not merely another element in a chain, but the purpose toward which all the other elements rise, in which they flower. Miss Deutsch may have had to get it in because of her option in the stanza's first line; but that doesn't alter the happy consequence that her climax sounds a little more climactic than in the other versions.

With regard to the second poem, all we have to do is look at the other versions (not to speak of the original) to see how pompously polysyllabic and imprecise Mr. Leishman's opening has come out. What, oh what, persuaded the unhappy man to call farmers "crop-attenders," ("shepherds," translated into this sort of translatorese, ought to be "wool-waiters"), and in what strange clime can one see "waters corrugated"? Miss Deutsch's opening lines, by contrast, show what translation of the lyric can be—not, perhaps, a jewel transformed into another jewel, but a glitter here and there, from which we can see what the quality and tone of the original are like. The poem has to march, inevitably; it does so in the version as well as (and—heresy!—maybe even a little better than) in the original. The pun on "plain" isn't really a pun; it simply conveys that the land is "einfach" in two reinforcing senses. The word "wrinkled" for the seas (perhaps it comes from Tennyson's little poem on the eagle, perhaps just from having flown over water in an airplane) is beyond praise. Mr. Peck is disqualified by such strained equivalents as "vales deep-riven" for "Talern," his use of fillers (*"just* like a fugitive") alternating with unnatural omissions ("like wounded beast deprived of liberty")—though indeed his standing in this poem rises a good deal vis à vis Mr. Leishman. A major problem of meaning, though, emerges in connection with the last stanza, where our three translators diverge widely on a matter of interpretation. As one reads Mr. Leishman's last line, the hands which are not to find us wholly new are inevitably those of death—the "his" of the last line is powerfully attracted to the "his" of two lines before ("to give even Death his due"). With Mr. Peck's version, on the other hand, there's no way of knowing what the "his" in his last line refers to, since death is referred to above as "itself" and "earthliness" doesn't seem enough of a personification to merit the masculine possessive adjective. When in doubt, one can always invoke God, and maybe that's what Mr. Peck wanted us to do here—but it seems like rather a large concept to slither into a poem through such a very small postern. Miss Deutsch plainly wants the hands to belong to earthliness, and this reading forwards a major theme of the poem, which is a rich and assured dwelling in the here and now. But she has taken more liberties with the literal sense of the passage than any of the other translators—and when we translate Rilke's sense as literally and explicitly as possible, we can perhaps see why. "That we may no longer be new to the hands of the earthly" just won't go easily into English; rather than twist and distort her To-language, the translator softened (and perhaps sentimentalized, by a shade or two?) the difficult play of abstractions and concretions in Rilke's ending.

Translators of poetry clearly court worse disasters than translators of prose; probably the compressed, enigmatic quality of poetic statement has more to do with the difficulty than the mechanics of meter and rhythm, not to think of rhyme. But whether prose or poetry is involved, it is plain that the old language surrenders its different levels and nuances of meaning reluctantly, the new one accepts them with many reservations and limitations, besides imposing on them adventitious observances of its own. Our language, like a very old person grown sot in his ways, can take in the new only under the guise of something familiar. The best conceivable translation is necessarily at least half-rooted in its new idiom; and for the ◄ other half, it is often divided between several possible objects of imita- • tion—between surface (overt statement) and undercurrent (buried con-• nective), between emotive tone and literal meaning, between formal pattern • and expressive variation. Indeed, when all the apologies have been made, ● an area for boasting remains too; taking the translational task at its hardest, the good translator at the peak of his form not only dodges pitfalls and disdains the too-facile reduction of his original, he takes creative advantage of opportunities in his new idiom, exercising a fine balance between his talent for docile obedience and his artistic impulse toward a wiry bounding line of his own.

Yet behind all this division of the praise-blame vocabulary, there remains something equivocal about the translator's achievement; when we admire him most, our admiration selects words that could equally well apply to a master forger. The best work he can do is that which makes us least aware of what he is actually doing, which enables (persuades, compels) us to forget that we are reading a translation. So there is something like an act of collusion in every reading of a translation; the translator offers, in lieu of his beloved original, a patched and specious false front, which the reader, if a man of any sophistication at all, accepts warily (with the recommended suspension of disbelief), as a token of the original. Perhaps if both sides knew exactly what was involved, there wouldn't be any transaction at all. But that needn't stop us from trying to see at least some of the things that can happen behind the necessary, shared pretence that *Madame Bovary* in English "is" *Madame Bovary*.

CHAPTER III

Homer and the Bible

Faulkner, Flaubert, and Rilke are relatively recent authors; none of the translations we have so far considered is much more than seventy-five years old, most are less than twenty-five, and all involve finding equivalences between a pair of Western-European languages. When we consider books that have been translated, and retranslated, not for decades, but for millennia, and from languages more distant linguistically than French, German, and English, we are forced into fresh notions of equivalence. Homer and the Bible are the great testing grounds of translation theory and practice; over the years they have been variously interpreted and adapted to varying ideas of literary taste, varying cultural demands. By virtue of their peculiar forms (an epic poem and prophetic-historical-visionary anthology) they offer extraordinary obstacles to the discovery of translational equivalents. Were they not books so deeply engrained in the languages, cultures, and literatures of modern Europe, there might be some force to the argument that one must know Greek and Hebrew to discuss translations made from those languages. Indeed, an array of such problems might easily be mounted, for which expertise in the original tongues is required. But there are others, almost as interesting, to which no more than a bare minimum of the basic tongue is pertinent—and to some of these questions, without further ado, we turn.

1. Tonal commitment: epic length

One of the great and traditional difficulties about composing an epic poem derives from the simple fact that it is so long. For translator, as for author, this means that the decisions made in the first hundred lines or so—the tonal values established there—must be maintained pretty much unaltered for the next 9,900. Naturally, different epics admit different degrees of variation on the chosen tone; when any measure of comedy is involved, as in Ariosto, the spread of verbal values is likely to be greater. But within particular versions of the major serious epics, there is not much room for variation. As he begins his task, the translator has an enormously wide range of choice; he may translate Homer for laughs or for common sense, for turbulent energy or high seriousness. But whatever choice he makes, he is permanently stuck with—he immediately finds it on his back, as heavy as history. Four versions of Diomede's contemptuous speech to Paris (*Iliad* XI, 385 ff.), two relatively old, two modern, suggest how remarkably a translator's choice of tonal values can alter the feeling of a single passage: *

Hide yourself and pull your bow!
Come and steal a wife and go!
Frizzle-head with pretty curls,
you can make eyes at pretty girls!

—Stand up and fight like a man, and much good will your bows and arrows be. This time you have just grazed my foot, and listen to the boasts! I care no more than if a woman shot me, or some fool of a boy—

Blunt, I tell you, is the shot
of a coward good-for-naught!
Mine is quite another thing—
one touch, and death is in the sting!

—Then the man's wife will have to tear her two cheeks, and his children will be orphans, while his blood reddens the earth and his body rots. More vultures than women about him then!

(Rouse)

He, dauntless, thus: Thou Conqu'ror of the Fair,
Thou Woman-Warrior with the curling Hair;
Vain Archer! trusting to the distant Dart,

You archer, foul fighter, lovely in your locks, eyer of young girls.
If you were to make trial of me in strong combat with weapons
Your bow would do you no good at all, nor your close-showered arrows.
Now you have scratched the flat of my foot, and even boast of this.
I care no more than if a witless child or a woman
Had struck me; this is the blank weapon of a useless man, no fighter.
But if one is struck by me only a little, that is far different,
The stroke is a sharp thing and suddenly lays him lifeless,
And that man's wife goes with cheeks torn in lamentation,
And his children are fatherless, while he staining the soil with his red blood
Rots away, and there are more birds than women swarming about him.

(Lattimore)

Bowman, reviler, proud in thy bow of horn (or rather, resplendent with thy lovelock), thou gaper after girls, verily if thou madest trial in full harness, man to man, thy bow and showers of shafts would nothing avail thee, but now thou

* Rouse, tr. Homer's *Iliad* (Mentor Books, 1956); Lattimore, tr. Homer's *Iliad* (Chicago, Phoenix Books, 1961); Pope, tr. Homer's *Iliad* in *Poems*, Twickenham ed., Vols. VII, VIII; Lang, Leaf, and Myers, tr. Homer's *Iliad* (London, Macmillan, 1911).

Unskilled in Arms to act a manly Part!
Thou hast but done what Boys or
    Women can;
Such Hands may wound, but not in-
    cense a Man.
Nor boast the Scratch thy feeble Arrow
    gave,
A Coward's Weapon never hurts the
    Brave.
Not so this Dart, which thou may'st one
    Day feel;
Fate wings its Flight, and Death is on
    the Steel,
Where this but lights, some noble Life
    expires,
Its touch makes Orphans, bathes the
    cheeks of Sires,
Steeps Earth in purple, gluts the Birds
    of Air,
And leaves such Objects as distract the
    Fair.

(Pope)

boastest vainly, for that thou hast
grazed the sole of my foot. I care not,
no more than if a woman had struck
me, or a senseless boy, for feeble is the
dart of a craven man and a worthless.
In other wise from my hand, yea, if it
do but touch, the sharp shaft flieth,
and straightway layeth low its man,
and torn are the cheeks of his wife,
and fatherless his children, and he,
reddening the earth with his blood,
rots away, more birds than women
round him.

(Lang, Leaf, and Myers)

Radically as they differ from one another, one can easily see that these
different versions are all rooted in the same soil; each brings out a tonal
element of the text which the others choose to minimize or neglect. Even
Rouse's version, which is surely the most radical, reminds us that the slang-
ing matches of Homeric heroes are not unlike the taunting and challenging
of little boys. In this version Diomede perhaps comes closer to sticking out
his tongue at Paris than our sense of Aegean warfare as a fearful occupation will comfortably accommodate; his singsong verges on the infantile.
Yet, given the general level of Rouse's version, his rendering of Diomede's
speech is just a little bit under the established level of verbal dignity. The
point is that Rouse's rendering of Diomede's speech was determined, in its
main outlines, when on the third page of his translation, he had Achilles say
to Agammenon, "Your Majesty, gettings are keepings with you, there's no
doubt about that. Pray how will our brave men give you a prize?" * If that

---

* For purposes of comparison, Lattimore's rendering is:

> Son of Atreus most lordly, greediest for gain of all men,
> how shall the great-hearted Achaians give you a prize now?

Pope has it:

> Insatiate King (*Achilles* thus replies)
> Fond of the Pow'r, but fonder of the Prize!
> Would'st thou the *Greeks* their lawful Prey shou'd yield,
> The due Reward of many a well-fought Field?

is how the chief Greek warriors address one another in public council, then Diomede, who's rather a rough diamond at best, is bound to use different, and lower, language to Paris, whom he despises.

Choice of tone is most obvious when one deals with sharply contrasting versions of a single passage, like those of Rouse and Pope; an interesting instance of crucial options in the middle range is provided by E. V. Rieu's *Odyssey*. This is a simple, sensible prose translation, in the tradition of Samuel Butler, whose sharply astringent version took a lot of Victorian fat out of Homeric translation. Yet its very middle-of-the-road position on a series of similar options has the cumulative effect of giving the poem a very distinct coloration, which can be illustrated easily by printing Mr. Rieu's version of several successive passages on the left, and a sampling of the many others on the right. For example, as he sacrifices a bit of slaughtered hog to the gods, we hear of

. . . the swineherd, who was a man of sound principles.	The swineherd did not forget the immortals, for he was a man of pious heart.
(XIV, 420)	(Rouse)

Telemachus, enumerating the suitors, tells his father:

Dulichium has sent fifty-two, the pick of her young men, with six valets in tow.	From Dulichium alone fifty-two, picked men, with armourers a half dozen.
(XVI, 250)	(Fitzgerald)

Pallas Athene, making conversation with Telemachus, says:

"But tell me, are you really Odysseus' son? How you have grown!"	"Are you real and very son to Odysseus, you who are so well grown of body?"
(I, 200)	(T. E. Shaw)

Odysseus invites Eumaeus to tell his life story:

"You surprise me," said Odysseus, "You must have been quite a little fellow, Eumaeus, when you came all that way from your parents and your home."	And Odysseus of many councils answered him saying: "Ah, Eumaeus, how far then didst thou wander from thine own country and thy parents while as yet thou wast but a child!"
(XV, 380)	(Butcher and Lang)

And Chapman:

> King of us all, in all ambition
> Most covetous of all that breathe, why should the great-souled Greeks
> Supply thy lost prize out of theirs?

Dryden gets the adjective in with characteristic neatness and lucidity: "Would'st thou the Grecian Chiefs, though largely Sould,/ Shou'd give the Prizes they had gain'd before?"

Athene speaks to Telemachus, warning him of an ambush:

". . . sooner than that, the earth will close over some of these lovelorn gentlemen who are wasting your wealth."	". . . some of them That waste thy fortunes, (shall) taste of that extreme They plot for thee."
(XV, 74)	(Chapman)

The tendency of Rieu's translation is clear enough from these examples; his is a very conversational, and a very middle-class, *Odyssey*. Note for example the difference between calling the swineherd "a man of sound principles," and calling him "a man of pious heart." The first is a vestryman's virtue, with a strong element of social solidarity involved; the second implies instinctive goodness of feeling, a "natural piety" if one will, such as the swineherd does continually evince throughout the poem. Or again, those "valets" in XVI, 250; six valets for fifty-two suitors is a very strange proportion indeed. If one thinks of them as valets in the usual sense—shiners of shoes, providers of clean linen, dressers of hair—it will be hard to see why they are mentioned at all in an enumeration of enemies. (T. E. Shaw adds a letter and makes them "varlets"—no particular improvement.) Chapman solves the matter of numbers with a fine sense of Elizabethan excess: "From Dulichius, fifty-two, and every one of these / Six men attend," but that multiplies out to 312 attendants, and what they were doing during Book XXII is likely to be felt as an embarrassing problem. So it is better to have just six of them, and then "valets" becomes an office too redolent of Louis Quatorze to have meaning in this context.

The effect of setting Mr. Rieu's translation, as it were, against the field is to show how a basic tonal decision, to which the translator must make an early commitment, deepens and reinforces itself in the course of the work. Athena telling Telemachus, "How you have grown!" is in effect a *dea ex suburbis,* and the swineherd then becomes a man of sound principles—a ratepayer, a churchgoer, and a thoroughly decent chap. To be sure, the terms of the comparison are grossly unfair to Mr. Rieu, as they would be to any other translator who had to stand single-handed against a field. A single line pursued consistently makes itself felt mostly in moments of strain or stress; precisely then one compares it with the most interesting or revelatory of the other options, as if the translator had had a completely free choice among them. He doesn't, he can't. But with a wide-minded poet like Homer, it's probably a fault in the right direction if a translator sins by adopting too bold, too rough, and too varied a tone—one more redolent of the courts of sea kings, Niarchos and Onassis, than of Kew Gardens and Wimbledon.

2. Names and epithets: epic depth

Preparing to depart the country of the Phaeacians, Odysseus is guest of honor at a splendid feast, which George Chapman's version describes zestfully:

> The thighs then roasting, they made glorious cheer
> Delighted highly; and amongst them there
> The honour'd-of-the-people us'd his voice,
> Divine Demodocus.

(XIII, 38)

In other words, the minstrel sang a song. His name, Demodocus, really does mean "people's honor" or "people's delight"; on this public occasion Homer and Chapman both want to emphasize the etymology, and, without doing away with the name as a name, remind the reader of what it means. Elsewhere in the poem, Demodocus will be simply Demodocus, as Alcinous is simply Alcinous.

These names and epithets with specific meanings are frequent enough in Homer; the name "Odysseus" itself is explained, in a preface to the story of his hunt on Parnassus with Autolycus, as meaning "the victim of enmity" (Rieu) or "the man-of-all-odds" (Rouse). Homer goes rather out of his way to furnish this etymology (XIX, 350); he evidently thought well of it. We note also, that the passage occurs long after the name "Odysseus" has been established as a name; there is no question of substituting the etymology for the name. The scar on his leg calls to mind the story of how he got it, Autolycus is mentioned in that connection for the first time in the poem, and this moment of recall brings back that instant of prophetic insight when Autolycus, half-foreseeing Odysseus' future career, christened him with the name of his adventures. Greeks of the Homeric age seem to have admired this sort of verbal cleverness. There are many other Homeric names and epithets which have equivalent meanings, more or less overt, and they are not always as easy to handle as in these passages, where Demodocus and Odysseus exist as established names and then are given explicit meanings by Homer himself. The translator's problem arises when the meaning is buried in, and inextricably confused with, the name—and it's simply the problem, Which does one translate?

Some perspective on the problem can be gained from the reflection that English names too often have generic "meaning" apart from their private proper-noun application. Smith, for instance, is one of a large class of occupational names, the force of which we suddenly feel when we list a lot of them together—Farmer, Miller, Taylor, Carpenter, Sawyer, Fisher, etc. Black, Gray, and Brown are as obvious as Freeman, Newman, and Freud.

Newcastle, Underwood, and Shakespeare line up alongside Robustelli, Du-
pont, Goldberg—and so forth, and so on. We don't normally translate these
names when we use them. (A man distressed at finding himself Goldberg
has sometimes been known to alter the name to Ormont, but that's an excep-
tion that proves the rule—Ormont isn't by any means the same as Goldberg
even though both names would translate to the same thing in a third tongue.)
Of course habit may be partly responsible for our readiness to accept names
simply as names—habit and mental torpor. A name is supposed to be a
surface, not a comment on life. We feel it as an artificial thing in Dickens'
world when names (like Gargery, Pumblechook, Murdstone) comment too
directly on, or express too precisely, the characters to whom they are assigned. In addition, there are severely practical reasons for taking names at
their face value. If we encountered Mr. Chickpea and Mr. John Bull in a
history of the Roman republic, there might be some problems about understanding that Cicero and Hannibal were being referred to.* The cantatas of
John S. Brooks and the operas of Joseph Green aren't particularly well
known.

Returning to Homer, it is true that Telemachus has a specific meaning—
it is a name whose components would be familiar to every hearer of the
Odyssey. *Tele* = distant and *machia* = struggle; Telemachus is a far strug-
gler, a warrior at a distance. By itself, this combination of names doesn't
seem to apply very closely to the young man, or to be very significant. But
when, in the course of proliferating legend, Odysseus is made responsible
for a son by Circe, he is given a name in the same pattern: Telegonus, the
far-born. That starts to look more deliberate and meaningful. One of Apollo's
epithets is the Far-Shooter, and the names of Odysseus' sons may have something to do with the rays of the sun, whom Odysseus emulates and represents, as well as with their physical remoteness from their father. On the
other hand, how to convey in English this quality of his name? It's out of the
question to have the young men walking around with a name like Far-
Fighter. Then his associates have to be Eat-'em-Alive and Never-Say-Die;
and the quality of his being a normal young prince with an unremarkable
name (so unremarkable that Homer never comments on it at all) is lost
entirely. The latent meaning of Telemachus is perhaps a little nearer the
surface than the latent meaning of English names like Stephen and Robert
(crown and red-beard); but not much nearer. Perhaps the closest parallel
is with certain girls' names in English—Grace, Victoria, Faith, Prudence—
but they don't help very much with the problem of Telemachus.

The universal choice, the only correct solution, is to leave Telemachus

---

* Life is already complicated by the practice of translating or modifying geographical names
to suit the language. Livorno for some reason has become Leghorn in English, Liége in Flemish
is Luik (pronounced Loyk), and when one refers to Monaco in Italian, it's never clear whether
one means München or Monte-Carlo.

Telemachus, and relegate the overtones of the name, either to the waste-
basket or to the scholiasts, or at most to a footnote appended to one's translation. But then must we forego translation of names where the element of
fantasy and invention is even more pronounced? The difficulty of drawing
a line is illustrated by two passages from the translation of Mr. Rouse, which
has gone furthest of all in the line of name-play. When he is listing the
participants in the Phaeacian sports, Mr. Rouse is in high form:

> Young champions were found in plenty: Topship and Quicksea and Pad-
> dler, Seaman and Poopman, Beacher and Oarsman, Deepsea and Look-out,
> Go-ahead and Upaboard; there was Seagirt the son of Manyclipper Ship-
> wrightson; there was Broadsea, the very spit of bloody Arês himself, and
> Admiraltidês, the finest man in stature and strength after the admirable
> Laodamas. And there were three sons of Alcinoös, Laodamas, and deep-
> see Halios, and Clytoneos of naval renown.
>
> (VIII, 110 ff.)

On the other hand, when Athena is giving Odysseus a quick genealogical
rundown of the Phaeacian royal house, before he enters the palace of
Alcinous, Mr. Rouse translates the names not at all:

> You see there was first Nausithoös, the son of Poseidon Earthshaker and
> the lovely Periboia, youngest daughter of Eurymedon king of the furious
> Giants. Eurymedon destroyed his own wild people, and he was destroyed
> with them. But Poseidon lay with Periboia, and their son was Nausithoös,
> King of the Phaiacians. Nausithoös had two sons, Rhexenor and Alcinoös.
> Rhexenor was killed in his own hall by Apollo with a silver bolt, while he
> was a young bridegroom and had no son as yet; but he left an only daugh-
> ter Arêtê, and Alcinoös married her. Alcinoös honoured her as no woman in
> the world is honoured by her husband. So she is honoured still by her
> husband and children, and the people think her divine, and cheer her
> loudly whenever she passes through the city. Aye, indeed, she has plenty
> of good sense. If her friends quarrel, she makes it up, even for men!
>
> (VII, 55 ff.)

Now we can hardly help being struck, when we compare the two passages,
that Arêtê's name cries out, more than anyone else's, for translation. She
couldn't be more explicitly named, her name is Virtue, and this is clearly
why Athene says people consider her divine, and why she is so good at
settling controversies, "even for men!" Yet her name, which is clearly and
pointedly significant, doesn't get translated at all. We notice further that the
first passage contains a name which in the Greek is very similar to one in
the second. That picturesque fellow Broadsea is, in the Greek original,
Euryalus. Euryalus and Eurymedon are not particularly far apart, as names;
Broadsea and Eurymedon are very different indeed. Is there some reason for
translating the name Euryalus = Broadsea which would not, with equal

force, impel one to translate Eurymedon = Broadreach, or something of the sort? Indeed, within the first passage itself, we note that the sons of Alcinous all have untranslated names, while the other personages mentioned include Poopman, Paddler, and Upaboard. It seems to be a social distinction almost as sharp as that between noble and common personages in certain plays of Shakespeare: Hippolyta and Theseus on one level, Snout, Flute, Starveling, and Bottom the Weaver on the other. As a matter of fact, Mr. Rouse's intent of producing a "lively" *Odyssey* seems to have controlled his decision where to translate and where not. Lower-class people can be translated into funny names; serious names, like Arêtê, get left in the Greek. If he wanted to, he could have translated all the names in the genealogical passage, as well as those on the athletic program.*

Apart from levels of social dignity, one sort of practical consideration is that the easiest names to translate are those which occur only once. Names that recurred again and again would quickly become tiresome if they carried an abstract meaning. At least under these circumstances, length is the mortal enemy of depth in translation; what one can't touch lightly and then drop, one is probably better off not touching at all. Since the Homeric poems are literally bottomless oceans of allegorical potentiality, the translator must be particularly wary of asking his version to absorb more of this watery stuff than the original makes unmistakably manifest. But that, alas, is a rule that sounds more definite than it actually is. Arêtê is unmistakably manifest; but no one's going to feel very grateful for having her converted to "Queen Virtue."

3. Priam's cart: epic detail

When he tells his nine surviving sons—not without some gafferly maledictions and complaints—to prepare a wagon for him to use in redeeming Hector's body from the Greeks (*Iliad* XXIV, 265 ff.), King Priam gets a prompt response. In describing how his orders were executed, Homer touches on a task the particulars of which are plainly dear to his poetic heart—he loves to describe processes, and does it well. Neither the poignant, climactic scene that is building between Priam and his son's iron-hearted killer, nor the approaching end of the entire epic, leads the poet to hurry over the least specific act in the preparation of the tackle. It's inconceivable that he would have gone out of his way to make explicit so many details, or that his audience would have listened to him patiently, if he hadn't known exactly how the job was to be done. But half a dozen different translations leave us with some very hazy ideas of how a Greek mule cart was prepared for use—and

---

* Eurymedon = Broadreach; Periboia = Herdrich (or "bride bought for many cattle"); Nausithoös = Shipborn; Rhexenor = Strong to Break the Ranks(?); and, of course, Arêtê.

with some reflections, too (if we care for them) on how technical details can be assimilated into an epic style. Let us begin with two versions of the passage, one by Rouse, the other by Pope:

> They were all startled by their father's outburst, and got to work. So they brought out a fine new mule-wagon with its wheels, and fastened on the top-carrier. They took down from the peg a box-wood yoke fitted with knob and rings for the reins. Then they brought out the yoke with its yoke-band, nine cubits long, and fitted it on the pole at the curving end and the ring over the pin; they tied it over the knob with three turns to left and right, and carried the rope back to the car-post tucking the tongue under the rope.

> The Sons their Father's wretched Age revere,
> Forgive his Anger, and produce the Car.
> High on the seat the Cabinet they bind:
> The new-made Car with solid Beauty shin'd;
> Box was the Yoke, embost with costly Pains,
> And hung with Ringlets to receive the Reins;
> Nine Cubits long the Traces swept the Ground;
> These to the Chariots polish'd Pole they bound,
> Then fix'd a Ring the running Reins to guide,
> And close beneath the gather'd Ends were ty'd.

The first part of the process is not too confusing in either translation—or in both together. There is a top carrier (either a receptacle to sustain a top, or a receptacle which fits on top), called a "Cabinet" by Pope, which has to be put on the wagon. But the boxwood yoke gets much more manipulation from Rouse than from Pope; though less elaborately ornamented, it has a more eventful career. It has a yoke-band (Pope makes it plural, and calls them "traces") which is nine cubits long * and is used to fasten the yoke to the pole. On this view of the matter, there are no proper traces at all. The yoke-band is a rope which wraps round yoke and pole (making use of an indefinitely located pin and ring connection and a knob fitted in the yoke), and is then carried back to the car-post. There's some confusion as to what tongue is tucked under the rope—the pole *is,* in contemporary terminology, the wagon-tongue, and how you can tuck a tongue of such dimensions and inflexibility under a rope is dim. But this is as nothing compared with the confusion engendered by a comparison with Pope. We have already noted that, as far as he is concerned, the yoke is already attached to the chariot somehow, or else it is attached by the traces, which are bound to "the Chariots polish'd Pole." Then there is some work with the reins, which Rouse had mentioned only in passing and then forgot entirely; for Pope they

---

* By comparison, Aias fights among the ships with a jointed pike that is twenty-two cubits long (Book XV).

apparently correspond to that extra piece of yoke-band that Rouse carried back to the car-post. Pope creates a ring for them to be drawn through and, for some reason, fastened or tied beneath. It's far from a clear picture.

Samuel Butler is a downright, clear-minded fellow; perhaps he can help get the operation in focus:

> They brought out a strong mule-waggon, newly made, and set the body of the waggon fast on its bed. They took the mule-yoke from the peg on which it hung, a yoke of boxwood with a knob on the top of it and rings for the reins to go through. Then they brought a yoke-band eleven cubits long, to bind the yoke to the pole; they bound it on at the far end of the pole, and put the ring over the upright pin making it fast with three turns of the band on either side of the knob, and bending the thong of the yoke beneath it.
>
> (Butler, tr. *Iliad* in *Works of S. B.* (Shrewsbury ed.), Vol. XIII.)

It's clear that Butler is much closer to Rouse than to Pope; he doesn't, indeed, draw the ends of the yoke-band back to the car-post, he simply bends it (if the thong of the yoke and the yoke-band are indeed the same thing) under the yoke itself. One detail surprises us; both the previous translators said the yoke-band was nine cubits long, but Butler tells us it was eleven. One would think that in conveying the measure of a yoke-strap, Homer could declare distinctly the difference between nine and eleven cubits. But on the whole, there's no faulting the lucidity of Butler's version. We understand just how the wagon was prepared, and that's fine. But the style; it's as dry and stodgy as the instructions on a box of cereal. "They brought . . ." "They took . . ." followed by a major variation, "Then they brought . . ." leading to "they bound . . ." Four consecutive assertions begin exactly the same way—as prose, it's flat, monotonous, and drab beyond extenuation. When Pope swept under the carpet all those grubby details involving thong and yoke and tongue and pin and ring, it was evidently because he sensed that explaining them in detail would make his verse mean; hence a wagon-bed became a "cabinet," and the tying together of a couple of pieces of wood with a bit of rope was transformed into a business with reins and traces—not a very distinct piece of business, indeed, but one clearly involving the central and dignified part of wagon preparation. Butler plainly doesn't care whether his prose is mean or not—at least, he hasn't taken the slightest pains to avoid a kind of creeping iteration that would get him red marks in an elementary composition course.

When in doubt, one always turns to Mr. Richmond Lattimore; he has translated the passage, handsomely as usual, and gives us something of a blend of previous renderings as follows:

> So he spoke, and they in terror at the old man's scolding
> hauled out the easily running wagon for mules, a fine thing
> new fabricated, and fastened the carrying basket upon it.

> They took away from its peg the mule yoke made of boxwood
> with its massive knob, well fitted with guiding rings, and brought forth
> the yoke lashing (together with the yoke itself) of nine cubits
> and snugged it well into place upon the smooth-polished wagon-pole
> at the foot of the beam, then slipped the ring over the peg, and lashed it
> with three turns on either side to the knob, and afterwards
> fastened it all in order and secured it under a hooked guard.
>
> Lattimore, tr. *Iliad* (Chicago, Phoenix, 1961).

There are all sorts of good things to say about this solution. Essentially the process described is about the same as in Rouse and Butler; the yoke is taken down and fastened to the wagon-pole. We have a new element in the "hooked guard" which apparently keeps the yoke band from slipping loose; but it's not a major change. A phrase like "then slipped the ring over the pin" does a particularly nice job of mentioning these little mechanisms, but as if they were familiar items to be mentioned in passing—and in fact, Mr. Lattimore seems deliberately to have made his sentences long and non-periodic to help us get the sense of many little tasks being performed *seriatim* as part of one big job. Still, there are spots even on the sun, and a translator shouldn't ever be satisfied. "Newly fabricated" isn't a natural expression to apply to a mule-wagon; "newly made" (Butler) is clearly better. You don't take a yoke "away from its peg" in normal English; you take it "off its peg," or "from the peg" (adding "on which it hung" if you want to be absolutely explicit or fill up your meter with something that Homer implies but doesn't say). And the parenthesis "(together with the yoke itself)" doesn't seem to be an altogether graceful way of handling an apparent redundancy in Homer; what they did was take down the yoke and carry it out, with its nine-cubit-long lashing, to be fastened on the pole, and the reader shouldn't be asked to shift his attention from yoke to lashing to yoke again with inconvenient abruptness. Finally, there are some blurs at the end of the passage. Which end of a wagon-tongue is the foot? One would think, the end at which it's attached to the wagon, especially since in Greek days the other end was often ornamented with a head; but the wagon-end is very much the wrong end to attach to a yoke. Mr. Lattimore has two "pegs" in his passage—which wouldn't matter so much if we had any notion where the other one, the one that *isn't* on the wall, was located; given the vagueness, it might be better to call one a "pin." The "it's" get a little out of hand, too; "snugged it well into place" should, in all syntax, refer to the yoke-lashing, though in common sense it must refer to the yoke; but then "lashed it" can refer to "yoke," "ring," "peg," or "beam" (as the knob is plainly part of the yoke, and the beam plainly is not, we should perhaps feel more secure about the whole rig if these were unequivocally the two things tied together). As for the two "it's" in the last line, I confess to a sense of total defeat in trying to figure out what they refer to.

Of course a niggling analysis of a nonniggling translation can always produce this sense of distress and confusion; Mr. Lattimore wants us to feel, as a result of his last line, that Priam's sons finished off the job and got everything about the cart's tackle tight and shipshape, and that sense is at least as important to a translation of the passage as our knowing where each rope and thong passed. In fact, it's his sense of the architecture of the passage that allies Lattimore with Pope; and we may feel he's driven a better bargain by a good deal (in the form of fewer sacrificed particulars) to get his finished shape. Two things seem to be involved here, subordination and pace; by stretching out the grammatical unit and reducing the specific detail to a fugitive element making toward a large point, one can accommodate more details with less sense of choking on them. On the other hand, full periodicity in the description of household chores would be too pompous; better a swift, paratactic sequence of short phrases, with the details buried as much as possible (by the use of the definite article, perhaps) in the swing and movement of the description.

If the reader isn't wholly sated by this plunge into the tack room, a last rendering of the passage will lead us toward a conclusion. It is by those much-abused and wholly disreputable fellows, Lang, Leaf, and Myers:

> Thus spake he, and they fearing their father's voice brought forth the smooth-running mule chariot, fair and new, and bound the body thereof on the frame; and from its peg they took down the mule-yoke, a boxwood yoke with knob well fitted with guiding-rings; and they brought forth the yoke-band of nine cubits with the yoke. The yoke they set firmly on the polished pole on the rest at the end thereof, and slipped the ring over the upright pin, which with three turns of the band they lashed to the knob, and then belayed it close round the pole and turned the tongue thereunder.

It's the second "thereof" and the "thereunder" in this passage that do the crucial damage; both of these forms are archaic with a Biblical overtone, and three such forms in two sentences start to sound pretty heavy. But, this failing apart, the Lang, Leaf, and Myers version is deft, clear, and dignified. Nothing is more common than to abuse this translation for its semi-Biblical Victorian overstuffing; and certainly in passages of high feeling, "quotha's" and "verily's" would be out of place. But in a passage of straight, exact exposition, like that involving Priam's cart, our Victorian translators acquit themselves manfully, and in "belayed," manage even a salty touch, suggestive of the open air and sea breezes, and highly appropriate to the scene.

Length, depth, and detail—the difficulties of the Homeric poem derive from the way it draws its translator in these three different ways at once. To sustain itself over long distances, it has to be mobile; in rising toward the sublime, it can't get pompous; and in dropping to the colloquial, it shouldn't get silly. It can't stay safely in the cozy range of the conversational. Its allegorical overtones have to remain overtones; when they start forming toward a big pattern, they drag the poem to a halt. And while the poet loves details, and the translator cannot slur over them, they too have to be kept moving. It's a large and very special order.

The difficulties of translating the Bible are different, but no less terrifying. Indeed, of all the books in the world which seem at first glance absolutely resistant to translation, the Bible is unquestionably a prime instance. It was written, in many different tongues and dialects, over a span of better than a thousand years; the text is often in deep disarray and confusion; the meaning of many words is wholly uncertain; enormous extraliterary pressures have often been brought to bear on the interpretation of a single word. One problem can stand for many: how shall we translate the word for the Lord— Yahweh: Adonai, Jehovah, The-Name-That-Is-Not-To-Be-Spoken? The Tetragrammaton, YHWH, apparently represents in the Hebrew text an unpronounceable collection of consonants, for which, when the text was read aloud, the name "Adonai" was regularly substituted, the substitution being sometimes (though by no means invariably) indicated by means of a marginal note. By a concatenation of errors over a period of years the vowels of "Adonai" came to be sometimes though not consistently interspersed with the consonants of "YHWH." Various translations use the resultant "Jehovah" with varying degrees of liberality in different passages; in addressing Moses, the Almighty Himself takes note of the confusion (Exodus vi); sometimes, He admits, He is the Lord, sometimes the Lord Jehovah; and the translators have variously compounded their Maker's bewilderment. Ephods and ephahs, shekels and cubits and hissop and shittim wood form another dense chevalde-frise of untranslatable concepts; some of them survive in all translations and a great many in some. It would scarcely be the Bible at all if it didn't reproduce the terms and concepts peculiar to the ancient Hebrews. The book is, after all, a history, and history is nothing if it is not faithful to the dense texture of its own particulars. But it is not just a history; as the names of its two sections (Old Testament, New Testament) indicate, it is a moral revelation (or revelations), a body of teaching, more or less coherent, describing the terms and conditions of man's developing contract with the deity, and for many years read as if it were and necessarily must be a seamless web, infused with a single, coherent, overriding intent. The same passage in the Bible may sometimes be read as historical report or as commandment. When Abraham returned from warring on the Chedorlaomer, he was blessed by Melchizedek, and gave him tithes of all (Genesis xiv, 17–20); for better than a millennium, the passage was regularly cited as evidence that tithing was the law of God, universally binding upon every Christian man unless for some reason exempted by positive law. (In England it was John Selden's clever, controversial *History of Tithes* that stood the argument on its historical head—though on its logical feet—by proposing that tithes were due only where positive law provided for them.) In passages less direct than this, the translator is still offered a choice between emphasizing or minimizing the typological parallels between Christ and Joseph, Christ and Moses, Christ and Samson, Christ and Josiah, Christ and Noah. Should a translator of Isaiah emphasize, minimize, or disregard the complex and subtle intertwinings of that prophetic book with the claims of Christ? How he translates will depend on what he thinks of primary importance in the text, and there his options are many as well as diverse. Simply in confronting individual words, because Hebrew is a richly metaphorical language, he is often presented with a variety of moral implications (from sparse to luxuriant), all legitimately derived from a single word, among which he has to choose according to his sense, obscure as it may be, of the original intent. One of Christ's hard sayings was that it is easier for a camel to pass through the eye of a needle than for a rich man to enter the kingdom of God (Matthew xix, 24); translator-interpreters with well-to-do congregations have been known to explain the passage by saying that there were a couple of tall rocks by a road near Jerusalem known popularly as "The Needle's Eye"; the space between them was narrow indeed, compared with the surrounding plain, but not so narrow that a fully loaded camel could not pass through quite comfortably. . . . Again, sectarian predilections have sometimes distorted in obvious ways the translation of words like love/charity, priest/presbyter, church/congregation, bishop/overseer. The great pun on which Christ founded the Christian church is a fine, operational pun in Latin (Petrus), Greek ($\pi\epsilon\tau\rho o\varsigma$), and Hebrew (Cephas); it translates nicely enough into Italian (Pietro) and French (Pierre), since in all these languages, *Peter* and *rock* are either identical or close enough to make a pun. But in English, German, and a variety of other tongues, the pun is lost. As for the scope of Christ's words, "aedificabo ecclesiam meam," they have been disputed since the Reformation and doubtless before, as well. Even the very boundaries of the Bible are ambiguous and subject to question. What is the dividing line between canon and apocrypha, and who drew it, on the basis of what knowledge or lack thereof? Suppose one accepts the distinction, the question still remains open, what value should be assigned the apocrypha—for it may be that the only light available to clarify a linguistic or doctrinal crux *within* the Bible may come from one of the apocryphal books *outside* it, as the reading of New Testament Greek has been much influenced lately by discoveries in the vernacular literature of the day.

The only conceivable conclusion to be drawn from this mass of difficulties —behind which lie range after range of further problems—is that the Bible cannot possibly be translated adequately. And doubtless this is right. But it has not prevented the Bible from becoming the most-translated book that ever was or ever will be.

4. Solomon's Song: omni-directional translation

With the Song of Songs we plunge into the heart of the storm. This short lyrical book has been taken as a pastoral eclogue, as epithalamium, as a drama in five acts and an epilogue, as an allegorical retelling of Exodus, a didactic poem on how to be a good wife, a mystic song celebrating the union of Israel and Yahweh or Christ and the church, as a jumble of many traditional, unrelated erotic songs and marriage poems, or as an ode written to celebrate the marriage of King Solomon with an attractive young person who brought her husband a portion valued at precisely £120 16s. 8d. per annum.* It has been described as a summary and compendium of all the other books of the Old Testament, and a prophetic foreshadowing of the New.

With this lavish array of interpretive possibilities to choose from, and given the inflammatory character of the imagery, it is hardly surprising that a great many translators have felt under an obligation to insulate the reader from the Song of Songs before he even gets to look at the text. The Geneva Bible, which made such a great point of marginal explanations that King James forcefully warned the Authorized translators against following *that* precedent, is particularly explicit in its headnote:

> In this Song, Solomon by moste swete and comfortable allegories and parables describeth the perfite love of Iesus Christ, the true Solomon and King of peace, and the faithful soul or his Church, which he hathe sanctified and appointed to be his spouse, holy, chast and without reprehension. So that here is declared the singular loue of the bridegrome toward the bride, and his great and excellent benefices wherewith he doeth enriche her of his pure bountie and grace without any of her deseruings. Also the earnest affection of the Church which is inflamed with the loue of Christ desiring to be more and more joyned to him in loue, and not to be forsaken for anie spot or blemish that is in her.

And as if this were not enough, there is a note to verse 1, "This is spoken in the person of the Church, or of the faithful soule, inflamed with ye desire of Christ, whome she loueth." Thus prepared and fortified, the reader turns to Chapter 1, verse 1, which is translated identically by Geneva and King James, yet conceals a number of problems within it:

> Let him kiss me with the kisses of his mouth: for thy love is better than wine.

It is obvious enough that the first part of the verse refers to the beloved in the third person, the latter part in the second. That may produce a certain

---

* *Song of Songs,* tr. John Mason Good (London, 1803), p. xiii.

confusion as to the setting, but it's no more than an abrupt change of perspective. When we turn to the Vulgate, however, the verse gets a good deal knottier:

> Osculetur me osculo oris sui, quia meliora sunt ubera tua vino.

> May (he, she, or it) kiss me with the kiss of (his, her, or its) mouth, since your breasts are better than wine.

Is it possible that Saint Jerome, creator of the Vulgate, understood Solomon to be speaking this verse to the spouse, that the speaker is male, not female? "Ubera" seems hard to understand on any other terms, unless the speech be assigned to a third party (identified, sometimes, with the virgins of verse 2: "therefore do the virgins love thee"). Overcome by this consideration, the great French Orientalist Renan moves us in his dramatization of the *Song* (which he describes unhesitatingly as "traduit de l'Hébreu") right into the middle of Solomon's harem, where the Sulamite is addressed by, and responds to the comments of, the other "odalisques." But even this solution, which adds more explanatory machinery to the song than there is song, does not satisfactorily explain the passage. And the fact remains that the subject of "kiss" and the gender of the possessive adjective modifying "mouth" seem to be as undefined and unexpressed in the Hebrew as in the Latin.

Other problems come crowding upon us as we reach the third verse:

> Draw me, we will run after thee: the king hath brought me into his chambers: we will be glad and rejoice in thee, we will remember thy love more than wine: the upright love thee.

Once again, what the Authorized version translates "love" ("we will remember thy love more than wine"), the Vulgate renders "breasts" ("memores uberorum tuorum"), sharpening even further our difficulty over the pronouns; in successive words ("me, we"), the speaker is singular and plural, thus perhaps a personified collective—Israel? As for the king, he may be Solomon or the bridegroom (but in that event, who is the speaker?), or he may be no less a figure than Yahweh himself. I find serious contemporary commentators of massive erudition assuring me that the situation in question is the Hebrew people in exile, imploring Yahweh to draw them back into Sion; it is apparently their numbers that justify a shift to the plural, and on these terms the king's chambers are nothing less than the Temple. Of course this allegory does not preclude the typical situation of a bridegroom leading his bride to the nuptial chamber—though to this reader it seem a little distracting. But there is also a reading of the Hebrew, as I find it recorded, which makes the verb "hath brought" ("introduxit" in the Vulgate) a form of the future: "he will introduce me," and this has been made grounds for reading the chambers as something like Abraham's bosom, or heaven.* And finally, there is an optional reading which provides a notable alternative to the (potentially phallic) phrase "the upright love thee" (Authorized) or "the righteous do love thee" (Geneva); it is given in the margin of King James as "they love thee uprightly," and in the French of Renan as "qu'on a raison de t'aimer." "They are right to love you" makes a very different meaning, and a still more different tone, from "the righteous do love thee."

It appears, then (to generalize briefly from the first three verses of the Song), that the speaker of these verses, and the situation in which the words are supposed to be spoken, not to mention the statement which is made, are in many ways undetermined and indefinite. The original seems to leave open a great many options which the various To-languages (Latin, English, French, German) require one to seal off. In these To-languages, the speaker and the person addressed have to be of one gender or another, have to be singular or plural; the tense of a verb can be past or future, but not both at once. The original text of the Song maintains decorum of speakers much less strictly than we are used to seeing it maintained—that is, the speakers are less distinctly nominated, and they alternate speeches much more abruptly than elsewhere. The many attempts to cast the poem in dramatic form bear witness to the difficulties which are felt in providing the speeches with a context where they will "make sense." During the heyday of the Pindaric ode in English, several attempts were made to convert the Song of Songs to that apparently outlandish form, on the score, evidently, that abrupt and irregular shifts of thought and diction are natural there. Verses 7 and 8 of this same first chapter raise the translator's difficulties close to the boiling point:

> Tell me, O thou whom my soul loveth, where thou feedest, where thou makest thy flock to rest at noon: for why should I be as one that turneth aside by the flocks of thy companions?

> If thou know not, O thou fairest among women, go thy way forth by the footsteps of the flock, and feed thy kids beside the shepherds' tents.

Pretty clearly in the first verse it is the bride who addresses the groom; that he should be king as well as shepherd creates no difficulty, but if he is also Yahweh being addressed by Israel, it is not easy to decide who his "companions" should be. Still, this is as nothing compared with the problems raised by the answer. Either the bridegroom is starting to find his bride a bit tiresome; or he is testing her devotion; or he is saying "I'm a shepherd and you'll find me among my fellow-shepherds;" or he could be saying, "You threaten to go off with the shepherds? Go!"; he may even be treating

---

* There is, we learn, a "prophetic perfect" in Hebrew, which enables one to describe a future event as having already been accomplished, and thus to express one's absolute assurance that it *will* be accomplished.

her with ironic contempt as a prostitute, who will be paid for her services with goats; he may be telling her to go back to her shepherdly village if she doesn't like it here in Jerusalem; any and all of these retorts may be addressed to her by her jealous fellow odalisques in the harem; or, lastly, she may be advised in all seriousness, perhaps prophetically, to seek her beloved among the shepherds, among the humble nomads where Truth is to be found. (I take this brief summary of a few of the various interpretations that have been proposed from Robert, Tournay, and Feuillet, *Le Cantique des Cantiques* (Paris, Gabalda, 1961, p. 81). Here, more than a social scene is undecipherable; it is the moral content of the passage which wavers as from north to south.

The Homeric translator can shrug off interpretive complications and dismiss moral implications and overtones to the scholiasts; what remains (the human scene) is still enough to occupy his verse completely. But the translator of the Song of Songs has no such recourse. Not knowing where to "point" a passage results in a kind of automatic, or woodenly noble version, where the general tone of the nearby diction is continued, but without any quality of expression behind it. The passage comes out neutral; the words are rendered, but their possible meanings are neither affirmed nor denied. Is the flock which the inquirer is told to follow (in verse 8) identical with or different from the "flocks of thy companions" that she does not want to be turned aside by (in verse 7)? The question can be answered one way or another, and the translation could steer us, without much effort, in either direction, but it refrains from doing so—holds back, in other words, from giving the passage any one preferred meaning. This hedging can be seen even more strikingly in the Geneva Bible, which knows precisely what it thinks the passage means, and says so in its glosses, but doesn't translate in such a way that one could get that meaning from the passage without their aid. According to the glosses, the "companions" of verse 6 are men "whom thou hast called to the dignity of pastures [pastoral care is implied] and they set forth their own dreams instead of thy doctrine." The answer is then explained as Christ's admonition to his church, "bidding them that are ignorant to go to the pastors to learn." The "companions" of verse 6 are false prophets, the "shepherds" of verse 7 are true teachers. But one would never get this meaning from the unaided translation.

In all this discussion of what the Song of Songs "means"—and the difficulties of interpretation have barely been broached, they are Talmudic in their infinite range of branching possibilities—we have of course bypassed the fact that the Song of Songs is, or can be made into, magnificent poetry. One doesn't have to be a budding theologian, a cultural historian, or even a frustrated dramatist to sense the passion of the verse, the majesty and boldness of the imagery. Any "interpretation" that denies or obscures the fact that this is splendid love poetry (whatever the gender and relation of the lovers) simply goes against the history of the human race, which has had the profound good sense to read the book as love poetry for thousands of years. (That tangle of allegorical footnoting thrown up by the Geneva parsons is not evidence that "the sixteenth century" read the Song of Songs allegorically, it is evidence that certain parsons felt the general public had to be argued into reading it allegorically.) If anything, current beliefs about the libido ought to render the diffuse and multiply directed eroticism of Solomon more accessible to the modern reader, and diminish the need for "interpretation." But this is just a way of saying that all of us—translators and readers of translations alike—can get a minimal sense out of the Song of Songs: in a blurred, omni-directional sense, it's erotic. What it is beyond that, apart from the fact that it's probably something, nobody seems too sure. As a result, the translator puts on his poker face, trusting to a sense of exaltation to atone for his own indecision over other sorts of sense.

5. "Modernized" Bibles: plain sense vs. exalted mood

It is commonplace in discussing Bible translation to say that one can understand the modern versions better, but that the older, established translations feel more noble, more "religious." There are several reasons to feel suspicious of that latter judgment. Many of the people who make it have simply got used to the phrasings and rhythms of the traditional Bible; they associate it with their childhood pieties, and cannot be reconciled to any other formulas. Something of the same thing is true of the culture; after more than 350 years, the Authorized version has passed into the language, carrying in its archaic terminology a rich patina of reverential feelings. A good deal of this archaic dignity is surely adventitious; the language of the King James version feels old and strange to us in a variety of ways that certainly did not appeal to its first hearers as old and strange. Yet after making all these discounts, there is still reason to think that the early translators, who were convinced that the text as they had it was the immutable word of God, did sometimes translate without being completely sure of what they were saying; and, perhaps to atone for this, they did aim at a relatively elevated prose tone—not "natural" speech at all, even by the somewhat stiffer standards of the seventeenth century, but speech of a deliberately artificial and resonant dignity. Bacon's prose in the *Essays,* or Jonson's in *Timber,* will remind us of what the seventeenth century sounded like when it was not striving for exaltation:

> It is an assured sign of a worthy and generous spirit whom honor amends. For honor is, or should be, the place of virtue; and as in nature things move violently to their place and calmly in their place, so virtue in ambition is violent, in authority settled and calm. ("Of Great Place")

> Poetry and picture are arts of a like nature; and both are busy about imitation. It was excellently said of Plutarch, poetry was a speaking picture, and picture a mute poesy. For they both invent, feign and devise many things and accommodate all they invent to the use and service of Nature.

Blunt, flat, workmanlike prose like this was within the reach of the Authorized translators if they had thought it appropriate; but the doctrine of stylistic decorum encouraged them to give the most lofty of books a properly lofty tone—not just where it happened to hit a high key, but throughout, because it was all the word of God. Nowadays, when we are less hieratic in our definition of the inherent dignity of subjects and less likely to think they can be elevated by what we consider "artificially" dignified style, it is only natural that plain, stripped prose should be the chosen vehicle of Biblical translation. But when one lowers the general level of the style, curious things happen to those passages where the inherent mood is exalted. In Matthew xviii, 17, Christ is telling his disciples what to do with an obdurate sinner who after private rebukes refuses to heed the voice of the church; and the Authorized version expresses the final condemnation: "let him be unto thee as a heathen and a publican." These two words carry finely complementary reverberations. A heathen, barbarous and outside the law, is an unclean idol-worshipper; concepts of cannibalism and savagery are woven into the fringes of the word. As for "publican," the word as it is commonly received has been contaminated (wrongly but powerfully) with the notion of keeping a public house, that is, profiting from the "low" impulses of mankind; while from its original sense of "tax-collector" it inherits other large connotations, of a worldly-minded person, who shouldn't be suffered to contaminate the holy places. But when the Revised Standard translates baldly, "let him be as a Gentile and a tax-collector," the impression is very different. The first thing that strikes us is the enormous gap between the two nouns. "Heathen" and "publican" complement one another; "Gentile" and "tax-collector" seem as oddly assorted as "postman" and "Presbyterian." I don't suppose anyone feels passionate devotion to tax-collectors as such, but we don't deny them access to the holy places; and "Gentile" is far more a descriptive word, in general usage, than "heathen," which still carries overtones of religious horror. As a matter of fact, quite a few of us are Gentiles ourselves; and what's so bad about that? "Heathen" and "publican" merge in the peripheral areas of connotation; "Gentile" and "tax-collector" don't.

One of Christ's more discouraging parables, to which Matthew gives a particularly sharp twist, describes how a certain king invited guests to a banquet, but when they didn't come gave his banquet to passersby whom his servants collected on the streets. The king, however, had strict standards for his new, and involuntary, guests; as King James describes it,

> he saw there a man which had not on a wedding garment: and he saith unto him, Friend, how camest thou in hither not having a wedding gar-

ment? And he was speechless. Then said the king to the servants, Bind him
hand and foot, and take him away, and cast him into outer darkness; there
shall be weeping and gnashing of teeth. For many are called, but few are
chosen. (Matthew xxii, 11–14)

Revised Standard makes the king's question read, "Friend, how did you get
in here without a wedding garment?" and the final fate of the wretch is that
the attendants are told to "Bind him hand and foot and cast him into the
outer darkness; there men will weep and gnash their teeth." The king's
question is perfectly natural—so natural that it might as well be asked by
an usher as by a king. And the outer darkness to which he condemns his
guest is less dark and terrifying than in the Authorized version, because the
translator is perfectly sure there are men there. Disembodied weeping and
gnashing of teeth pose a tremendous, unspecified threat—what one will be
regretting in hell is precisely one's loss of humanity. The naturalism of the
modern version detracts from its power. We see the limiting power of a
concrete noun again in the passage where St. Paul says, according to the
Authorized version: "For this corruption must put on incorruption, and this
mortal must put on immortality." The Revised version gives it, "For this
perishable nature must put on the imperishable, and this mortal nature must
put on immortality" (First Corinthians xv, 53)—as if somehow, the presence
of an anticipated noun were a stronger rhetorical effect than its absence. (The
substitution of "perishable" for "corruption" is another softening of the text—
it implies that the body will perish, not that it *is* perishing and corrupting
right now.) One even sees the more modern version turning away from, and
carefully softening, a strong metaphor which the old translation swallows
whole. "If after the manner of men," St. Paul says, "I have fought with
beasts at Ephesus, what advantageth it me, if the dead rise not? let us eat
and drink; for tomorrow we die." But the Revised Standard uses the first
phrase to soften the second: "What do I gain if, humanly speaking, I fought
with beasts at Ephesus? If the dead are not raised, 'Let us eat and drink for
tomorrow we die.' " (First Corinthians xv, 32) "Humanly speaking"—quite
apart from the tone, which is deferential and apologetic just when the apostle
is expressing his most profound and agitated concern for the central meaning
of his mission, the phrase is altogether unclear. Does it mean, "metaphorically speaking?" Certainly the sense of the passage that would paraphrase it,
"that I stood up like a man against the beasts at Ephesus—what was the
point of it if there is no resurrection?"—such a sense is by no means outside
the apostle's range. "By the grace of God," he says in a nearby passage,
whose multiplied "but's" suggest a deeply troubled modesty, "I am what I
am: and his grace which was bestowed upon me was not in vain; but I
laboured more abundantly than they all: yet not I, but the grace of God
which was with me." So should it be "humanly speaking" or "like a man"?
Plainly, the decision depends on one's estimate of the dramatic situation.

Would the apostle be more likely to qualify his metaphors or to dramatize himself? There is a danger, of course, that if one translates in the bolder style, simple minded readers will get an image of St. Paul fighting barehanded with lions at Ephesus, like Charlton Heston. But it's conceivable that the saint himself, who had a strong sense of the dramatic, would not have worried too much about that.

In talking of modern versions of the Bible, one can scarcely avoid paying one's respects to the most recent, which, as of this writing, is the so-called New English Bible. (What it will be called when it has become the old New English Bible will be the next generation's problem.) This most recent updating has appeared in two installments, the New Testament first and the Old Testament second; looking at the results with this distinction in mind, it seems clear that once more the modern style, which is flat, unaccented prose, works to best advantage in simple descriptive or narrative contexts, where plain facts are to be laid out in a plain order. For example, Mark, describing one of the appearances of Jesus after his crucifixion, takes the following form in King James and NEB:

After that he appeared in another form unto two of them, as they walked and went into the country.	Later he appeared in a different guise to two of them as they were walking, on their way into the country.
And they went and told it unto the residue: neither believed they them.	These also went and took the news to the others, but again no one believed them.

Mark xvi, 12, 13

It's just an unhappy accident for King James that "residue" has taken on its present connotations; but the complicated pronouns and word order of the second verse provide a gratuitous difficulty that the modern English version easily avoids. Again, when the women come to the tomb and find the stone rolled away, King James has a logically ungainly sequence of thought that NEB effortlessly smoothes out:

And when they looked they saw that the stone was rolled away: for it was very great.	. . . when they looked up and saw that the stone, huge as it was, had been rolled back already.

Mark xvi, 5

If one simply supposes that the King James Version implies some such expression, after the colon, as "and they were amazed"—the passage can be read into perfect plain sense; but it clearly demands more energy on the reader's part, and on a point where it isn't particularly well repaid. Similarly, and even more patently, in the matter of time-telling: when King James says "and it was the third hour and they crucified him" (Mark xv, 25), the modern reader will be largely at sea. Even if he knows about the canonical hours, it will be hard for him to imagine them applying to an event that occurred before the establishment of the Christian church. (The anachronism is like that which, in many old paintings, shows Christian saints, with crosses and halos, kneeling in prayer before the baby Jesus.) NEB is unexceptionable in saying simply, "the hour of the crucifixion was nine in the morning."

For passages of a higher strain, however, modern prose is persistently unsatisfactory—or at least, "modernized" prose has proved hard to manage. Witness the first of the Beatitudes:

Blessed are the poor in spirit; for theirs is the kingdom of Heaven. <div align="right">Matthew v, 3</div>	How blest are those who know that they are poor; the kingdom of Heaven is theirs.

The "poor in spirit" are, one supposes, generally understood as the spiritually retiring, the nonarrogant; that would be in line with the tone of the Beatitudes generally, and seems a value significant enough to merit the kingdom of heaven. But to be poor and know it doesn't seem like much of an achievement; a higher sort of *sancta simplicitas* might well be to be poor and *not* know it. To be poor and know it includes the possibility, even the probability, of feeling bitter about it—surely this is not what Christ is recommending.

Plain style, in short, has trouble making large, indefinite gestures. A recurrent phrase in the Sermon on the Mount is Christ's ominous warning to the hypocrites:

Verily I say unto you, they have their reward. <div align="center">Matthew vi, 2, 5, 16</div>	I tell you this: they have their reward already.

The whole point of the menace, as King James expresses it, is that the hypocrite has been written down for a reward that he does not expect; it is inevitable now and will be terribly surprising to him when it comes. If he has it "already," things cannot be any worse than they are now—the word truncates a whole vague spectrum of sinister possibilities.

But there is an obverse side to the atmospheric superiority of the older over the newer translations; it is the fact, already noted, that the old translators felt such reverence for the text that they often preserved what they thought they found there, whether it made sense or not. Modern translators, with a greater range of manuscripts to collate and a sharper suspicion of corruption and contamination, are quicker and more resourceful (sometimes more ruthless) to modify their text in the direction of coherence: Isaiah, chapter xv, for example, contains a unit which the Authorized Version calls "The burden of Moab," but which NEB titles "Moab: an oracle."

My heart shall cry out for Moab: his fugitives shall flee unto Zoar, an heifer of three years old: for by the mounting up of Luhith with weeping shall they	My heart cries out for Moab, whose nobles have fled as far as Zoar. On the ascent to Luhith men go up weeping;

go up it: for in the way of Horonaim   On the road to Horonaim there are
they shall raise up a cry of destruction.   cries of "Disaster!"

Isaiah xv, 5

The King James translators are disturbed by the heifer of three years old, and not unnaturally; the contorted syntax of the rest of the verse mirrors their distress. We can learn from Revised Standard what happened here:

My heart cries out for Moab; his fugitives flee to Zoar, to Eglath-shelishiyah.

The Authorized translators simply translated a place name; but the NEB, with its concern for neatness, threw the phrase out altogether. Again, we observe the fate of violent imagery when the prophet turns to denounce the misdeeds of Ephraim:

Woe to the crown of pride, to the drunkards of Ephraim, whose glorious beauty is a fading flower, which are on the head of the fat valleys of them that are overcome with wine!

Oh, the proud garlands of the drunkards of Ephraim
and the flowering sprays, so lovely in
their beauty,
on the heads of revellers dripping with
perfumes,
overcome with wine!

Isaiah, xxviii, 1

It may be that there is linguistic reason to convert those difficult "fat valleys" to "dripping with perfume"; certainly the effect, with most readers, will be to convert a grotesque and meaningless metaphor into a readily accessible and rather poetic image. As for the plural verb which the Authorized translators throw so joltingly into their version ("which *are* on the head of the fat valleys"), it is one more symptom of confusion and distress. Whatever the idiom may be in Hebrew, the plural verb apparently controlled by a singular pronoun can only yield dismay in English.

One reason that there are so many and such violent differences of judgment over Biblical translations is doubtless that people read the Bible in such a variety of different ways—as a text to be intoned or murmured privately, as a record to be critically investigated, as a legal document to be interpreted, and so on. And of course people who become familiar with one version early in life can hardly help feeling that all other versions are just parodies of that one, or incompetent efforts to reproduce it. (Among the curses of having a fairly good record library is that one gets used to the way Elizabeth Schwarz-kopf, say, sings Strauss *lieder,* and everyone else thereafter sounds wrong— as, in fact, they probably are, but their only cure is to be Elizabeth Schwarz-kopf.) Thus opinions polarize, and enthusiasts for one version barricade themselves behind a wall of horrible examples culled from the others. Actually, though, if one were to look at the two versions (Authorized and NEB) with relatively uncommitted eyes, it's by no means clear that one could even distinguish them over a short run, let alone establish a categorical superiority of either over the other. As an experiment, one might take that opening passage of Isaiah's Chapter lx which, in the King James version, Professor George Saintsbury pronounced vehemently to be the absolute high-water mark of English prose style.* Printing the King James version in the left-hand column and the modern version in the right, one doesn't feel that the page is radically out of balance.

1 Arise, shine; for thy light is come, and the glory of the Lord is risen upon thee.

Arise, Jerusalem, rise clothed in light, your light has come and the glory of the Lord shines over you.

2 For, behold, the darkness shall cover the earth, and gross darkness the people: but the Lord shall rise upon thee and His glory shall be seen upon thee.

For, though darkness covers the earth and dark night the nations, the Lord shall shine upon you and over you shall His glory appear;

3 And the Gentiles shall come to thy light, and kings to the brightness of thy rising.

and the nations shall march towards your light and their kings to your sunrise.

4 Lift up thine eyes round about, and see: all they gather themselves together, they come to thee: thy sons shall come from far, and thy daughters shall be nursed at thy side.

Lift up your eyes and look all around: they flock together, all of them, and come to you; your sons also shall come from afar, your daughters walking beside them leading the way.

5 Then thou shalt see, and flow together, and thine heart shall fear, and be enlarged; because the abundance of the sea shall be converted unto thee, the forces of the Gentiles shall come unto thee.

Then shall you see, and shine with joy, then your heart shall thrill with pride: the riches of the sea shall be lavished upon you and you shall possess the wealth of nations.

6 The multitude of camels shall cover thee, the dromedaries of Midian and Ephah; all they from Sheba shall come: they shall bring gold and incense; and they shall show forth the praises of the Lord.

Camels in droves shall cover the land, dromedaries of Midian and Ephah, all coming from Sheba laden with golden spice and frankincense, heralds of the Lord's praise.

7 All the flocks of Kedar shall be gathered together unto thee, the rams of Nebaioth shall minister unto thee: they shall come up with acceptance on mine altar, and I will glorify the house of my glory.

All Kedar's flocks shall be gathered for you, rams of Nebaioth shall serve your need, acceptable offerings on my altar, and glory shall be added to glory in my temple.

---

* *A History of English Prose Rhythm* (London, Macmillan, 1912), Chap. VI.

8   Who are these that fly as a cloud, and as the doves to their windows?

Who are these that sail along like clouds, that fly like doves to their dovecotes?

9   Surely the isles shall wait for me, and the ships of Tarshish first, to bring thy sons from far, their silver and their gold with them, unto the name of the Lord thy God, and to the Holy One of Israel, because He hath glorified thee.

They are vessels assembling from the coasts and islands, ships from Tarshish leading the convoy; they bring your sons from afar, their gold and their silver with them, to the honour of the Lord your God, the Holy One of Israel; for He has made you glorious.

10   And the sons of strangers shall build up thy walls, and their kings shall minister unto thee: for in my wrath I smote thee, but in my favor have I had mercy on thee.

Foreigners shall rebuild your walls and their kings shall be your servants; for though in my wrath I struck you down, now I have shown you pity and favour.

Reading the two versions over consecutively, it is not hard to sense that the rhythms of the King James version are a good deal stiffer and more repetitious than those of NEB. The specific contrasts don't by any means go all one way. Take verse 5: there is no doubt that "thrill with pride" is a cliché and a flat one; but "thy heart shall fear and be enlarged" is not very felicitous either—a modern reader will think of aneurysm. I have considerable difficulty in understanding the first phrase in the Authorized version of verse 9; that the isles (*which* isles?) shall wait for the Lord doesn't seem to connect with the procession led by the ships from Tarshish, nor is the relation of verse 9 to verse 8 a clear one. Finally, in verse 7, it seems very clear that "glory shall be added to glory in my temple" outdoes, not only in clarity but in ease and poise of assertion, "I will glorify the house of my glory."

The point of this little exercise is not that one version is categorically better than another; over a short haul, it's not easy to distinguish one from the other. Another consideration is that, in translating old books, as in restoring old paintings, a first problem confronting the workman is whether he's trying to get his finished product to look fresh or archaic. As a matter of practical fact, we distinguish one version from another by means of the "thee's" and "thou's," the "unto's," the "hath's." Discounting these differences, we are left with a certain archaic stiffness on the part of King James, a sort of suppleness on the part of NEB. Which comes closest to the "reality" of the original—a rendering of the passage as it may have appeared to its first viewers, or as it has now become to modern perceivers of an ancient original? We know for sure that the first hearers of Homer and Isaiah did not bring to the experience that antiquarian reverence which for us is inescapable; they may have brought, on the other hand, different sorts of reverence, for which our "modern" antiquarian feelings are a sort of equivalent.

Indeed, it is perfectly possible that nowadays certain "ultimate" feelings like reverence, nostalgia, or ecclesiastical devotion are only to be evoked by means of archaic language, though in Homer's day, or Isaiah's, they required no such specialized vocabulary.

These considerations apart, Homer and the Bible provide two different sorts of problem to the translator in search of equivalents. In Homer the problem is that of combining details into a sustained narrative, of carrying forward the action while getting into the substructure or periphery as many specific details and allegorical overtones as possible. The best Homeric translations, it appears, are able to cling to the hard specifics, but incorporate them in a strong, clear, and, above all, active sweep of assertion. The Bible too has its literal and symbolic levels of language, but the space between the two is wider, and the short-breathed paratactic sentences give no opportunity to insert details along a long arc of suspended syntax. The great dimensions of Biblical translation are vertical, so to speak; those of Homeric translation are horizontal. In both instances, we who are ignorant of the original can scarcely do with fewer than two translations, one taking the low road and one the high road—and more, we can be sure, wouldn't hurt.

CHAPTER IV

Transplanted Translations

When one translates Homer or the Bible, one assumes an automatic position of inferiority before the great works of the past; at every point, one is trying to reach up to the level of one's mighty original, to efface one's self in order to enhance the light of the ancient author. But translation can imply another relation entirely between original and imitator, may be a way for the translator to define his self, to assert his own distinct identity by showing the ways in which he is, and is not, like a "classic." During the Renaissance particularly it became common practice for poets to stitch translations into the midst of poems otherwise original. They aimed thereby at a variety of special effects, depending on the quantity of material translated, the faithfulness of the rendition, the public reputation of the original, and the openness with which obligation was acknowledged or the subtlety with which it was concealed. But the motive frequently declared itself in the decision to imitate precisely when the translator was declaring his personal artistic purpose.

On a very small scale the passing, subsurface translation may amount to little more than an allusion. When Milton warns us at the beginning of *Paradise Lost* that he is about to enter on new themes, "things unattempted yet in prose or rhyme," he is echoing Ariosto, who in the second stanza of the first canto of *Orlando Furioso* promises us "cosa non detta in prosa mai, ne in rima." The echo is an overtone which both affirms and modifies the poet's audacity. On the one hand, it says what Milton must very much have wanted to say ("there's never been a poem in the world like the one I have in mind"); on the other hand, it invites the knowing reader to recall that Ariosto thought himself original—and was—long before Milton wrote. This is very frequently the form taken by Milton's allusive translations, perhaps because he worked so consistently in traditional forms, into which he breathed fresh, individual strains of feeling. Thus he wanted readers to be conscious of both elements and their polarity; his allusions are made by words which simultaneously carry the poem forward and recall us to an earlier and perhaps remote perspective. In "Lycidas" we find the lines:

> Return, Alpheus, the dread voice is past
> That shrunk thy streams; return, Sicilian Muse. . . .

Milton is calling back the pastoral tradition, which has been in abeyance during Saint Peter's angry denunciation of the degenerate clergy. He invites Alpheus, the Arcadian stream, to flow again, and the Sicilian Muse (patroness of Theocritus, Sicilian by origin and the first great pastoral poet) to resume surveillance of his poem. We are returning to the vein of imagery and feeling with which the poem began. One can play with the notion that Alpheus, when he appears in line 132, is bobbing up in pursuit of Arethusa in line 84; the classic myth had it that he dived into the Ionian sea in pursuit of her, followed her underground all the way to Sicily, and there bubbled up through the spring of Arethusa, on the island of Ortygia, in Syracuse harbor. But the words "Sicilian Muse," through a translation, make another connection, which works in quite a different way. For the words hark back to a phrase with which Vergil announced his *departure* from the pastoral vein: "Sicelides Musae, paulo majora canamus." It is the first line of the Fourth Eclogue, devoted (as Milton and his age read it) to the same sort of prophetic religious truth as St. Peter's speech in "Lycidas." So that at the very moment, and in the very phrase with which Milton is inviting the pastoral muse back, he is reminding the reader that she has sometimes been dismissed for a time by the very greatest of pastoral poets. In describing and justifying the interruption of poetic tradition, he reaffirms its continuity.

In the very first lines of this inexhaustible poem, Milton has woven an allusion, in the form of a translation, which invites us to see the poem in a double focus:

> Yet once more, o ye laurels, and once more
> Ye myrtles brown, with ivy never sere. . . .

The "yet once more" here might be excessively egotistical if all it did were to assert that John Milton is about to write another poem. But it has a longer perspective, that is conveyed by the invocation of those traditional, mythologically rich evergreens. It reminds the reader of this poem that laments for lost shepherds have been written for a long time now, and specifically by Vergil, in the Second Eclogue, which, though it is a poem of love, not death, includes the lines:

> Et vos o lauri carpam, et te proxima myrte
> Sic positae quoniam suaves miscetis odores.

> And I shall pluck you, o laurels, and you, neighboring myrtle,
> since when placed side by side you mingle such sweet odors.

So that the laurels and myrtles which are appearing "yet once more," though they do imply that John Milton is going back to the well again (and "yet once more" has in fact been used as the title of a book about Milton's notable tendency to self-reproduction), also serve to place the poem they head within a long tradition of elegiac poems, poems about love and death.

Milton's allusions are subtle and private; they scarcely ruffle at all the surface of his poem, and one has to look at "Lycidas" through Vergilian-tinted glasses to make these phrases stand out in their true stereoscopic dimensions. Though I am not sure how noble a pleasure it is (there is something about reading poetry for its allusions which is like belonging to an "exclusive" key club—a lot of the pleasure comes from the sense of who is being excluded), still there is an undeniable pleasure in catching allusive subtleties on the fly. It is the swift economy of the transaction, combined with its complexity, that delights.

Much more public and ostentatious about its translational borrowings is Pierre Ronsard's famous poem "A Sa Lyre" (Odes, I, xxii), in which the poet, with characteristic Renaissance exuberance, glories that he has already become, in his youth, one of the famous literary lights of France. Indeed, he says, he has not hesitated to ransack antiquity in order to fit out a French lyre with the tones and melodies which are requisite to make it a noble instrument; and the very poem in which he makes this claim is itself an extraordinary patchwork of passages imitated from classical antiquity, chiefly Pindar and Horace. By printing Ronsard on the left and his sources on the right, we shall get a quick visual impression of the poet's debts to Thebes and Apulia:

Lyre dorée, où Phébus seulement	Golden lyre, held of Apollo in common
Et les neuf Soeurs ont part également,	possession
Le seul confort qui mes tristesses tue,	with the violet-haired Muses: the dance
Que la danse oit et toute s'évertue	steps, leaders of festival, heed you;
5 De t'obéir et mesurer ses pas	the singers obey your measures
Sous tes fredons mignardés par compas	when, shaken with music, you cast the
Lorsqu'en sonnant tu marques la ca-	beat to lead choirs of dancers.
dence	You have power to quench the speared
De l'avant-jeu, le guide de la danse,	thunderbolt
Le trait flambant de Jupiter s'éteint	of flowing fire. Zeus's eagle sleeps on
10 Sous ta chanson, si ta chanson l'atteint;	his staff, folding his quick wings
Et au caquet de tes cordes bien jointes	both ways to quiet,
Son aigle dort sur sa foudre à trois	lord of birds; you shed a mist on his
pointes,	hooked head,

---

4. oit = entend   8. l'avant-jeu = le prélude
6. par compas = en mesure

Abaissant l'aile; adonc tu vas charmant
Ses yeux aigus, et lui, en les fermant,
15 Son dos hérisse et ses plumes repousse,
Flatté du son de ta corde si douce.
　　Celui ne vit le cher mignon des dieux
A qui déplaît ton chant mélodieux,
Heureuse lyre, honneur de mon en-
　　fance!
20 Je te sonnai devant tous en la France
De peu à peu, car, quand premièrement
Je te trouvai, tu sonnais durement,
Tu n'avais fût ni cordes qui valussent
Ni qui répondre aux lois de mon doigt
　　pussent.
25 Moisi du temps, ton bois ne sonnait
　　point:
Lors j'eus pitié de te voir mal en point,
Toi qui jadis des grands rois les vi-
　　andes
Faisais trouver plus douces et friandes.
Pour te monter de cordes et d'un fût,
30 Voire d'un son qui naturel te fût
Je pillai Thèbe et saccageai la Pouille,
T'enrichissant de leur belle dépouille.
Lors par la France avec toi je chantai
Et jeune d'ans sur le Loir inventai
35 De marier aux cordes les victoires
Et des grands rois les honneurs et les
　　gloires.
　　Jamais celui que les belles chansons
Paissent, ravi de l'accord de tes sons,
Ne se doit voir en estime pour estre
40 Ou à l'escrime ou à la lutte adextre;
Ni marinier fortuneux ne sera,
Ni grand guerrier jamais n'abaissera
Par le harnais l'ambition des princes,
Portant, vainqueur, la foudre en leurs
　　provinces.
45 Mais ma Gatine et le haut crin des bois

dark and gentle closure of eyes; dream-
　　ing, he ripples
his lithe back, bound in spell
of your waves.

Pindar, First Pythian, tr.
Richmond Lattimore

Quem tu, Melpomene, semel
　　Nascentem placido lumine videris,
Illum non labor Isthmius
　　Clarabit pugilem, non equus impiger
Curru ducet Achaico
　　Victorem, neque res bellica Deliis
Ornatum foliis ducem,
　　Quod regum tumidas contuderit
　　　minas.
Ostendet Capitolio;
　　Sed quae Tibur aquae fertile prae-
　　　fluunt,

---

13. adonc = alors
17. vit = est (du verbe "vivre")
31. Thèbe, ville de Pindar; Pouille, province
　　d'Horace, i.e., Apulie

38. paissent = nourissent
40. adextre = adroit
45. ma Gatine = la forêt de Gatine

Qui vont bornant mon fleuve vendô-
　mois,
Le dieu bouquin qui la Neufaune en-
　tourne
Et le saint choeur qui en Braye sé-
　journe
Le feront tel que par tout l'univers
50　Se connaîtra renommé par ses vers
Tant il aura de grâces en son pouce
Et de fredons, fils de sa lyre douce.
　　Déjà, mon luth, ton loyer tu reçois
Et jà déjà la race des François
55　Me veut nombrer entre ceux qu'elle
　loue
Et pour son chantre heureusement
　m'avoue.
O Calliope, ô Cleion, ô les soeurs
Qui de ma Muse animez les douceurs,
Je vous salue et resalue encore,
60　Par qui mon prince et mon pays j'ho-
　nore.
　　Par toi je plais et par toi je suis lu,
C'est toi qui fais que Ronsard soit élu
Harpeur français et, quand on le ren-
　contre,
Qu'avec le doigt par la rue on le mon-
　tre;
65　Si je plais donc, si je sais contenter,
Si mon renom la France veut chanter,
Si de mon front les étoiles je passe,
Certes, mon luth, cela vient de ta grâce.

Et spissae nemorum comae
　Fingent Aeolio carmine nobilem.
Romae principis urbium
　Dignatur suboles inter amabiles
Vatum ponere me choros
　Et iam dente minus mordeor invido.
O testudinis aureae
　Dulcem quae strepitum, Pieri, tem-
　peras,
O mutis quoque piscibus
　Donatura cycni, si libeat, sonum,
Totum muneris hoc tuist,
　Quod monstror digito praetereun-
　tium
Romanae fidicen lyrae:
Quod spiro et placeo, si placeo, tuumst.

Quodsi me lyricis vatibus inseris,
Sublimi feriam sidera vertice.
　　　　Horace, Carmina IV,iii and I,i

Translated below:
　　　　　　The man, Melpo-
mene, on whose birth you once look
with favor, may not make himself famous boxing at the Isthmian games, or
drive tireless horses to victory in a
Greek chariot race; perhaps his warlike
deeds won't earn him a palm wreath
on the Capitol for having repelled the
haughty aggressions of kings. But the
streams that flow before fruitful Tibur,
and the thick tufts of leafy groves shall
weave his name into an Aeolian song.

---

47. entourner = rôder autour
53. loyer = récompense

54. jà déjà = comme le latin jamjam

Thus the sons of Rome, chief of cities, have been kind enough to place me in the choir of poets; and now I suffer less from the sharp tooth of envy. O you Pierian Muses, who govern the sweet tones of the golden shell—you who could endow mute fishes with the song of the swan if you wanted to— all this is your gift to me, that I'm pointed out by the finger of the passer-by, as the bard of the Roman lyre: that I breathe, that I please (if I do) is your doing.

If you include me among the lyric poets, with head raised high I shall strike the stars.

There is a pleasant irony in that the chief passage where Ronsard is (in our modern sense) "original" is that in which he explicitly professes his debt to antiquity. Lines 21–28 of the French poem may indeed owe something to Horace, Carmina III, xi, where a phrase describes the lyre as having once been neither tuneful nor pleasant, but adds that now, thanks to Mercury, it is welcome at temples and at rich men's feasts. It would be agreeable enough if Ronsard had had in mind this tribute to the patron saint of thieves, but the resemblances are scarcely striking enough to record. And in any event, it would be more in line with the symmetry of the poem to have it begin with Pindar and end with Horace, enclosing a little bit of original Ronsard in between.

Given that he makes no secret at all of his borrowings, what does Ronsard gain by the presence of Pindar and Horace? Most obviously, a justification of poetry which cannot be dismissed as the special pleading of a parvenu or an opportunist. Ronsard, though an innovator in France, urges by the very process of his imitations that he is restoring to the lyre powers which in civilizations of unimpeachable dignity it once had. His aim is wholly conservative. The poet neither has nor aspires to powers beyond the limits of his art; and those limits are, as the adaptation from Horace deliberately indicates, pastoral rather than imperial. Poets aim at no practical power, and Ronsard is even more modest than Horace. His carefully chosen French equivalents for the Latin poet's literary landscape (the "forêt de Gatine," "fleuve vendômoise," "Neufaune," and the "saint choeur qui en Braye séjourne") all have a deliberately provincial and reductive tone. Ronsard claims to be only a mock Horace, as France is a mimic Rome; while Horace mentions Tibur, a fashionable summer resort in which emperors had villas, Ronsard's "forêt de Gatine" is humble enough to be almost parodic. Proportions conserved, if Charles IX is going to have a Horace, it will evidently have to be Ronsard. Thus, for all the modesty of the poet's powers and pretensions in practical matters, his art can be in its own sphere sublime and eternal, raising both poet and patron to the stars. And in this way the last little snippet from Horace brings us back to the original, eaglelike perspectives of Pindar, having passed through a humility which may be mock, but never allows us to forget that good poets can make big things out of little ones.*

A less personal but no less interesting translation-in-passing is that in which Spenser, at the heart of Acrasia's bower of bliss (Book II, Canto xii, stanzas 74, 75), reverts to a song composed by Tasso for a remarkably talented bird to sing, in *Gerusalemme Liberata,* at the heart of the garden of Armida (Canto XVI, stanzas 14 and 15). The song is framed, in Spenser's British lay, by a galaxy of words like "false," "sorcery," "witchcraft," "wanton," "lewd," "lascivious," "licentious," and "lust," so there's not much chance of mistaking the author's moral stance: the texts of the song, in original and translation, compare as follows:

The whiles someone did chant this
  lovely lay:
"Ah see, who so fair thing dost fain to
  see,
In springing flower the image of thy
  day;
Ah see the virgin rose, how sweetly she
Doth first peep forth with bashful
  modesty,
That fairer seems the less ye see her
  may;
Lo see soon after, how more bold and
  free
Her barèd bosom she doth broad display;
Lo see soon after, how she fades and
  falls away.

"So passeth in the passing of a day
Of mortal life the leaf, the bud, the
  flower,
No more doth flourish after first decay,

"Deh mira," egli cantò, "spuntar la
  rosa
dal verde suo modesta e verginella,
che mezzo aperta ancóra, e mezzo ascosa,
quanto si mostra men, tanto è piú bella.
Ecco poi nudo il sen già baldanzosa
dispiega: ecco poi langue, e non par
  quella,
quella non par, che desïata avanti
fu da mille donzelle e mille amanti.

"Così trapassa al trapassar d'un giorno
de la vita mortale il fiore e 'l verde;
né perché faccia indietro april ritorno,
si rinfiora ella mai, né si rinverde.
Cogliam la rosa in su'l mattino adorno

---

* It is interesting to parallel Ronsard's adaptation of Pindar's First Pythian with Thomas Gray's use of the same original in "The Progress of Poesy." Both later poets coöpt Pindar to represent the power and majesty of the lyric tradition, but Ronsard accepts a "political" heritage as well, as the national poet of praise and blame. For him Pindar and Horace are natural allies in defining the new world of public poetry in France. But for Gray the tradition is strictly literary, and the past as much a reproach as an inspiration. It is the presence of the mediating present, Ronsard's exuberant acceptance of his real milieu, that makes his use of the past the reverse of nostalgic.

That erst was sought to deck both bed
  and bower
Of many a lady and many a paramour.
Gather, therefore, the rose whilst yet is
  prime,
For soon comes age that will her pride
  deflower.
Gather the rose of love whilst yet is
  time,
Whilst loving thou mayst lovèd be
  with equal crime."

di questo dí, che tosto il seren perde;
cogliam d'amor la rosa: amiamo or
  quando
esser si puote rïamato amando."

Both Tasso and *his* original, Catullus,* play along the delicate balance of feelings about growing old and staying desirable—a balance which indicates that by loving we forfeit that innocence which makes us desirable—but that it was given us only to be lost, and can't be better lost than in mutual enjoyment, *and right now*. Spenser imposes several notable changes on his original. He does full justice to the modesty of the virgin rose; but, in the first of his notable departures, he omits the "mille donzelle e mille amanti" whom Tasso took over from Catullus's "multi pueri . . . multae puellae," putting them off to lines 4 and 5 of the second stanza. But Spenser does more than defer their appearance, he changes their function, making them, instead of sexual wooers of the rose, esthetes busy decking an apartment for some very indefinite encounter between "many a lady and many a paramour." Tasso's beautiful cadence,

> e non par quella,
> quella non par, che desïata avanti
> fu . . .

---

* Catullus, Carmina lxii:

Ut flos in saeptis secretus nascitur hortis,
ignotus pecori, nullo contusus aratro,
quem mulcent aurae, firmat sol, educat imber;
multi illum pueri, multae optavere puellae;
idem cum tenui carptus defloruit ungui,
nulli illum pueri, nullae optavere puellae;
sic virgo, dum intacta manet, dum cara suis
  est.
cum castum amisit polluto corpore florem,
nec pueris iucunda manet nec cara puellis.
Hymen o Hymenaee, Hymen ades o Hymenaee.

(As the flower is born, hidden in a secret garden, unknown to the crowd, never bruised by the plow, and grows amid gentle breezes, sunshine, and rain, so that many boys love her and many girls as well; but when she is cut down, plucked by a slender finger, then no boys love her nor any girls: so the untouched virgin is dear to her friends, but when she loses the flower of her chastity, the purity of her body, she no longer pleases the boys nor is dear to the girls. Hymen o Hymenaee, be with us, Hymen o Hymenaee.)

The verse is part of a dialogue; it is sung by the girls, and the boys answer with a verse arguing that the vine is fruitless and undesired when alone, but fruitful when married to the elm, and so prized.

  Also in the background are Poliziano, *Stanze* I, 78 ff., and Ariosto, *Orlando Furioso* I, stanzas 42–44.

thus fades into the flat statement of Spenser's first alexandrine. Virginity for Spenser is solitary, he doesn't think of it flourishing amid "mille donzelle" (all jealous) and "mille amanti" (all hotly desirous); and the loss inflicted by time is not, therefore, the loss of those admirers, it is a fading and falling away which is made explicit in the second stanza by the word "decay." The flower and the leaf of mortal life, says Tasso, don't renew themselves any more than April, once past, can be repeated; but "first decay" sees death already at the heart of the budding rose. And the two other strong words that Spenser introduces, "deflower" and "crime" complete the darkening of the picture. In a pun worthy of Marvell, old age "deflowers" the rose; and the point of loving equally is not to get pleasure from giving it, but to share the guilt. The total direction of these various changes is to lighten the sexuality of nature, making the rose in its innocent state more innocent, but darkening, and rendering more ultimate, its fall. We knew before that Spenser was a chiaroscuro author, fond of glittering highlights and somber blacks; his dealing with Tasso's little poem confirms this quality of his vision.

Why, then, if he was going to change the tone of Tasso's poem so markedly, did Spenser copy it at all? A first effect of the stylized song is to draw a veil over action which is already as sexy as Spenser's decent British temper will endure. Much in the manner of Volpone's song to Celia, which estheticizes an attempted rape, a piece of Catullus here represents passionate erotic sentiment, but formalized in an art form and more than a millennium and a half old. Tasso is also appropriate, because Spenser wanted his reader, just when the Bower of Bliss was at its most seductive, to think of the analogous situation in Armida's garden, where Rinaldo lies oblivious to his military duty. Spenser's story gives us no occasion to think of Verdant as neglectful of his responsibilities; he has stacked his arms indeed, but we have no real sense of an actual task in which he would have used them. The recollection of Tasso gives us the overtone that the redemption of Jerusalem itself and the triumph of our holy faith are being held up by the knight's dereliction. As a result, we may feel less distress at the rigor of those wayfaring, warfaring Christians, Guyon and his Palmer, when they proceed at the end of the canto ruthlessly to rip apart the Bower of Bliss.

A last consideration is simpler. The description of Acrasia's garden, deeply rooted as it is in the Homeric garden of Alcinous and the enchanted islands of Circe and Calypso, is a beautiful and richly eclectic piece of writing. Garden descriptions tend naturally to become *florilegia*—elaborate comparisons, direct and indirect, with other famous gardens, as for a climactic example, in Milton's description of Eden. Thus nature could be described through the artifice of literature and the marriage of both celebrated. In fact, Spenser took over from Tasso a stanza celebrating precisely this marriage (*FQ* II, xii, 59: *GL* XVI, 10) which Tasso had laboriously and ingeniously constructed out of Ovid (*Met.* III, 157 ff.). Mr. C. S. Lewis, a latter-day Puritan in episcopal clothing, would persuade us that this wedding of art and nature in the Bower of Bliss should be read as an indictment of the whole place as false and unnatural. There are plenty of such denunciations elsewhere (none more pointed and conscious than II, xii, 83); one might want to keep an open attitude here toward a process which seems to be the process of the poem itself.

But no English author is so adept in managing this sort of flimflam as Shakespeare, who took care to introduce a translation (or at least a paraphrase of a translation) into *Antony and Cleopatra* Act II, where it serves to enrich, deride, authenticate, and entangle the otherwise rather heavy-footed Roman business of the act. Indeed, Shakespeare got the entire fable of his play from Plutarch (as translated by North from Amyot's French)—not only its outlines, but hints for many of the lesser characters, episodes, and some actual phrases of the dialogue. But there is no such extended passage of close paraphrase as that in which Enobarbus describes, for a couple of admiring Roman colleagues, the first meeting of Antony and Cleopatra at Tarsus on the river Cydnus. Even this framing of the passage is so skillfully tendentious as to invite a moment's comment. In the first part of the scene, "downright" Enobarbus (who has, in Plutarch, no name and only a shadowy existence) has been present at the diplomatic negotiations in which Antony's marriage with Octavia is arranged; his free and cynical comments on the unctuous professions there put forth establish his position with the audience as a knowing, natural fellow, who will tell the truth. Maecenas, who is glad that the business of the meeting between the great men is "so well digested," has evidently been reading Plutarch too; for he asks Enobarbus if that story is right about extraordinary feastings in Egypt. Eight wild boars roasted and only twelve people to eat them! It is clear that the Roman imagination dwells upon such gluttonous gut-stuffing as the sublime of decadent debauchery. But Enobarbus has been in Egypt, where nature far outdoes the Roman fancy—and, not without the relish of a man with an inside story to tell, he begins:

(She resolved) to take her barge in the river of Cydnus, the poope whereof was of gold, the sailes of purple, and the owers of silver, which kept stroke in rowing after the sounde of the musicke of flutes, howboyes, citherns, violls, and such other instruments as they played upon in the barge. And now for the person of her selfe: she was layed under a pavillion of cloth of gold of tissue, apparelled and attired like the goddesse Venus, commonly	I will tell you. The barge she sat in, like a burnish'd throne Burn'd on the water: the poop was beaten gold; Purple the sails, and so perfumed that The winds were love-sick with them; the oars were silver, Which to the tune of flutes kept stroke, and made The water which they beat to follow faster,

drawen in picture: and hard by her, on either hand of her, pretie faire boyes apparelled as painters doe set forth god Cupide, with little fannes in their handes, with the which they fanned wind upon her. Her ladies and gentlewomen also, the fairest of them were apparelled like the nymphes Nereides (which are the mermaides of the waters) and like the Graces, some stearing the helme, others tending the tackle and ropes of the barge, out of the which there came a wonderfull passing sweet savor of perfumes, that perfumed the wharfes side, pestered with innumerable multitudes of people. Some of them followed the barge all alongest the rivers side: others also ranne out of the citie to see her comming in. So that in thend, there ranne such multitudes of people one after an other to see her, that Antonius was left post alone in the market place, in his Imperiall seate to geve audience.

As amorous of their strokes. For her own person,
It beggar'd all description: she did lie
In her pavilion—cloth of gold, of tissue—
O'er-picturing that Venus where we see
The fancy outwork nature. On each side her,
Stood pretty dimpled boys, like smiling Cupids,
With divers-colour'd fans, whose wind did seem
To glow the delicate cheeks which they did cool,
And what they undid did.
Agr.   O, rare for Antony!
Eno. Her gentlewomen, like the Nereides,
So many mermaids, tended her i' the eyes,
And made their bends adornings. At the helm
A seeming mermaid steers: the silken tackle
Swell with the touches of those flower-soft hands,
That yarely frame the office. From the barge
A strange invisible perfume hits the sense
Of the adjacent wharfs. The city cast
Her people out upon her; and Antony,
Enthron'd i' the market-place, did sit alone,
Whistling to the air; which, but for vacancy,
Had gone to gaze on Cleopatra too,
And made a gap in nature.

In passing, we note that where an animating image lifts the level of the speech, or a flourish of fanciful energy opens it out, the source is generally Shakespeare. Instead of telling us that Cleopatra had a gilt barge, he says that it "burn'd on the water." That the sails were perfumed as well as purple, so that "the winds were love-sick with them" is Shakespeare's addition; so is the assertion that the water, adoring her rowers' oars, became "amorous of their strokes." (Masochistic water! a fine conceit.) Especially in depicting the lady sailors, Shakespeare plays the roughness of the work against the delicate sexuality of the workers: there's not-very-latent intercourse in the tackle swelling under those flower-soft hands "that yarely frame the office"—the phrase says they perform a seaman's task and perform it well, but "framing the office" is vague enough to accommodate another sort of preparation as well. The thronging out of the people is reduced from North's two weak phrases to a single active one,

> The city cast
> Her people out upon her—

the first "her" being necessary because Shakespeare didn't yet have an "its" to work with, but "her" also because *urbs* is a feminine noun (we're never, in fact, told by the play what city was involved, and are likely to think it Alexandria out of sheer audience inertia), and finally because the supreme tribute to a lady's attire is given only by another lady. Thus, the maliciously developed picture of Antony, the confident, authoritative male reduced to absurdity by female elegance, is reserved for the end, where it can lead us to generalize on our sense that Rome is a man's world, Egypt a woman's— that Rome is a world of land, Egypt a world of water (Antony's veterans will warn him against fighting by sea, when they are accustomed to fight and win on dry land)—that Antony in Egypt is trusting himself to an alien and treacherous element, which yet yields rewards of delight beyond any that prudent, practical, masculine Romans can even imagine.

The first point of Enobarbus' speech, and an obvious reason for using Plutarch so directly in it, is to gain historical authenticity at what looks like a supreme moment of romantic fantasy. "Rome"—i.e., two English actors labeled "Maecenas" and "Agrippa"—is on stage before us; they are devotees of the gut and the groin very much like the Elizabethan audience (as Shakespeare defines it in this play) of gross mechanics. In effect, they are lewdness and prudence; while voluble, ingratiating Enobarbus is, in terms of a parallel, the poet himself. At the moment when his story most amazes the gaping Roman listeners, and the still more widely gaping Wat and Giles in the pit, because it's past the shape of dreaming (their dreaming)—at that point, it is to Shakespeare's interest that we be reminded that we read this story somewhere before, in a history book. Thus the play's biggest theme is fulfilled, that the imagination is more real than mere reality; and Enobarbus, who acquired our trust as a downright truthteller, serves as a peephole opening momentarily on a world far richer than anything in Rome or London or the sphere of practical sense. It is just one more duplicity in Shakespeare's assertion of his superior authority that Plutarch can be invoked as authentic because he is seen through the eyes of imagination. I think one can feel, behind the very closeness with which his verse follows the prose of North-Amyot-Plutarch a kind of Shakespearean derision—"with only a touch of imagination, look what this image can become!"

At its most naïve, stitching a snippet of someone else's admired original into one's own homespun can be not only a confession of incompetence but a shortcut to patchwork. By softening and disguising the procedure, by clouding the attitudes involved in it, the translating imitator maintains a certain vertical distance above what is, if closely considered, not much better than petty larceny. Pope, for example, had the highest admiration for Sarpedon's great speech to Glaucus in the twelfth Iliad (371 ff.); he admired just as warmly his own translation of that speech. For that very reason, when he chose to adapt it for use as Clarissa's speech to Belinda in the second version of *The Rape of the Lock,* he was careful to soften and blur the points of resemblance. The verbal parallels are few and not particularly striking; what Pope did retain was the rhetorical and logical structure, a feeling of the passage's rhythm. And, much as he admired it, his attitude toward the speech in its final mock-heroic incarnation is predominantly derisive. The more we are aware of its heroic originals, the more comic it seems. For adapting such a speech from its original to its ultimate circumstances is really an act of dominance over Homer, a miniature rape. From beginning to end, *The Rape of the Lock* is busy compressing heroic amplitude into miniature equivalents while retaining the original shapes. To cut Sarpedon's statement of the warrior's creed down to a housewife's profession of good humor is such an exercise of power. Yet in its own right, Clarissa's speech is a proper comment on the poem's actors and action; though it's perhaps too sensible to end the poem effectively, and is therefore subordinate to another climax, it gathers a lot of moral feeling into a perfectly worthy formula. The derision enters only when we are aware of what lies in the background.

Pope is particularly expert at this business of making a minimal, an almost contemptuous allusion to some peripheral point of an original. What he achieves thereby, though he generally calls it an "imitation," seems to merit some other name—it isn't even a "parody" but more like a game of allusive tag. For example, in his imitation of the first satire of Horace's second book, Pope follows Horace into the not very complex thought that "Different people have different tastes in amusement." Horace illustrates the commonplace from mythology:

> Castor gaudet equis, ovo prognatus eodem
> Pugnis. . . .

Castor is mad for horses, his brother, born of the same egg, is a boxer. . . .

Pope twists the passage into a sneer at Lord Hervey, retaining nothing more of Leda's egg than a catch phrase for the private amusement of those who know their Horace:

> A boy Lord Fanny loves, a wench his brother,
> Like in all else, as one egg to another.

The English egg here is rather a triumph, after all; simply by being present, it triumphs over the strangeness of the mythological story. It doesn't parody

Horace in any degree, or add malice to the mention of Hervey, it simply uses the same word, touching off the very minimum reverberation of a parallel. It is so gratuitous that Pope, when he rewrote the passage to adapt it to another set of enemies, could retain the egg unchanged:

> Fox loves the senate, Hockley Hole his brother,
> Like in all else, as one egg to another.

In the sense that it's a game played for the sake of its arbitrary difficulties, Pope's dealing with Horace in this poem is like a parody of parody—the shape of the parallel has to be preserved without any of the reason for it. Indeed, the more ingeniously Horace's irrelevancies are preserved while his central point is perverted or obscured, the more successful Pope's game must be judged.

Another instance of the same nature comes up in the same poem in connection with the theme of public poetry. Horace is advised by his friend Trebatius that he might win favor at court with a few poems on the military triumphs of the regime, but he demurs:

> cupidum, pater optime, vires
> deficiunt: neque enim quivis horrentia pilis
> agmina nec fracta pereuntis cuspide Gallos
> aut labentis equo describit volnera Parthi.*

Pope turns the idea of military poetry into sneers at Sir Richard Blackmore and Eustace Budgel, while saving the horse of Horace's last line for a Parthian shot at George II's equitation:

> What? like Sir Richard, rumbling, rough, and fierce,
> With ARMS, and GEORGE, and BRUNSWICK crowd the verse?
> Rend with tremendous sound your Ears asunder
> With Gun, Drum, Trumpet, Blunderbuss, and Thunder?
> Or nobly wild, with Budgel's fire and force,
> Paint Angels trembling round his falling Horse?

He has of course turned Horace's wounded and dying enemy upside down; fat, ungainly George II is the object of heavenly solicitude because of his own inept horsemanship. But a horse there is, in Pope as in Horace. The parallel is a parallel only in that it involves the same prop. Horace has faded to the remotest shadow of a pretext. The counterpoint of parody with original has been attenuated to the status of a Cheshire cat—a disembodied grin, without any feline attached to it. One couldn't ask for a better instance of adaptive translation as an act of conquest and domination; Pope has practically posed himself with his foot on Horace's lolling, lifeless neck.

---

* I'd like to, dear friend, but I'm not up to it; it's not everyone who can describe battle-formations bristling with javelins, Gauls perishing on their broken lances, the wounded Parthian falling from his horse.)

CHAPTER V

The Low and the Lofty

❧

A classic problem exercising eighteenth-century translators of the *Iliad* is presented by a passage in Book XI, where Ajax, sullenly retreating before masses of menacing Trojans, is compared to an intruding ass being driven out of a field by a crowd of boys. Pope invokes a good deal of circumlocutory tact in handling this passage, with the aim of preserving the dignity of the hero:

> In some wide Field by Troops of Boys pursu'd,
> As the slow Beast with heavy Strength indu'd,
> Tho' round his Sides a wooden Tempest rain,
> Crops the tall Harvest, and lays waste the Plain;
> Thick on his Hide, the hollow Blows resound,
> The patient Animal maintains his Ground,
> Scarce from the Field with all their Efforts chas'd,
> And stirs but slowly when he stirs at last.
> On *Ajax* thus a Weight of *Trojans* hung,
> The Strokes redoubled on his Buckler rung.
>
> (682–691)

There can be no question that Ajax is here being compared to a donkey; but Pope creeps up on the similitude with infinite precaution. "The slow Beast with heavy Strength indu'd" could perfectly well be an ox or even a plow horse. It is only through the "patient Animal" that he is definitely, though still allusively, identified with the donkey. Homer is perfectly literal and matter-of-fact about the word; ὄνος is the unadorned, vulgar phrase for donkey or ass (XI, 558), and Pope's artful elegance in dodging the direct English equivalent may seem like an effort to lend artificial dignity to his author. But in fact the translator has made no effort to gloss over his problem; he has explained it, at considerable length, in a footnote, and his argument is not that he is trying to improve on his author, but that he is trying to be faithful to the original intent. In English, for a modern reader, the connotations of "ass" or "donkey" are strongly comic; the animal is known for laziness, stubbornness, stupidity, recalcitrance, and the humble tasks to which it is assigned. But in Homer's time it was not so; and Pope cites Mme. Dacier in evidence that in those days the ass "was a Beast upon which Kings and Princes might be seen with Dignity," and that Jacob, in blessing his children, is made by Scripture itself to say that "Issachar shall be as a strong Ass." To these arguments for the basic dignity of the passage, Pope adds some others of his own. Eustathius, who wrote a commentary on Homer strongly defending his author's taste wherever it was impugned, says nothing at all about this passage—a fact which is presumed to show that in antiquity the simile was not felt to be improper or undignified. Furthermore, the immediate context shows no sign that Homer intended Ajax's behavior to be thought comic or unheroic. Quite the contrary; Hector himself is shown to be fearful of encountering Ajax again, and the Greek hero gives way before his enemies only because Zeus himself casts terror into his heart. Just before he is compared to an errant, hungry ass under attack from boys, he is compared to a lion being assailed by a circle of dogs and farmers. Thus, the argument runs, the comparison of Ajax with an ass carries for Homer few grotesque or comic overtones, such as customarily attach to the comparison in modern English; and the translator, in seeking an equivalent, is bound to avoid such overtones. Pope might therefore be expected to take a dim view of a modern translator like W.H.D. Rouse, who accepts gratefully the comic aspects of Ajax in confusion and the Trojans in terror of him, putting them very much in evidence:

> You may have seen a stubborn ass in a cornfield, who is too much for the boys. They may break many sticks on his back, but he goes on cropping the corn; they beat away with their sticks, but what is the strength of a child! They can hardly drive him out when he has eaten all he wants. So the crowds of Trojans hung upon the heels of mighty Aias, poking his shield with their poles all the time.

Indeed, Pope is not above adding touches of wit to the poem himself; the "wooden Tempest" raining on the sides of the ass evidently vents a sense of the grotesque, but it is directed against the ass, not the hero. Boileau, who is not above using his Greek as a club against a Greekless opponent (Perrault), pushes the point even further, and by undertaking to defend the ass as well as the hero puts the cause of both in doubt:

> On voit donc par là le peu de sens de ces critiques modernes, qui veulent juger du grec sans savoir de grec, et qui, ne lisant Homère que dans des

traductions latines très-basses, ou dans des traductions françoises encore plus rampantes, imputent à Homère les bassesses de ses traducteurs. . . . Ces messieurs doivent savoir que les mots des langues ne répondent toujours juste les uns aux autres, et qu'un terme grec très-noble ne peut souvent être exprimé en françois que par un terme très-bas.

Oeuvres de Boileau (Paris, 1873), III, 378.°

The generalizations are splendid in their assurance; but they have carried Boileau into several very doubtful particulars. That the Greek word for "ass" is one of resonant dignity will be hard for anyone to maintain who simply looks up in Liddell and Scott the range of usage cited there. ὄνος is used repeatedly in proverbs illustrating stupidity, loudness, stubbornness, ugliness, laborious indignity, and various other disagreeable qualities. These passages are all post-Homeric, to be sure, and weak evidence of Homer's intent, since the reputation of the ass may have sunk with time. But in fact the Homeric age hardly discussed donkeys at all, and Homer nowhere else except in *Iliad* XI, 558. So how to judge the word's tone? Eustathius does not discuss the passage at all, and perhaps his silence is evidence, as Pope suggested, that antiquity saw little to question in it. On the other hand, the Homeric scholiast denominated "B" discusses it, though not without ambiguity. He says that Homer did well to compare Ajax to an ass, not as the ass is a beast of burden, but as it is ungainly, powerful, and accustomed to blows. In other words, he gives little overt attention to the highness or lowness of the image, but only to its accuracy. Yet he defends it; and that may imply some sense that it needs defence—on what level is not explicit. The most we can say is that serious questions exist about the tone of the central word used by Homer to describe Ajax; and Boileau, though he knows Greek, is really no better judge of this question than a man who doesn't.

Wider and more important than any question involving the word ὄνος is the general matter of Homeric *noblesse*. Did the poet try to represent his heroes as *chevaliers sans peur et sans reproche?* Did their bravery and skill on the field of battle preclude ungainliness and stupidity? It is curious that the man compared with an ass is Ajax, who in post-Homeric mythology degenerated so thoroughly into a mindless plugugly—as Shakespeare, for example, represents him. But perhaps this very comparison was responsible for his later degeneration. In the *Iliad* itself, though by no means as sharp or imaginative as Ulysses, he is not made remarkable for stupidity. Hector calls him, to be sure, an "inarticulate ox" (Lattimore) or a "blundering lout" (Rouse), but these are battlefield insults (XIII, 824). The presence of Zeus

---

° This makes clear the absurdity of those modern critics who pretend to pass judgment on Greek without knowing any, and who, because they read Homer only in Latin translations of a low order, or in even more groveling French versions, lay to Homer's account all the vulgarities of his translators. . . . These gentlemen ought to be told that the same words in different languages are not always of equal force, and that often a very noble Greek word can only be expressed in French by a very humble word.

in the near proximity of the ass comparison raises further problems. If Zeus as all-powerful father of the gods is personally intervening in mortal affairs and casting a literal cloud over Ajax's mind, it is no disgrace for the hero to be confused; but if Zeus's cloud is a euphemism for Ajax's own mental incapacities (as we sometimes feel the presence of Athena in a particular scene to be simply a way of accounting for Odysseus' quick wit), then we must assume something is being said about the state of Ajax's intellectuals that isn't altogether complimentary.

Largely speaking, there seems no way to maintain seriously that Homer's notions of *noblesse* corresponded even approximately with M. Boileau's. The Iliadic heroes (like their gods, for that matter) gorge, lecher, murder, loot, and squabble without bringing into question their own heroic characters or the grandeur of their enterprise. Theirs is a terrible enterprise but a noble one; Homer's broadness of vision was quite capable of seeing Ajax as a warrior of great courage and simplicity of heart, strong to endure blows as to give them, but capable of being stunned and bewildered by the very multiplicity of his enemies, and behaving under these circumstances like a large awkward animal at bay. The metaphor is hardly "funny," but it isn't "noble" either, as the comparison with the Biblical metaphor suggests that it is. Rather, it is very much in the modern taste in its realism and strength; perhaps that is the best argument for a translation here that breaks a few of the heroic decorums—without that verbal violence we would not get the full sense of men in battle, where they do not comport themselves, customarily, with the poise and esthetic assurance of marble statues.* Literary

---

* A handy six-language compendium of the *Iliad*, published at Florence in 1837, gives (in addition to Pope) the following renderings of the crucial passage:

Ut vero asinus in arvum praevalet pueris,   C. G. Heyne into Latin prose

Ac veluti, pueris nequidquam obstantibus, arvum
Ingressus tarda quadrupes de gente rudentum,   R. Arnich into Latin verse

                    E quale interno
Ad un pigro somier, che nelle messe
Si ficcò, s'arrabattano i fanciulli,   V. Monti into Italian

Wie wenn am Feld' ein Esel geführt obsieget den Knaben,   Voss into German

Ou tel cet animal, à qui Cybèle avare
Abandonne à regret un chardon maigre et rare
Dans un champ, couronné des présens de Cérès,
S'est enfoncé; sa faim dévaste les guérets.
Vainement sur son corps des enfants avec rage
Brisent leur bois noueux. . . .   Aignon into French

Cual asno tarde, á quien pueril caterva
Echar procura del sembrado fértil
Con repetidos golpes. . . .   Garcia-Malo into Spanish

The German and Spanish translators seem perfectly at home with the metaphor; Latin prose absorbs it easily, but in verse it is felt to require dignified circumlocution. The French translation elocutionizes the ass out of existence, and Monti, in Italian, faces the fact, but takes the edge off it by using the relatively obsolete form "somier" instead of the vulgar "asino."

nobility, in a word, may be weakened by appearing too effortless and un-flawed; the noble image, like the noble hero, must have something gritty and powerful to dominate; it is narrowed, not exalted, by being made too smoothly successful. Given the general aim of the metaphor, the unfamiliar-ity of modern readers with farm animals, and the possibility of confusing donkeys, asses, and burros, conceivably a solution for a twentieth-century translator might be found in the deliberate inaccuracy of a "mule."

But it is never safe to modulate one's author into another tone, particu-larly a higher one; trying to make him seem better than he wanted to be is a first step toward looking foolish oneself. Inevitably we smile at a translator who has committed himself to a "noble" style and then finds something in his author that doesn't live up to that nobility. Perhaps we secretly, instinc-tively sympathize with the author against the translator—he being as genuine as we are, while the translator is a mere secondhand word-artificer. Or per-haps it is just a matter of the portentous, top-hatted banker slipping on a banana peel and falling on his prat. In any event, the problem is not one which time has outworn. André Gide, translating *Hamlet,* clearly found the lucidity and abstraction of his native tongue drawing him away to a level of diction well above Shakespeare's turbid imagery. A classic instance of his difficulty may be found in that passage (I, 2) where Hamlet turns on his mother's use of the word "seems" with a sharp rebuke: "Seems, madam! Nay, it is; I know not *seems.*" Here the clean Cartesian dichotomies of M. Gide's native idiom betray him into a famous flounder: "Apparence? Eh! non, madame! Réalité. Qu'ai-je affaire avec le 'paraître'?" Evidently, it's the assurance and sharpness of the "apparence-réalité" dichotomy that make Gide's version of the passage seem so incongruous with Hamlet's brooding, doubtful mind. The old-fashioned, early-nineteenth-century version of Le-tourneur may have been tongue-tied, but it did not click off the contrast so mechanically: "Cela me semble, madame! non, cela est. Je ne sais ce que veut dire 'semble'."

M. Gide could thus transform a passing phrase; but his patience with Shakespeare's taste for low and vulgar metaphor was stretched to breaking by the player's speech in Act II, scene 2. Hamlet himself has a number of commendatory things to say about this speech and the play from which it pretends to be taken, calling it

> an excellent play, well digested in the scenes, set down with as much modesty as cunning. I remember one said there were no sallets in the lines to make the matter savoury, nor no matter in the phrase that might indict the author of affectation, but called it an honest method, as wholesome as sweet, and by very much more handsome than fine.

But no sooner has Hamlet begun to recite this elegant and correct composi-tion than Gide begins to retrench him:

The rugged Pyrrhus, he, whose sable arms,
Black as his purpose, did the night resemble
When he lay couched in the ominous horse,
Hath now this dread and black complexion smear'd
With heraldry more dismal; head to foot
Now is he total gules; horridly trick'd
With blood of fathers, mothers, daughters, sons,
Bak'd and impasted with the parching streets
That lend a tyrannous and damned light
To their vile murders: roasted in wrath, and fire,
And thus o'er-sized with coagulate gore,
With eyes like carbuncles, the hellish Pyrrhus
Old grandsire Priam seeks.

L'âpre Pyrrhus, dont l'arme et l'écusson de deuil
Imite par sa nuit la noirceur de son âme,
Dans le fatal cheval étendu, se prépare
A teindre son blason d'un flot de sang vermeil.
O massacre des fils, des femmes, des vieillards!
Un ruisseau cramoisi coule de vos blessures,
Victimes d'un tyran que le carnage enivre
Dont les yeux sont luisants des flammes de l'enfer.
C'est l'ancêtre Priam qu'il poursuit....

Baked, impasted, roasted, and o'er-sized with coagulate gore—when Gide has deprived poor Pyrrhus of all these fat kitchen-metaphors, he hardly retains enough energy to get out of the horse at all. And when the First Player takes up the recitation, we find the excisions become even more extensive, the speech is trussed down to a shadow of its former self. Priam is not knocked flat by the wind of Pyrrhus' sword, nor does the crash of senseless Ilium take prisoner Pyrrhus' ear. There is no outcry, "Out, out, thou strumpet fortune," and the description of Hecuba is reduced to a pale and shrunken thing.* M. Gide explains his doings in a thoroughly uneasy footnote:

---

* We note, by contrast, that Letourneur is not much daunted by these explosive pomposities:

Son fer frappe à côté. Sa fureur est trompée;
Mais le souffle de l'air agité par l'épée
Suffit a renverser le viellard défaillant.
Tout ainsi que son prince, Ilion succombant
Frappé du même coup, tombe en ruines fumantes.
De ce fracas affreux, pour un instant ému,
Pyrrhus s'arrête. . . .

. . . Pyrrhus at Priam drives; in rage strikes wide;
But with the whiff and wind of his fell sword
The unnerved father falls. Then senseless Ilium,
Seeming to feel this blow, with flaming top
Stoops to his base, and with a hideous crash
Takes prisoner Pyrrhus' ear: for, lo! his sword,
Which was declining on the milky head
Of reverend Priam, seem'd i'the air to stick:
So, as a painted tyrant, Pyrrhus stood. . . .

Admiration for the courage with which he tackled them must, of course, be qualified by amusement at the results. The fall of Troy-town a "fracas affreux"! One can only be grateful that the meter didn't permit "épouvantable."

Me pardonnera-t-on d'avoir, ici, grandement simplifié un texte dont l'intérêt nous échappe aujourd'hui en grande partie, sur ce point. Faut-il voir, dans la tirade déclamée par Hamlet d'abord, puis par l'acteur, une satire de Nashe ou de Marlowe? Est-ce une citation de quelque pièce plus ancienne, encore que récente, dont Shakespeare lui-même, rivalisant avec Marlowe, serait l'auteur, ainsi que le suggèrent quelques critiques? Tous, presque tous, s'accordent sur ceci: la tirade est de Shakespeare; mais on doute si Shakespeare l'approuve et la donne en exemple, ou la livre à la moquerie. C'est d'un subtilité d'intention qu'aucune traduction ne saurait rendre. Et comme, ici, le sens des mots importe beaucoup moins que le ton et que l'allure des vers, c'est là ce que, du moins, j'ai tâché de maintenir; fût-ce aux dépens de la signification exacte. (A. G.) *

All sorts of doubt cluster round this little between-the-acts declaration. If indeed Shakespeare intended the speech as a parody, it surely was not gratuitous parody; its artifice reflects on Hamlet's perception of himself in his reactions to the player and to the murder of his father. The audience too, with this Trojan rhetoric ringing in its ears, has reason to think of Hamlet's already highly figured blank verse as more "natural." A particularly odd feature of Gide's note is that "le ton et l'allure des vers" are precisely what he *hasn't* rendered, the mere "sens des mots" what he has. What he objects to is bombast, and he has cut it down. It's possible to think the French are more sensitive to bombast than we Anglo-Saxons are, and therefore get more flavor from a modest sampling; the basic fact may or may not be correct, but at least there is some logic to the argument. The worst thing about Gide's position, however, is that it gives the translator almost unlimited privileges over his victim. If we accept it, there is not really any way we can cast a disapproving eye on the Abbé DeLille, famous as a translator of the classics into French Alexandrines during the late eighteenth and early nineteenth centuries. One of his main ventures was a translation of Vergil's *Eclogues* (1805), into which he had not advanced very far before he encountered a very Gidean problem in the second,

> that horrid one
> Beginning *"Formosum pastor Corydon."*

Life evidently ran high among the shepheds around Mantua, and the shepherd Corydon is described as bursting with affection for the handsome boy

---

* May I be excused for having here greatly simplified a text whose interest in this context largely escapes us of the present day. Should we perhaps see in the declamation recited first by Hamlet, then by the actor, a satire on Nashe or on Marlowe? Or is it a quotation from some even older, though still recent, play, which Shakespeare himself might have written during the days of his rivalry with Marlowe—as various critics suggest? Everyone, or almost everyone, agrees on this point: the declamation is by Shakespeare, but we are not sure whether Shakespeare approves of it, and gives it as an example, or delivers it up to satiric mockery. It is a subtlety of intention that no translation could possibly render. And as, here, the sense of the words matters much less than the tone and deportment of the verse, I have tried to maintain at least the latter; even at the expense of the exact sense.

Alexis, whom he wants to carry off to his humble cot for use as a room-mate. Given the feelings of his day and age about homosexuality, given the perfect, simple frankness of Vergil's poem, and given his own rather namby-pamby style, the Abbé DeLille found Eclogue Two much too strong a dose; • so he changed the young lad Alexis to the young lady Lycoris, and made • Corydon sigh for a shepherdess with a very minimum of fictitious femininity. • One can imagine the good Abbé arguing (somewhat to M. Gide's perplexity, one would think) that, after all, the "ton et allure" of Vergil's verses are what matter, not the mere "sens des mots," and since homosexual affairs now (1805) have a very different "ton et allure" than they used to, hand-some Alexis must be translated across the sex barrier. As a matter of fact, that is the substance of the note—almost as shamefaced as M. Gide's own—which constitutes Abbé DeLille's only recognition of the problem. Practically speaking, the matter of conversion was simplicity itself, amounting to little more than the exchange (sexchange?) of a few pronouns and the renaming of a rival:

> Ne valait-il pas mieux, de l'altière Corinne
> Endurer les dépits et la fierté chagrine! *

But when translators start taking liberties like these, they obviously aren't to be trusted in anything. Particularly nowadays, when practice and familiarity have made it easy for us to adjust to different mores, it is hard to imagine a set of verbal or social conventions so distressing that the mere act of falsify-ing them would not be more distressing. The greater problem of a modern • translator is likely to be the apparently excessive reaction of characters (in • nineteenth-century novels or plays, for instance) to facts of life which are • now generally viewed more calmly. The problem centers, as often as not, on the original's setting too "high" a tone, rather than too "low."

When a fiction had had the misfortune to fall into a completely antiquated • and artificial dialect, of course, there may not be anything whatever to do • about it. Lord Lytton's *Eugene Aram* is written in a kind of nineteenth-century novelistic lingua franca of which there are many less horrible examples—unless one undertakes to rewrite it from the ground up, there is no remedy for *Eugene Aram*, it is a dead pigeon. But when the problem is less massive, there are some things that a translator can do to camouflage the linguistic warts and blotches of his original, without actually rebuilding its whole face. Generally speaking, Stendhal needs no favors from his twen- • tieth-century translators; by comparison with the inflated and emphatic • styles that Romanticism fostered, his tone is sharp, hard, factual. That is • exactly the style that modern taste finds most congenial. And yet there are

---

* Or, as we might write it in English:
> Better, no doubt, to put up with the mean
> And arrogant snubs of the lofty Corinne!

passages of Stendhal himself which, if one translated them literally, would strike a modern reader as intolerably fatuous and inflated. When, in *The Red and the Black,* Mme. de Rênal's little boy Stanislas is recovering from fever, Stendhal tells us: "Enfin le ciel eut pitié de cette mère malheureuse" (Book I, Chap. 19). Doubtless it is half a paraphrase. In his defence, one can say that perhaps Stendhal is giving us the situation as it appears to Mme. de Rênal, half crazed by piety and guilt. But the novelist has not guarded us sufficiently against taking the conventional, exaggerated words as his own. If the translator doesn't care about his author, or about the impression that his reader gets, nothing is easier than to translate *correctly:* "At last heaven took pity on this unhappy mother." But that isn't an artistic or an adequate translation. The French are more at ease than the English with this casual invocation of "le ciel"; the nineteenth century accepted that sort of idiom more naturally than the twentieth. One has to soften it in some way; my own version, "At last the clouds lifted for the wretched woman" tries for such a softening.

The fact is that levels of diction change over the years. What the nineteenth century thought scandalous may be for the twentieth century merely commonplace—as what the eighteenth century thought commonplace, the nineteenth century thought scandalous. Such a fearful fuss in Bernard Shaw's *Pygmalion* over Liza Doolittle's spectacular word, "bloody"! If we had to translate *Pygmalion* into another language (French, for example), we should certainly feel obliged to alter the equivalent word, from generation to generation, in order to keep up with changing standards of the outrageous. With the disadvantage of having to read *Pygmalion* in its original English, we must exercise our imaginations to guess what that word "bloody" must have felt like back in 1912. In effect, the extremes of language (high as well as low) are decaying nowadays—words like "love," "sublime," "passion," and "heroic" taking on a sardonic tone, while the so-called four-letter words, through sheer frequency of usage, are rising to respectability. This seems like a joke, but it is a serious matter for an author who wants to have some words in reserve for specific effects. Where is he to find the sacred or the taboo word that for a nineteenth-century author was easy—perhaps all too easy? The problem takes other forms too: nothing looks sillier than a detour where there's no longer an obstacle. Circumlocutions for legs or breasts, asses or cocks, look completely foolish in this day and age. Should one bestow on one's author the frankness of which he was incapable, or make him look extraordinarily prissy? When he represents the speech of a Jew or a Negro, should one reproduce the gross distortions which were conventional in his day or modify him into the no less arbitrary conventions of our own time? Changing conventions represent a linguistic problem for which, in the history of the individual language, there is probably no solution save historical awareness. But in the jolt of passing the language barrier, via translation, one is bound to adjust also for cultural and temporal differences; thus obsolete or obsolescent terminology becomes the translator's problem as it isn't necessarily, or at least not so pointedly, for the native speaker.

The problem of language erosion manifests itself most plainly in extremes —wherever speech strains after emphasis, it has to transgress (go above, below, beyond) norms set by convention, and by so doing it changes those norms. But all language values are interrelated. If extreme words become norms, then old norms become subnorms, words negatively valued or even despised for their weakness and neutrality.* Whether the search for extreme language is cause or consequence, it accompanies the erosion of language devoted to the middle range of experience. A result is that a good many nineteenth-century novels have become in effect untranslatable, except as period pieces. Naturally, the difficulty is not just the translator's. If some novel has ceased to be viable in its own right, translators are under no obligation to redeem the ravages of time and changing taste. Still, we do wrong to pretend that language, as it opens up one set of expressive possibilities, doesn't necessarily close off others. And when this change appears, as it does nowadays, to be aimless and accidental—not directed toward a standard of any sort, but simply a consequence of successive social accidents—the only significant distinction among usage-levels starts to be sensed as "the latest" versus "all the others." That is in effect a tyranny of the present over the past, and one expression of it is the readiness of translators to work only with those originals that they can readily get into a modern dialect. That means essentially a preference for hard style over soft.

As an age, we have done far better at translating Homer and Dante than Vergil and Petrarch (and we have done better with *Inferno* than with *Purgatorio* or *Paradiso*); Flaubert has been many times translated, Balzac much less, George Sand hardly at all. It implies too much assurance by far to say that what we have found amenable to translation is inherently superior to what we haven't. In effect—provincialism being one major ingredient of what we call "taste"—we have translated what could be made to accord with current prejudices and used it to flatter ourselves into the belief that we are cosmopolitan. Mr. Robert Graves gave away the procedure all too plainly in the preface to his fine translation of Apuleius' *Golden Ass*. Apuleius, as Mr. Graves takes note, wrote in a highly mannered, elaborately

---

* A neat contemporary instance of a word reversing its connotations is provided by "square." At the beginning of the present century, George M. Cohan could write a song in praise of the name "Mary," in which the word "square" was used as a term of unequivocal praise:

> For there is something there
> That sounds so square,
> It's a grand old name.

In less extreme reversals, "nice" and "cute" have worn out their positive connotations, and taken on satiric or sardonic tonalities.

metaphorical style of late Latin preciosity. Clearly a modern translator doesn't want to write anything like that—least of all a translator like Mr. Graves, whose own poetry and prose are of a spectacular limpidity. How to surmount the impasse? "Paradoxically," says Mr. Graves, "the effect of oddness is best achieved in convulsed times like the present by writing in as easy and sedate an English as possible." Paradoxically, indeed—and a most convenient paradox it was for Mr. Graves, who is rarely at a loss for reasons to do exactly as he pleases. As for Apuleius, he's been dead for some time now, and can't protest that his times were convulsed too, and if he wrote as he did, it was because he wanted to.

Making a translation sound "modern" is sometimes as much of an incubus, and gets as much in the way of seeing the real original, as the use of an old-fashioned and outmoded dialect. Especially as it is usually performed, jazzing up the classics leads us a giant stride away from the classic experience; and one need not turn to the real vulgarizers to illustrate the fact. The occasional gratuitous and half-hearted colloquialism, the touch of factitious liveliness where it's not called for, are what do the real job of destruction. C. Day Lewis, for example, could hardly fail to produce a spotty *Aeneid* when, seeking to enliven a slow passage, he had Mercury ask Aeneas,

> What do you
> Aim at or hope for, idling and fiddling here in Libya?
>
> (IV, 270)

Or again, when he had King Latinus address the Trojans, presenting themselves before him,

> Trojans—oh yes, your city and line are not unknown to us,
> We'd heard of you before you sailed this way—pray tell me
> What you would have.
>
> (VII, 195)

A weighty burden borne by English poetry since Yeats is that it shouldn't try too hard, or take itself too seriously. This conflicts automatically with the epic demand for sustained exaltation. Just how hard Day Lewis worked to get his *Aeneid* casual may be seen by looking at the two passages above in the original, or in literal translation:

Quid struis? aut qua spe Libycis teris otia terris?

What is your scheme? what is your aim wearing out your leisure in Libya?

Dicite Dardanidae (neque enim nescimus et urbem
Et genus: auditique advertitis aequore cursus)
Quid petitis?

Tell me, Trojans (for we know both your city and lineage: you come
here at the end of a much-talked-about voyage), What do you want?

As a matter of fact, the requirement that a modern translation must
sound modern to a modern audience rests on some pretty shaky assumptions
and leads to some fairly disagreeable conclusions. Not every original sounded
"modern" to its first readers; quite apart from deliberate archaisers like
Milton and Spenser, the very concept of individual originality was not always
prized, so that authors sometimes strove to sound as if they were retelling
ancient and well-known fables, and in terms of style as if they aimed at
the steady and familiar rather than the striking. Apart from sounding modern
in general, there are all sorts of particular requirements involved in sounding
modern *now,* one instance of which is the casualness with which we saw
Day Lewis energetically inoculating the *Aeneid.* To say that we don't want
the classics translated in a stuffy old-fashioned style may be a way of saying
that if they can't be made colloquial, ironic, textured, structured, paradoxi-
cal, and easy for us to admire without any shifting of our literary sights,
they probably aren't classics. Vergil can evidently be made to sound more
or less colloquial, but it is quite apparent to anyone who looks at the
original that nothing was farther from the poet's thoughts when he composed
ceremonial words of welcome for King Latinus' speech. It is a grave and
dignified occasion on which he speaks; his intent is not to put his guests
at their ease, or to show that he is suave himself. He has just come from
consulting with his gods, who have told him how important these visitors
are for his future and that of his people. We do him grievous wrong in rendering his grave words as if they were an offhand response to an introduction at a cocktail party. Or, to shift to the other instance, even if we have
reason to think that Stendhal was dissatisfied wih the dialect that circumstance demanded he use to express passionate feeling, we are on thin ice
in giving him what we consider a better one, since splotching his work with
modernisms will disfigure it at best, and we have no way of knowing what
effect the missing idioms (if he had possessed them) would have had on
other elements of his style. This is not an argument for the brown nineteenth-century uniform of archaic nonspeech in which the classics were so
often, and so suffocatingly, shrouded; but rather for a decorum in translators
and readers of translations that will balance the chosen idiom of the original
against the demand of the "lively," the "contemporary," and the "immediate." In some of their Old-Testament moods, my colleagues have been
known to say that students of literature nowadays form their tastes entirely
on writing done since 1920 and on Shakespeare; and that these two supports
for a sense of literary taste and judgment are in effect one, since Shakespeare is generally read through the strongly tinted glasses of modern criticism, for the values approved by it. And those values turn out to be, if we

look into the backgrounds of Eliot's criticism, or Pound's,* the slogans under which "modern literature" pushed forward to claim its place in the sun.

As social generalization, this Jeremiadry may or may not be accurate, but it carries a worthwhile warning about translation, which, as it is currently practiced, seems sometimes to lend universal authority to what is in fact a rather narrow concept of taste and literary judgment. A student might very well complete a course titled "Literary Masterpieces in Translation," or some such title, with a strong sense that the world's great literary artists were all trying to write like Mr. Ezra Pound, and were occasionally so fortunate as to succeed. The very experience which could correct narrowness of mind and limitation of perspective would thus serve to reinforce those qualities.

An irony in connection with Pound is that he himself has been narrowed by the success of his own process. If not the onlie, he is at least a major begetter of the colloquial, free style of translation-imitation, which flourishes under the rubric of "Make It New." All sorts of licensed liveliness has sprung up in the wake of his Propertius—Rouse's Homer, and Lowell's *Imitations,* for example. But though the "Homage to Sextus Propertius" and the controversies over it have established him as primarily a colloquialist, Pound did at least as much eftsoonery-work as the next fellow. A sonnet by Ronsard's contemporary Joachim DuBellay (we note in passing that DuBellay himself translated his "original" sonnet from a poem by the fifteenth-century neo-Latin writer Janus Vitalis Panormitanus) does not sound too different in a version by Ezra Pound than it does in a version by Edmund Spenser:

O thou new comer who seek'st Rome in Rome	Thou stranger, which for Rome in Rome here seekest
And find'st in Rome no thing thou canst call Roman;	And naught of Rome in Rome perceiv'st at all,
Arches worn old and palaces made common,	These same old walls, old arches, which thou seest,
Rome's name alone within these walls keeps home.	Old Palaces, is that which Rome men call.
Behold how pride and ruin can befall	Behold what wreak, what ruin, and what waste,
One who hath set the whole world 'neath her laws,	And how that she, which with her mighty power
All-conquering, now conquerèd, because	Tamed all the world, hath tamed herself at last,

---

* I don't suppose here that Eliot and Pound are the last word in modern criticism, just that what is said against their provincialism bears, *a fortiori,* against narrower and more extreme provincialisms. It scarcely seems worth while to spell out the case aganist the more pedestrian and mechanical varieties of Marxism, which are so far from being able to understand the historic past that they don't even understand their own.

She is Time's prey, and Time consu-
meth all.

The prey of Time, which doth all
things devour.

Rome that art Rome's one sole last
monument,
Rome that alone hast conquered Rome
the town,
Tiber alone, transient and seaward
bent,
Remains of Rome. O world, thou un-
constant mime!
That which stands firm in thee Time
batters down,
And that which fleeteth doth outrun
swift time.

Rome now of Rome is th'only funeral,
And only Rome of Rome hath victory;
Nor aught save Tiber hastening to his
fall
Remains of all: O world's inconstancy!
That which is firm doth flit and fall
away,
And that is flitting, doth abide and
stay.

The point of these observations is not that Pound's practice was inconsistent and therefore bad, but that he had some sense of decorum in translation, and was therefore good. Catullus often goes very well into the flip
modern style, but there is no way to get DuBellay's (or Panormitanus's)
ornate wordplay to sound either modern or casual, and no reason why it
should be made to sound either way. The theme of the sonnet is simple
nostalgia, its style is unalterably florid; and though there is no pretending
that either version is a mighty advance over the other, both convey a very
decent sense of what the original is like.* "The prettiest girl in the world,"
say the knowing French, "can give no more than what she's got." This may
be true of girls; it's less true of literature, where we don't sometimes know
what a work has to give till we've tried it out in a whole variety of odd, and
at first glance wrong-headed, ways. But the fact that some works seem in-
finitely pliable and adaptable may mislead us into thinking that all works
can or should be so, or that works which aren't are somehow inferior. And
when we start thinking that way, we've taken a couple of long steps toward
transforming translation from a vehicle of wider and more varied literary
experience into a vehicle of flat, uniform, and shallow cosmopolitanism—
which is, in fact, the ultimate provincialism.

A final instance, lending credibility to this melancholy reflection. In the
history of poetic imitation, it has been customary for the imitation to stand

---

* Nouveau venu, qui cherches Rome en Rome,
Et rien de Rome en Rome n'apperçois,
Ces vieux palais, ces vieux arcz que tu vois,
Et ces vieux murs, c'est ce que Rome on
nomme.

Voy quel orgueil, quelle ruine: et comme
Celle qui mist le monde sous ses loix,
Pour donter tout, se donta quelquefois,
Et devint proye au temps, qui tout con-
somme.

Rome de Rome est le seul monument,
Et Rome Rome a vaincu seulement,
Le Tybre seul, qui vers la mer s'enfuit,

Reste de Rome. O mondaine inconstance!
Ce qui est ferme, est par le temps destruit,
Et ce qui fuit, au temps fait resistance.

in a defined and considered relation to its original. Fidelity wasn't necessarily the point, nor even consistency, but a constant and controlled tension between original and imitation was felt to be desirable. When the original appeared strongly through the imitation, that implied one thing; when it was abandoned—by a certain measure, in a certain direction—that meant something else. The reader steered toward an understanding of the imitator's heading by measuring his tacks and veers along the line laid down by his original. But there was never anything sacrosanct about these assumptions, and in 1961 Robert Lowell called most of them into question with a book of *Imitations,* where the relation between original and imitation was loose to the point of being sometimes inverted. By way of explanation, Mr. Lowell declared in his Introduction that he had tried "to do what my authors might have done if they were writing their poems now and in America." But this is not much of an explanation. What François Villon or Charles Baudelaire —not to mention Homer—might have done if born to poor-but-honest parents of Mormon beliefs and agricultural vocation, domiciled in Tucumcari, New Mexico, is certainly hard to imagine. The one sure thing is that they would not have been much like Villon, Baudelaire, or Homer. The liberty assumed by the imitator is so great, by virtue of the indefiniteness of what he imagines he's imitating, that there's an imaginable reason for putting anything into the imitation or leaving anything out. (Two severe sentences in Matthew Arnold's essay on translating Homer suffice to dispose of the whole notion.) But the modern imitators make no bones about their unlimited authority over the past. When the imitator tells us explicitly that he has felt free to modify, combine, transpose, omit, simplify, substitute, and in addition to disregard altogether the intent of the poem he is imitating, we are quite prepared for his next assertion: that though they are called "imitations," the poems of his volume do not depend on their originals in any obvious way. His book, says Mr. Lowell, is "partly self-sufficient and separate from its sources, and should be read first as a sequence, one voice running through many personalities, contrasts, and repetitions." * Homer and Baudelaire thus become phases in a sequence constructed by Lowell's "voice," variations on Lowell, aspects of his impressively varied personality. In a sense that Mr. Lowell obviously wouldn't want to avow but that comes through anyhow, *they* imitated *him,* and with a little readjustment (drop a third of this poem, add a few stanzas to that, overscrawl a few loud metaphors) can be made to talk a common language—a Lowell-common-denominator of twentieth-century American dialect. Under the circum-

---

* The manifold difficulties of reading Mr. Lowell's poems against their originals when the latter have been dismembered and occasionally mistitled, make clear that the words "partly" and "first" are face-savers—that reading Lowell against his originals isn't really contemplated, and wouldn't be particularly rewarding—as in fact it isn't. A hazy, conventional idea of the original works better against Mr. Lowell's imitations than an exact and specific one.

stances, it's rather beside the point to berate Mr. Lowell for inaccurate representation of his sources, or obtuseness to what they happen to be saying; by the terms of the game he's playing, these are virtues, not defects.

About the merits of the poems that result, I won't try to pronounce. It is very hard to dissociate a judgment of them, as pronouncements of Mr. Lowell's voice, from a sense that they are pretending to be something they're not. This is more than a matter of name and title, it is a question of a poem's fundamental motivation.* But of the pernicious confusion of the process that produced them, it seems there cannot be much doubt. It amounts to an evocation of the great figures of the heritage for a cultural Halloween party, a convocation of ventriloquist's dummies.

In the old, old days, men used to distinguish literary styles according to their relative elevation, as lofty or low or middling. Obviously, there were disadvantages to getting stuck in any one of these channels; but certain effects could be achieved either by playing them straight or by deliberately crossing them up. There are two things to do with any decorum: observe it or violate it. Either way one gets a calculable effect. Nowadays we don't recognize the distinctions strictly, and so are limited in the use we can make of them. Verbal garbage is a standard material of fine literary art ("Eumaeus" and "Nausicaa" in *Ulysses;* pop prose in a dozen different guises), and the idea of a heroic "vein" is so absurd that even for parodic purposes it feels obsolete. One of the last remaining places where we can make stylistic discriminations and gain the effects of stylistic contrast is in translation. Here at least the relation between now-writing and then-writing includes the possibility of setting something distinct against something else. The unsuspicious reader of translations may not appreciate the glints and exploits and hairbreadth escapes of this counterplay—the clash of idioms, the thrust of one formula against another. But a good translator does not translate, any more than a good writer writes, for the unsuspicious reader. If he enters this arena at all, he comes with the imagination that a good friend of the text will always be standing behind him, with a knife at his throat. His relation to the original maybe close or distant, emulative or derisive, without violating the code of the game; but it has to be defined, and a defined

---

* To take a single instance: I think I understand pretty well the reasons for Baudelaire's animus against the yawning, complacent reader in the great poem that stands before *Les fleurs du mal.* That is a confessional book, in which Baudelaire is giving his raw soul to the unknown and ferocious cannibal audience, about which he knows only that it is bored and passive. He has good reasons for both shame and hatred, of which the poem is full. But why Mr. Lowell should get so frenetically exercised, I haven't the faintest idea. He is no pariah, he confesses nothing (his raw soul is the last thing we either get or want), he is a respectable gentleman poet using a traditional dialect (down to and including the ritual, obligatory "bad word") in a wholly conventional pastime. If there is anything in the poem that embarrasses him, he can always put it off on Baudelaire. In effect he has transposed and loudspeakerized the rhetoric but muffled out of all recognition the controlling reasons for it. His poem reads *empty* where Baudelaire's is full.

relationship presupposes distinct and independent entities. If you hold (and exercise) absolute power over an antagonist, you do wrong to invite the public to witness a fencing contest between the two of you.

One might extend the reflections here with some observations about pastiche and masquerade as persistent modes of romantic and postromantic (or neoromantic, which is much the same thing) style; by making any personality available at will to any performer, masquerades have a clear tendency to erode all sense of authentic identity in the not-very-long run. Even if extempore roles don't dissipate formed identities, they distract from the slow, secret work of forming one. By the terms of his vocation, the translator, that licensed artist in counterfeit, has a special call to confront the words of several different tribes, and do what he can to give them the purest sense of which they are capable. It would be ironic indeed if the confidence man of literature became a guardian of stylistic discrimination and authenticity, but we've seen stranger and stronger ironies.

CHAPTER VI

Imitations

Since we have touched on a set of imitations which do not seem too clear about what they are imitating, or indeed about who's imitating what, there seems reason to cast a retrospective eye on some earlier instances of the imitator's art, their intents and accomplishments. As a widespread, recognized and *named* literary activity, imitation does not seem much to antedate the English Restoration. Of course authors had been imitating one another for thousands of years before that; what is distinctive about the new form of imitation which came into such vogue in the early eighteenth century is that it is named for its *non*-imitation of the original. Of the three different methods of translation that Dryden distinguishes in his Preface to the translation of *Ovid's Epistles* (1680), imitation is the freest. Metaphrase and paraphrase imitate the original far more closely; imitation assumes a freedom to depart from the words and sense of the original whenever it chooses to do so. Yet it insists upon reminding us persistently of the original, and it makes consistent literary capital out of both its departures and its reminders, using them to sustain a coherent attitude toward its primary topic, which is contemporary or timeless. And, though one doesn't find anything about this written into the ground rules, the predominant feeling of the imitation is generally on the serious side of ironic. Wry, passing allusions tend to fall into the vein of sardonic discord; when one commits oneself to a sustained relationship like imitation, something weighty and unequivocal is generally involved. What one is "translating" for is not an equivalence of surface impressions (these are incidental at best and often frankly at variance), but an equivalence of significant social configuration. Even when both the original and the imitation are witty and ironic, the relation between them can involve a good deal of specific gravity.

There is no lack of gravity in the triad of Juvenal, Dryden, and Dr. Johnson. We can perhaps begin by distinguishing between the two imitators. Dryden came to Juvenal late in life, after his loss of the laureatship in the great overturn of 1688. Translation had become his central occupation, in this last decade of his life; and while he had reasons enough for satire, Juvenal must have appealed to him primarily as a splendid rhetorician. Johnson, on the other hand, came to Juvenal as a young man, a very poor man, and a social outsider; for him, Juvenal's intellectual scorn of sycophants and plutocrats must have counted heavily. Both had reason to be specially intrigued by the theme of the Tenth Satire of Juvenal, best summarized in the title of Dr. Johnson's imitation as "The Vanity of Human Wishes," but they went at it in very different ways. A passage near the beginning describes, in Juvenal's Latin and Dryden's English, the bad old day of Nero's reign:

Temporibus diris igitur iussuque Neronis

Longinum et magnos Senecae praedivitis hortos

clausit, et egregias Lateranorum obsidet aedes

tota cohors; rarus venit in cenacula miles.

Pauca licet portes argenti vascula puri,

nocte iter ingressus gladium contumque timebis,

et motae ad lunam trepidabis arundinis umbram:

cantabit vacuus coram latrone viator.

For this, in *Nero's* arbitrary time,
When Virtue was a Guilt, and Wealth a Crime,
A Troop of Cut-Throat Guards were sent, to seize
The Rich Mens Goods, and gut their Palaces:
The Mob, Commission'd by the Government,
Are Seldom to an Empty Garret sent.
The Fearful Passenger, who travels late,
Charg'd with the Carriage of a Paltry Plate,
Shakes at the Moonshine shadow of a Rush;
And sees a Red-Coat rise from every Bush:
The Beggar Sings, ev'n when he sees the Place
Beset with Thieves, and never mends his pace.

Though he professes to be translating an original, Dryden deals with it after his customary casual fashion. He blithely ignores, we note, the particulars of Nero's confiscation—the gardens of the Longini and of Seneca, the palaces of the Laterani. On the other hand, a single word ("miles" = soldier) is expanded into "The Mob, Commission'd by the Government," and this is Dryden's usual practice, to inflate. Twice Juvenal sums up a moral observation on the practical advantages of poverty in five dry words ("rarus venit in cenacula miles" = "it's a rare soldier that ransacks a garret", and "cantabit vacuus coram latrone viator" = "the traveler who's broke can whistle before a thief"); both times Dryden draws the *sententia* out into a full couplet. Though he made no consistent effort to translate Juvenal's social conventions into contemporary terms, Dryden was not above converting an uncostumed Roman bandit into a seventeenth-century English "Red-Coat." But on the whole, he translates not so much from one particular social milieu to another, as out of Juvenal's particularities and into general terms. Another observable, and perhaps connected, tendency is to melodrama and exaggeration. "When Virtue was a Guilt and wealth a Crime"— one looks in vain for anything equivalent in the Latin. Certainly "diris Temporibus" does not equal this elaborately counterpointed line.

Taking the poem as a declamation, Dryden imposes a special kind of rhetorical symmetry on Juvenal's already rather assured judgments and thus (with whatever implications for his own sceptical temperament and training) makes the moral cases sound open-and-shut. Johnson in his imitation moves in precisely the opposite direction, departing from Juvenal's text, as we would expect, more freely than Dryden, but pushing it toward the statement of more complex, and sometimes insoluble, moral dilemmas:

> Let hist'ry tell where rival kings command,
> And dubious title shakes the madded land,
> When statutes glean the refuse of the sword,
> How much more safe the vassal than the lord;
> Low skulks the hind beneath the rage of pow'r,
> And leaves the wealthy traytor in the Tow'r,
> Untouch'd his cottage, and his slumbers sound,
> Tho' confiscation's vultures hover round.
> The needy traveller, serene and gay,
> Walks the wild heath, and sings his toil away.
> Does envy seize thee? crush th'upbraiding joy,
> Increase his riches and his peace destroy;
> New fears in dire vicissitude invade,
> The rustling brake alarms, and quiv'ring shade,
> Nor light nor darkness bring his pain relief,
> One shews the plunder, and one hides the thief.

Instead of blackhearted tyranny, Johnson presumes a political situation much closer to the English experience, a disputed succession, such as Shakespeare's history plays often describe, and, for that matter, such as the houses of Stuart and Hanover were agitating at the moment of Johnson's writing. (We note that line 6 above, in the first edition read "bonny traytor," in allusion to four Scots leaders jailed and then executed for their part in the Jacobite rising of 1745.) A line like "When statutes glean the refuse of the sword," is altogether devastating in its implication that the law is simply a sharper, closer-cutting implement for slashing down what few crops war has left behind. Thus it isn't particularly a lawless monarch (as in Juvenal), nor a lawless mob commissioned by a lawless government (as in Dryden) that threatens the subject; by an interesting maneuver Johnson escapes altogether from the political dilemma, rising above it on wings of meaphor and abstraction, to lay the blame broadly and grandly on "confiscation's vultures." Likely this is the consequence of his having posed a problem (the choice between kings *de jure* and kings *de facto*) which was morally and legally too difficult, and practically too urgent, for a poem to pretend to solve it at all.

Elevation and perspective are the effects at which Johnson's poem aims, as we can see from the way he controls our view of the "vacuus viator." For Juvenal this fellow is simply a traveler with empty pockets, and his song may very well be a prudent way of advertising that fact; Dryden exaggerates him into a whistling vagabond, a merry beggar; Johnson places the reader far above him, as a disinterested investigator above a guinea pig, and proposes an experiment like that the Devil was allowed to try on Job:

> Does envy seize thee? crush th'upbraiding joy,
> Increase his riches and his peace destroy;
> New fears in dire vicissitude invade,
> The rustling brake alarms, and quiv'ring shade,
> Nor light nor darkness bring his pain relief,
> One shews the plunder, and one hides the thief.

That image of the newly enriched traveler quaking helplessly between imaginary perils sustains the poem's theme that we cannot pursue our own advantage. But as readers we stand between and above Johnson's moral examples, aware that they have been manipulated for purposes of display, conscious of what makes the difference in their behavior, and balancing impersonally the values involved. Johnson himself as arranger of scenes and formulator of moral problems enters more specifically within the frame of the poem—not as Sam. Johnson, LL.D., to be sure, but as the weighty voice of cumulative human experience from Juvenal to the present. His mind is felt in a mannerism of style peculiar to this poem: an assertion tends to be made in abstractions (as if immense quantities of experience had been compressed into one tightly knotted apothegm); often it is so general and remote, the words are applicable to so many different situations and persons, that the apothegm by itself seems to have no distinct meaning at all, until it is given specific content by what follows, often as the second half of a line or the second line of a couplet. The converse of this scheme is to give the examples, then raise them to a general law, epigrammatic sometimes to the point of enigma. Thus the poem rises from example to precept and slants down again; unusual only in this, that the gap between the two levels is so striking, and apparently so deliberate:

> *Love ends with hope,* the sinking statesman's door
> Pours in the morning worshiper no more;
> For growing names the weekly scribbler lies,
> To growing wealth the dedicator flies,
> From every room descends the painted face,
> That hung the bright Palladium of the place,
> And smoak'd in kitchens, or in auctions sold,
> To better features yields the frame of gold;
> For now no more we trace in every line
> Heroic worth, benevolence divine:
> *The form distorted justifies the fall,*
> *And detestation rids th'indignant wall.*

Viewed in isolation, the phrase "Love ends with hope" could perfectly well mean either "Love ends when hope begins," or "Love ends when the lover can no longer hope for success." These are polar opposites. Only the three examples explain to us what sort of "love" Johnson is concerned with, and what sort of "hope"; in fact, they turn out to be remarkably close to the same thing. The poet's transition to the next series of thoughts is slight but significant; not only do people repudiate their former loves and loyalties in the realm of politics, they repudiate their own families. The theme is the same, the application somewhat different, and it is not altogether clear how far and in what way Johnson expected his reader to be aware of the Juvenalian suggestion behind the entire passage. Yet an original there is, and thinking about its relation to Johnson's poem does not lead us to a dead end. Johnson is building on Juvenal's description of Sejanus' abandonment by all his former supporters at the first signal from Tiberius; the portraits being taken down from the wall parallel a rush of the mob to tear down and dismember an equestrian statue of Sejanus, and their sudden discovery, when he no longer has power, that they always thought his features ugly:

> mergit longa atque insignis honorum
> pagina; descendunt statuae restemque sequuntur.
> Ipsas deinde rotas bigarum impacta securis
> caedit, et immeritis franguntur crura caballis. . . .

> Gaudent ommes. "Quae labra? quis illi
> vultus erat? nunquam, si quid mihi credis, amavi
> hunc hominem."

> Down go the Titles; and the Statue Crown'd,
> Is by base Hands in the next River Drown'd.
> The Guiltless Horses, and the Chariot wheel
> The same Effects of Vulgar Fury feel. . . .

Sejanus with a Rope is dragged along,
The Sport and Laughter of the giddy Throng!
Good Lord, they cry, what Ethiop Lips he has,
How foul a Snout, and what a hanging Face:
By Heav'n, I never cou'd endure his Sight. . . .
　　　　　　　　　　　　　　　(translated by Dryden)

Of course, getting rid of Sejanus, a tyrant and a usurper, is one thing; throwing away one's ancestors because their portraits are out of fashion is quite another. Johnson, with his concern (already noted) for real cases of moral decision, has picked one involving loyalty to the past which might have actually presented itself to a prosperous bourgeois of the period of George III. But one can use the Juvenalian connection in various ways: Sejanus was a usurper of false authority, like one's family, and throwing down such figures is a moral necessity; on the other hand, he was a genuine and authentic figure of authority, like one's family, and its's the "modern" fashion to be afraid of live lions and courageous with dead ones. On the whole, Johnson opts for the second of these alternatives, though a thin ironic vein runs through his imagery, favoring the first. On the one hand, the man who takes down his ancestor's portraits is paralleled with the weekly scribbler and the venal dedicator—odious associates indeed. The phrase "better features," too, is surely ironic; it's the modern who, in his complacency, decides that his own features are more seemly than those of his ancestors. Further, heroic worth and benevolence divine were evidently once to be traced in every line (genealogical as well as pictorial) of our ancestors; if "we" don't feel impelled to trace them now, it's because we are degenerate. The "form distorted" of the last couplet may, therefore, be either the ancestral portrait, which looks distorted to a modern eye, or modern man himself, who looks distorted when seen as the last manifestation of a line which once possessed noble qualities. The last line goes both ways so dexterously as to yield no preferred meaning. It could say that the master's detestation of the old portraits rids the walls of them so thoroughly as to leave the walls gasping in indignation. Or again it may be that the pictures detest the master as a degenerate representative of their line, and quit the wall in indignation because it and its owner are unworthy of them. On either basis, it seems conceivable that Johnson wanted the parallel to be felt, even though he did not rigidly define it: in a word, imitation not only counters and reaffirms points made in the original, it may leave a little undefined space between for readerly speculation and reflection.

　　Dryden is a restless, feisty translator, always ready to snatch up a hint from his author and gallop away with it; he likes verbal business of any sort. Cicero's line of bad poetry, "O fortunatam natam me consule Romam" (Juvenal, 122) blossoms under his florid hand into a veritable garden of false wit:

> Fortune foretun'd the dying Notes of Rome
> Till I, thy consul sole, consol'd thy doom.

It is beneath Johnson's dignity to notice such buffoonery. On the other hand, he is not the man to reject wit when it lies to hand and serves his purpose, and a tremendous passage about the last days of the senile millionaire makes telling use of a pun for which even Dryden, had he thought of it, might have been willing to forego some of his bawdy invective:

> The still returning tale, and ling'ring jest,
> Perplex the fawning niece and pamper'd guest,
> While growing hopes scarce awe the gath'ring sneer,
> And scarce a legacy can bribe to hear;
> The watchful guests still hint the last offence,
> The daughter's petulance, the son's expense,
> Improve his heady rage with treach'rous skill,
> And mould his passions till they make his will.

The whore in whose favor Juvenal's miser disinherits his own children, and whom Dryden seizes on with all-too-evident relish of disgust, has no place in Johnson's poem. This is less, perhaps, for reasons of moral tone than because she represents too extreme and obvious a moral perversion. And this sort of omission, quite as much as the more positive changes imposed on Juvenal's poem, helps define Johnson's dealings with antiquity. He is not really seeking witty equivalents in modern life which can be hung on and played against Juvenal's poem; it is not the distance from Roman times that he wants his reader to appreciate, so much as a continuity. His own poem, moving as it does freely and swiftly from ancient to modern instances, subjugates them all to a law that is abstract, immutable, universal, and sometimes (because of those very qualities) gnomic. Juvenal serves Johnson as a sounding board, to give his moral judgments resonance; he confirms the modern poet from time to time in the cosmopolitanism of the disabused. The truly subdued will is universal; it wants, and has always wanted, only what is never out of its power to possess—conscious virtue. Though there's no major unit of Juvenal's poem for which Johnson hasn't supplied an analogue, he doesn't push point-for-point comparisons at the reader, or demand that one have a continual sense of counterparts. His moral point is continuity, sameness; witty points would come from the discovery of unexpected equivalence, and that's not to the purpose at all. Johnson cultivates the subdued style as a more persuasive way of preaching the subdued will. That is all human nature can achieve now, says Johnson, and Juvenal contributes the authoritative assurance that it was the limit in a much greater civilization than ours.*

---

* In passing, mention should be made of Robert Lowell's contemporary rendering of the Tenth Satire (in *Near the Ocean*, New York, Farrar, Straus, 1963, pp. 69–106); unlike Lowell's

When we turn from Johnson and Dryden in their dealings with Juvenal
to Ezra Pound and his dealings with Propertius, we have a variety of new
problems to take into account. Before stepping into that turbulence, it's to
be observed that the fundamental issues of imitation are really unchanged.
Dr. Johnson uses Juvenal to sustain and reinforce a stance that relates to
English as to Roman circumstance; Pound uses Propertius in the same
essential way. As a poet, Propertius is a good deal less solemn than Juvenal;
as an imitator, Pound is just as serious as Dr. Johnson.

Pound's handling of Propertius is not, and does not claim to be, an
exact translation; it includes units of direct translation, but departs freely,
as Dryden said it was the privilege of imitation to depart, from both the
words and the sense of the original. The device of the imitation is, essentially to enliven and modernize Propertius, to "bring him up to date," by
emphasizing one set of elements in him, and minimizing another. There
can be no question that the quality Pound chose to emphasize is present
in the original; it is a wry, sophisticated, erotic humor. And to bring
out this quality, the imitator has assumed remarkable but not necessarily
excessive liberties. He transposes freely from Roman to modern terms,
extends Propertian hints into explicit assertions, introduces colloquialisms
without specific warrant, omits whatever is inconvenient, rearranges the
poems or fragments of poems to his own taste—and only in the latter detail
does he start to overstep the traditional liberties and privileges of imitators,
and then not by much. In principle, of course, patchwork imitation is not
imitation at all. If one handles the materials freely enough, one is simply
composing a new original out of old materials—a process very popular in the
Byzantine period particularly, when fantastic *centos* were created out of
elaborately rearranged lines and half-lines of the *Iliad* or the *Aeneid*. Far
from being imitative, these exercises aimed at displaying the compiler's ingenuity in applying familiar tags to wholly unexpected situations, never
dreamed of by the original author. (Constructing lives of Christ out of materials supplied by Vergil or Homer was a favorite pastime.) But Pound by
no means carries his cutting and patching of Propertius to these lengths.
When two Propertian poems are related thematically, he often straps one to
the other; and in Unit 7 of the "Homage" (based on Propertius II, 15) he
homogenizes his original by reproducing the lines of Propertius' poem in the
following order:

---

imitations, this is a reasonably straightforward version, with little bombast, few pointedly
"modern" equivalents, and no excessive cuts or transpositions. The indicated comparison is
with Dryden, who, like Lowell, was interested in Juvenal as a rhetorician, and translated
the Latin rhetoric for its broad effects and large gestures. Lowell perhaps exaggerates a little
the moralistic, hortatory side of Juvenal, and his transitions sometimes need to be cleared up
by reference to the original; but his is a perfectly viable contemporary Juvenal.

lines 29–34
line 49
lines 51–54
line 50
lines 35–40

(We note in passing that lines 41–48 are omitted altogether. It would be interesting to know why: Campion used them as the second verse of his "translation" of Catullus' "Vivamus, mea Lesbia.")

But, generally speaking, these liberties are not those for which Pound's version of Propertius has been most liberally denounced—nor, indeed, after the first shock of finding Wordsworth, frigidaires, and erasers in ancient Rome, have Pound's deliberate anachronisms been much of a stumbling block. The things that stick in readers' craws have to do with the close texture of Propertius as Pound represents him, the passages where translation seems to be proceeding with least overt skewing. For example, we may compare Pound's first section with its original, in the first poem of Propertius' third book:

> Shades of Callimachus, Coan ghosts of Philetas
> It is in your grove I would walk,
> I who come first from the clear font
> Bringing the Grecian orgies into Italy,
>   and the dance into Italy.
> Who hath taught you so subtle a measure,
>   in what hall have you heard it;
> What foot beat out your time-bar,
>   what water has mellowed your whistles?

> Callimachi Manes et Coi sacra Philetae,
>   in vestrum, quaeso, me sinite ire nemus.
> primus ego ingredior puro de fonte sacerdos
>   Itala per Graios orgia ferre choros.
> dicite, quo pariter carmen tenuastis in antro?
>   quove pede ingressi? quamve bibistis aquam?

A careful Latinist would point to the way in which Pound has removed all the religious overtones of Propertius by translating "sacra" (line 1) as "ghosts" instead of "rites," by not translating "sacerdos" ("priest," line 3) at all, by translating "antro" ("grotto," line 5) as "hall," and by turning "quamve bibistis aquam" ("what water did you drink," line 6) as "what water has mellowed your whistles?" But these are all liberties within the traditional scope of imitation; there are even good grounds for arguing that the last line comes closer to conveying the full meaning of Propertius' question than a bald inquiry. Asking about the water suggests, in context, that it was water of Helicon, Aganippe, or some other sacred, inspiring spring; this overtone is eked out if we translate "antro" as "grotto" with the special implication of a god-haunted, god-inspired cavern (cf. also "nemus," "grove"). Pound has let slide the religious overtones which are so strong here; with "what water has mellowed your whistles?" he can recapture at least a jocose sense of the water being useful for purposes of song.

Serious doubts about Pound's version start to arise in connection with line 4. "Bringing the Grecian orgies into Italy" suggests the introduction of some sort of riotous, ecstatic religious dances, as if Propertius were claiming to have brought new sexual liberties, new religious observances out of Greece into Roman life. No such thing at all in the Latin. It is the Italian orgies (i.e., the mysteries of love in a Latin setting) that he is bringing into Greek rhythms. The very syntax, "Itala orgia—ferre—per Graios choros" cries out against the English version. Pound has added a sexy, suggestive overtone to Propertius, but it is factitous in itself and grates on the essentially literary relation to Callimachus and Philetas which the rest of the poem describes.

The next five lines represent an extract and recombination of some eight lines of Propertius:

> Out-weariers of Apollo will, as we know, continue their Martian generalities,
> We have kept our erasers in order.
> A new-fangled chariot follows the flower-hung horses;
> A young Muse with young loves clustered about her ascends with me into the aether, . . .
> And there is no high-road to the Muses.

The first two lines are reasonably close to Propertius:

> a valeat, Phoebum quicumque moratur in armis!
> exactus tenui pumice versus eat,—

but the next two lines are built about equally of materials supplied and invented. There is nothing in the original about a new-fangled chariot; the Muse, Propertius' daughter, triumphs with garlanded horses (coronatis equis), and Propertius himself is carried off by Fame (terra sublimis) far above the earth; he is accompanied in his chariot by little loves.

> quo me Fama levat terra sublimis, et a me
> nata coronatis Musa triumphatequis,
> et mecum in curru parvi vectantur Amores, . . .

If we are following the comparison closely, we may be curious at this point to see how Pound's last line grows out of what precedes; from a young Muse in a chariot ascending the heavens, how do we get to the statement that "there is no high-road to the Muses"? Above all, how do we get there by means of the conjunction "And"? In fact, two lines of Propertius have been left out, the first describing a crowd of writers who follow after the poet's rapidly receding chariot wheels, the second addressing a warning to them:

> scriptorumque meas turba secuta rotas.
> quid frustra missis in me certatis habenis?

Why do they loosen the reins in an effort to overtake him? Their efforts are bound to be "frustra," in vain, because there's no wide road to the Muses' home:

> non datur ad Musas currere lata via.

The width of the road matters only because the chariot being hurried aloft is the poet's, not the Muse's, and there are a crowd of other chariots trying to pass it. The extraordinary logical discontinuity of the English verse is Pound's contribution, and in no perceptible degree Propertius'.

A final set of remarkable and perhaps deliberate cross-purposes cluster around the four lines which conclude Pound's paraphrase of Propertius III, 1:

> And I also among the later nephews of this city
> > shall have my dog's day,
> With no stone upon my contemptible sepulchre;
> My vote coming from the temple of Phoebus in Lycia, at Patara, . . .

> meque inter seros laudabit Roma nepotes:
> > illum post cineres auguror ipse diem.
> ne mea contempto lapis indicet ossa sepulcro
> > provisum est Lycio vota probante deo.

"Nepotes" can indeed mean "nephews," but it also means "descendants" (as in Catullus, LVIII, 5 "magnanimi Remi nepotes") and in fact the time scheme demands that "inter seros nepotes" modify "Roma," not "me." Rome, in its later generations, will praise me. Pound omits the next line entirely: "I myself foresee that day beyond my ashes" (i.e., funeral). But how does he get from this assurance of Propertius' that he will be remembered and honored in future days to the line, "With no stone upon my contemptible sepulchre"? Only one way, by misconstruing the Latin. What Propertius says is: "Let not the grave be neglected where a headstone marks my bones! such is the decree of Lycia's god (Apollo), for he has approved my vows." It is by no means a contemptible grave without a headstone that the poet foresees, quite the contrary. And the "vote" of Lycia's god (Patara is Pound's original contribution) is really the "vota" = vows of the poet himself.

Errors and confusions of these massive proportions and primitive simplicity are quite sufficient to justify Pound's standing among classical scholars, which could scarcely be lower; they have been many times exposed and deplored. Of the various excuses and explanations put forward on his behalf, most are feeble enough. For example, there has been some effort to say that when he translated words like "vota" = vote or "contempto sepulcro" = contemptible sepulchre, Pound was responding like a poet to the surface of the Latin language as it strikes the eye. Pretentious nonsense: the same justification would serve for Pig Latin or Fractured French, just as well as for garbled Propertius. Perhaps Pound was just making private jokes; but, if so, his stubborn refusal to correct them, explain them, or define the sort of enterprise to which they would be appropriate throws one back on the simplest of explanations. He is trying to write a poem based on Propertius, making use of Propertius; many of his departures from the sense, structure, and tone of his original were purposeful and completely valid, but some were careless or perverse. And the irrelevance or absurdity of the latter materials is the less apparent to an uncritical reader because of the erratic and discontinuous style of the poem throughout. (Incidentally, it is the uncritical reader who is most likely to feel he's been duped when the nature of Pound's shell game is made clear to him.) Confronting these facts does not disqualify one, in any way that I can see, from admiring Pound's poem as a poem, or from accepting its basic method of dealing with the original material as traditional. Carelessness is not an essential part of that method, any more than ignorance is.

"Homage to Sextus Propertius" is very high-class *vers de société;* in being such, it fulfills much of the Propertian spirit. Where it offends against that spirit is in being more tangled, more elliptical, more confused than its original; the idiotic errors are just part of that confusion, painful not because they're errors but because they're pointless and distracting. Still, the balance has to be positive. At his best, Pound gives his English Propertianoids extraordinary qualities of poetic relief and energy, as a glance at a few lines of Section III will show:

> Midnight, and a letter comes to me from our mistress:
> Telling me to come to Tibur:
>
>   *At* once!!
> "Bright tips reach up from twin towers,
> Anienan spring water falls into flat-spread pools."

Nox media, et dominae mihi venit epistula nostrae: Tibure me missa iussit adesse mora,	'Twas midnight when a letter came to me from my mistress bidding me come without delay to Tibur where the

candida qua geminas ostendunt culmina turres,
  et cadit in patulos nympha Aniena lacus.

white hills heave up their towers to right and left and Anio's waters plunge into spreading pools. (Loeb Library)

A nice little question of etiquette and accuracy is involved in the possessive adjective of the first line, "dominae . . . nostrae." Translating "my mistress" conveys what Propertius means but carefully doesn't say; translating "our" is not only literally accurate, it doesn't mislead anyone as to the real situation, it compels the reader into complicity ("that mistress you've heard me talk about so often"), and it shades the poet's attitude toward the lady from complacent possession to polite deference. Her letter, in requesting haste, is categorical and idiomatic: *missa mora* is as strong as an ablative absolute can be. Pound's version gives the sputter of the pen, the peremptory staccato of an agitated lady. But ladies in such a mood do not generally indulge in flowery phrases descriptive of the locale where they want their gentlemen to appear. What to do with the third and fourth lines of Propertius' poem? Pound's solution is to put the passage in quotation marks, as if it were being recalled by the poet from a description made in another context. The touch of diffused irony (we have no way of knowing what or who is being cited) alters the poem all the more because it replaces a somewhat flat and redundant passage; it's an equal but opposite deviation from prevailing norms. One could quarrel also with the rendering of line 10; "in me mansuetas not habet illa manus" contains no such strained construction as "Her hands have no kindness me-ward." And "in the via Sciro" doesn't convey any sense of peril; in fact, Sciron was a legendary highwayman, destroyed by Theseus, and "via Sciro" is the public highway between Megaris and Attica (see Ovid, *Metamorphoses* VII, 440 ff.). So Pound's poem has its considerable weaknesses; but it has equivalent strengths. The poet's elegant wit exercises itself at the expense of his own timidity; having proved to his own satisfaction that nobody would be so mean as to do in a purehearted lover, he proceeds to work out in carefully stilted, decorous verse plans for his own funeral, with a mourning mistress seated by the pyre (Pound's version brings her closer to suttee than Propertius does), and a final expression of preference for a rural, rather than an urban, grave.

Casting up the balance on Pound, we see his departures from the original are variously determined and so variously defensible. When he departs through ignorance or carelessness, and so produces a random effect, a blurred or diffused focus, there is not much to be said in his defence at all. When he exaggerates or minimizes to bring out a particular quality in the original, he is well within his rights as an imitator, and there is no use looking down one's nice-nelly nose at him. When he creates willful discontinuities and changes the structural units as well as patterns of Propertius, he may be on dangerous ground; but his principle is a good deal worse than his practice. One thing he does not do at all is conscript Propertius into the service of his own poetical voice; it is an authentic "homage" that he has written. And the freedom he claimed for a translator to seek out cultural equivalents—however it may have been abused, whatever its side effects in fostering amid readers of translations an appetite for cross-cultural wisecracks—can scarcely be overvalued.

CHAPTER VII

Texture and Polish: Milton and Racine

An ancient rudiment of wiseacre wisdom, handed down through the family of translators from generation to generation, proposes that it is easier to find an equivalent for some piece of business, some knot or gnarl of an original (however deeply fixed in the grain of a peculiar dialect), than to render a placid and relatively unruffled surface. For deep texture, there is always some sort of equivalent; and when the general level of verbal energy is high, minor discords pass unnoticed. But on a smooth pond a single pebble makes a lot of ripples that cannot very well be concealed.

Of course a good deal depends here on what other qualities one is trying to capture, if any. Translating Rabelais is mostly a matter of getting a rich salmagundi of stylistic devices to work with—there are nuances to be preserved, but not a great many. Translating a merely torpid and monotonous poet into a dialect of equivalent somnolence can't be very hard. It is when the rough poem must also maintain dignity, when the tightly controlled poem must also seethe with latent passion, that the dimensions of the translator's task become apparent. The differing fates of Milton's *Paradise Lost* in French and Racine's *Phèdre* in English illustrate, not only translational problems, but some special oddities of differing national tastes.

With the help of M. Addison's appreciations, *Paradise Lost* first crossed the linguistic Channel into French when N. F. Dupré de Saint Maur, with the assistance of C. J. Chéron de Boismorand, produced in 1727 a version in French prose with notes. This respectable rendering in the safe middle style had a long and various history during the eighteenth and nineteenth

centuries; it was revised, it was annotated, it was fitted out with a translated biography of Milton. Until 1755 it went quite unchallenged; then
Louis Racine (Racine *fils,* in effect) turned off a version in Alexandrines;
and thereafter rivals came thick and fast. The last quarter of the eighteenth
century and the first quarter of the nineteenth produced at least half a
dozen different translations of Milton's poem, generally in verse, and commonly more elevated than exact. Among these laborers in the vineyard
we note the Abbé LeRoy (1775), M. Beaulaton (1778), M. Mosneron
(1786), the Abbé DeLille (1805), M. Salgues (1807) and M. Delatour
de Pernes (1813). In addition, I find Chateaubriand referring to a relent-
lessly (and incomprehensibly) literal, interlinear version by M. Luneau
de Boisjermain, of which I have not been able to find any other biblio-
graphical trace; and we may note a version by M. Deloynes d'Auteroche
(1808) in which Milton's poem was happily "dégagée des longueurs et
superfluités" which had previously afflicted it. Whether they said so explicitly or not, that in fact was what a lot of these poetical versions were
doing—or, rather, they undertook to substitute some of their own *longueurs*
for Milton's. Convinced that the epic was and should be an exalted form,
they emphasized exaltation; and to lighten themselves for flight, they cast
aside the heavy burden of Milton's meaning—as well as a good deal else.
The opening lines of the poem as rendered by Abbés LeRoy and DeLille
exemplify this sort of airy levitation:

Je chante la révolte & la chûte de
l'homme,
Le coupable larcin de la fatale pomme,
Du genre-humain naissant, qui changea
l'heureux sort,
Sema dans l'Univers la douleur & la
mort,
Produisit tous ces maux dont la terre
est couverte,
Et du charmant *Eden* nous fit pleurer
la perte:
Jusqu'à ce qu'un Sauveur, un Dieu
meme incarné,
Eût reconquis pour nous un séjour
fortuné.
　　Descends, fille du Ciel, de ton bril-
　　lant empire,
Je prendrai de tes mains la trompette
& la lyre;
Muse, qui sur les monts embrasés &
fumans,
Oreb & *Sinaï* célebres monuments,

Je chante l'homme en proie aux pièges
tentateurs,
Et le fatal péché de nos premiers
auteurs
Qui, par le fruit mortel privés de l'innocence,
Nous léguèrent le mal, le crime et la
souffrance,
Jusqu'au jour où, calmant le courroux
paternel,
L'homme-dieu nous rouvrit les de-
meures du ciel:
Sujet vaste et sacré, dont jamais la
génie
N'enchanta les bosquets des nymphes
d'Aonie.
Toi donc qui, célébrant les merveilles
des cieux,
Prends loin de l'Hélicon un vol auda-
cieux;
Soit que, te retenant sous ses palmiers
antiques,

Inspiras ce Berger dont le crayon
  champêtre
Dessina le tableau du Néant & de
  l'Etre,
Peignit un monde entier sortant du
  noir cahos,
Et l'œuvre de six jours, & le sacré
  repos:
Toi-même au peuple saint, par sa
  plume divine,
Tu racontois des tems la première
  origine . . .
Ou, si tu préféras d'autres lieux plus
  chéris,
Soit de riants côteaux, soit des vallons
  fleuris,
La sommet de *Sion* entouré de mira-
  cles,
Les bords du *Siloé* retentissans d'oracles;
De ces lieux je t'invoque, osant pren-
  dre un essor
Que nul autre avant moi ne s'est
  permis encor.
Soutiens mon vol hardi, Reine de l'har-
  monie,
Je franchis sur tes pas la cime d'*Aonie.*

  Et toi, divin Esprit, protecteur des
    mortels,
Dans les cœurs droits & purs qui
  choisis tes autels,
De lumière & d'ardeur inépuisable
  source,
Viens m'ouvrir la carriere & diriger
  ma course:
Toi qui sais tout, anime, embellis mon
  pinceau;
Ta présence du monde honora le ber-
  ceau:
Ainsi que la Colombe en son nid soli-
  taire
Étend sur sa famille une aile tutélaire,
De ton ombre couvrant l'abîme illi-
  mité,
Tu lui soufflois la vie & la fécondité:
Sur ses germes glacés, sur ses froides
  semences

Sion avec plaisir répète tes cantiques;
Soit que, cherchant d'Horeb la tran-
  quille hauteur,
Tu rappelles ce jour où la voix d'un
  pasteur
Des Hébreux attentifs ravissant les
  oreilles,
De la création leur contoit les mer-
  veilles;
Soit que, chantant le jour où Dieu
  donna sa loi,
Le Sina sous tes pieds tressaille encor
  d'effroi;
Soit que, près du saint lieu d'où par-
  tent ses oracles,
Les flots du Siloé te disent ses mira-
  cles:
Muse sainte, soutiens mon vol pré-
  somptueux!
Jamais sujet plus grand et plus majes-
  tueux
Des poëtes divins n'échauffa le délire:
Viens, sous l'archet sacré déjà fremit
  ma lyre.
Et toi, toi qui, planant sur le sombre
  chaos
Où dormoient confondus l'air, la terre
  et les flots,
Couvois par la chaleur de ton aile
  féconde
La vie encore informe et les germes
  du monde,
Esprit saint! remplis-moi de ton souffle
  puissant;
Et si ton plus beau temple est un
  cœur innocent,
Viens épurer le mien, viens aider ma
  foiblesse;
Fais que de mon sujet j'égale la noblesse,
Et que mon vers brûlant, animé de
  ton feu,
Venge aux yeux des mortels la justice
  de Dieu!
            tr. Abbé Jacques DeLille
                    (Paris, 1805)

Ta chaleur répandoit ses douces influences.
Viens, dessille mes-yeux, seconde mes
efforts,
A ce noble sujet mesure mes accords;
Je veux venger d'un Dieu la providence auguste
Et le montrer à l'homme aussi bon
qui'l est juste.
    tr. Abbé LeRoy (Rouen, 1775)

A simple way to see what these "translations" did to Milton is to line up the
original text with literal retranslations, back into English, of the two Abbés:

Of Man's first disobedience, and the
fruit
Of that forbidden tree whose mortal
taste
Brought death into the World, and
all our woe,
With loss of Eden, till one greater
Man
Restore us, and regain the blissful
Seat,
Sing, Heavenly Muse, that on the
secret top
Of Oreb or of Sinai didst inspire
That Shepherd who first taught the
chosen seed
In the beginning how the heavens and
earth
Rose out of Chaos: or, if Sion
hill
Delight thee more, and Siloa's brook
that flowed
Fast by the oracle of God, I thence
Invoke thy aid to my adventurous
song
That with no middle flight intends to
soar
Above th'Aonian mount, while it pur-
sues
Things unattempted yet in prose or
rhyme.
And chiefly thou, O Spirit, that dost
prefer
Before all temples the upright heart
and pure,

I sing man, a prey to the tempting
snares,
and the fatal sins of our first parents
who, deprived of innocence by the
mortal fruit,
bequeathed us evil, crime and suffering
until the day when, calming his father's
wrath,
the man-god will reopen for us the
house of heaven,
a vast and sacred theme, with which
genius
never delighted the groves of Aonian
nymphs.
Thou therefore, who celebrating heavenly marvels,
take bold flight far above Helicon,
whether Sion, holding you under her
ancient palms,
takes pleasure to repeat your songs,
or Horeb's quiet heights invite you
to recall that day when a shepherd's
voice,
ravishing the ears of the listening
Hebrews,
recounted to them the marvels of
creation;
or if, as you sing the day when God
gave his law,
Sinai still trembles with fear under
your feet;
or if, near the holy place of her
oracles,

Instruct me, for thou knowest; thou from the first
Wast present, and with mighty wings outspread
Dovelike sat'st brooding on the vast abyss,
And mad'st it pregnant: what in me is dark
Illumine, what is low raise and support;
That to the height of this great argument
I may assert Eternal Providence
And justify the ways of God to men.

Siloa's waves speak of her miracles,
Holy muse, support my bold flight!
Never did subject more bold and majestic
warm the madness of the divine poets,
come, my lyre already trembles under the sacred bow.
                    (so far DeLille)
And thou, divine spirit, protector of mortals,
who place your altars in upright and pure hearts,
inexhaustible source of light and warmth,
come open my course and direct my way.
You who know all, animate and fortify my pencil;
your presence honored the world's cradle:
just as the Dove in his lonely nest
extends over his family a tutelary wing,
so you, covering the endless abyss with your shade
blew into it life and fecundity:
on its frozen germs, its chilly seeds,
your warmth spread its gentle influences.
Come, open my eyes, sustain my efforts,
equal my powers to this noble subject;
I wish to justify the lofty providence of God,
and show him to man as good as he is just.
                    (above, LeRoy)

Instead of soaring high over the Aonian mount, like Milton, with an easy, remote gesture toward the Muses living down there, Abbé DeLille gets us right into the middle of its nymph-haunted bosks; Abbé LeRoy, still more literal, fits Milton out with musical instruments and artistic trappings to the point of making him look like a one-man band. He has a trumpet, a lyre and bow (the Abbé seems to think a lyre works on the principle of a double-bass), and, presumably in the other hand, a painter's brush or pencil. Where Milton's Holy Spirit

> with mighty wings outspread
> Dove-like sat'st brooding on the vast abyss
> And mad'st it pregnant,

LeRoy converts the entire scene to one of avian domesticity:

> Ainsi que la Colombe en son nid solitaire
> Etend sur sa famille une aile tutelaire . . .

In a word, the elevation is not where Milton puts it, in the point of view, the extended perspective, and the suspended syntax: it is in adjectives ("sujet vaste et sacré," "jamais sujet plus grand et plus majestueux," "à ce noble sujet mésure mes accords,"—not to mention "charmant Eden," and those "Hébreux attentifs"); it is in a balanced antithesis that sometimes verges on the tick-tock:

> Ou, si tu préféras d'autres lieux plus chéris,
> Soit de riants côteaux, soit des vallons fleuris,
> La sommet de Sion entouré de miracles,
> Les bords du Siloé retentissans d'oracles. . . .

The overflowing impetus of Milton's lines couldn't be more remote from the staid antithesis of these regular verses. Above all, we miss the far-flung suspensions of Miltonic syntax, like that which holds the first five lines of Milton's poem balanced on one side of the abrupt imperative, "Sing, Heavenly Muse," and then balances it on the other side with the dependent clauses of lines 7–16. Finally, the translators seek elevation in fleshing out Milton's allusions, and making more explicit concepts that he glances at in passing, expanding Oreb and Sinai with explanations, omitting those crucial words "In the beginning" (line 9) which bring Genesis before us, and stuffing the verse, instead, with a summary of the hexameral tradition. The problem is not that Abbés LeRoy and DeLille are indifferent to Milton's elevations, but that they seek elevation through a set of devices quite different from those Milton used, requiring the abandonment of many of his distinctive textured particulars.

It was in revulsion from versions like these that the Vicomte de Chateaubriand undertook to translate *Paradise Lost* into French prose in the years following his retirement from politics as a result of the 1830 Revolution. The new version appeared in the same year (1836) as his *Essay on English Literature,* with which it was intimately linked; both exercises aimed to tear down the veils of intercultural misunderstanding. The first and decisive choice for his translation was to abandon all French forms of dignity, emphasis, correctness, and symmetry, in favor of a version as literally accurate as might be. As he described the principles of his version, in a set of incisive prefatory "Remarques," he valued no quality more highly than word-for-word, phrase-for-phrase, nuance-for-nuance accuracy;

and in detailing some of the ways in which he had pursued this elusive quality, he opened up new areas of awareness. For example, though he forcefully declined to reproduce what he considered grammatical and syntactical anomalies, he refused to impose more clarity on Milton than Milton himself had sought; and he pointed to the confusions of Adam's last speech to Eve on the topic of her desire to work alone (IX, 343 ff.) as one of the genuine beauties of the poem:

> But, if thou think trial unsought may find
> Us both securer than thus warn'd thou seem'st,
> Go. . . .

In order to gain effects that he thought the original intended (and whether he was right or wrong in the details hardly matters), Chateaubriand cheerfully violated French idioms, French decorums, French word order, French high style. Seeing that Milton had based much of his diction on the English Bible, Chateaubriand phrased his translation after the French authorized version of Sacy. He was attentive to Milton's deliberate repetitions, as of the word "praise" in the morning prayer of Adam and Eve (V, 153 ff.); he prided himself on making use of theological terms like "synodes" (for "assemblées"), "mémoriaux" (for "emblèmes"), and "conciles" (for "conseils"); in emulation of Milton, he ventured now and then a modest neologism. In pursuit of the Miltonic nuance, he cast aside not only rhyme but verse, and abandoned altogether the *pointe assassine,* the antithetical balance on which "fine writing" traditionally depended, in prose as well as in verse. A triple comparison, made in the course of his "Remarques," sets a passage of Milton's original (A) against the early prose of Dupré de Saint Maur (still, a hundred years after its first appearance, the traditional version) (B), and then against Chateaubriand's own translation (C):

(A)   . . . Through many a dark and dreary vale
        They passed, and many a region dolorous,
        O'er many a frozen, many a fiery alp,
        Rocks, caves, lakes, fens, bogs, dens, and shades of death,
        A universe of death, which God by curse
        Created evil, for evil only good,
        Where all life dies, death lives, and Nature breeds,
        Perverse, all monstrous, all prodigious things,
        Abominable, unutterable, and worse
        Than fables yet have feigned, or fear conceived,
        Gorgons, and Hydras, and Chimeras dire.

                        PL II, 618–628

(B) En vain traversaient-elles des vallées sombres et hideuses, des régions de douleur, des montagnes de glace et de feu; en vain franchissaient-elles des rochers, des fondrières, des lacs, des précipices et des marais empestés, elles retrouvaient toujours d'épouvantables ténèbres, les ombres de la mort, que Dieu forma dans sa colère, au jour qu'il créa les maux inséparables du crime; elles ne voyaient que des lieux où la vie expire et où la mort seule est vivante: la nature perverse n'y produit rien d'énorme et de monstrueux; tout est horrible, inexprimable, et pire encore que tout ce que les fables ont feint ou que la crainte s'est jamais figuré de gorgones, d'hydres, et de chimères dévorantes.

(C) . . . elles (the *bandes aventureuses*) traversent maintes vallées sombres et désertes, maintes régions douloureuses, par dessus maintes alpes de glace et maintes alpes de feu: rocs, grottes, lacs, mares, gouffres, antres et ombres de mort, univers de mort, que Dieu dans sa malediction créa mauvais, bon pour le mal seulement; univers où toute vie meurt, où toute mort vit, où la nature perverse engendre des choses monstrueuses, des choses prodigieuses, abominables, inexprimables, pires que ce que la fable inventa ou la frayeur conçut: gorgones et hydres et chimères effroyables.

A reader of Chateaubriand's version by no means gets the impression that he is reading elegant prose by the author of *Mémoires d'Outre-Tombe;* yet it is not devoid of melody. Turning Chateaubriand back into English as literally as possible, one would fall inevitably into a certain number of blank-verse lines, a not-contemptible rhythm somewhere between prose and free blank verse—and one certainly gets the rough, jolting texture of a line like

> Rocks, caves, lakes, fens, bogs, dens, and shades of death,

while from Dupré de Saint Maur one would never guess its existence.

Whether Chateaubriand was able to capture what he clearly regarded as Milton's rude, Gothic nobility is a question we will confront shortly. Let us for the moment glance askance at his professions of slavish accuracy; for in this matter, his bark is a good deal worse than his bite. Though he makes a great point of all the sleepless hours and multiple revisions that precise accuracy has cost him, in fact he stumbled over a Miltonic archaism in translating the very first verse-paragraph of *Paradise Lost:*

or if Sion hill Delight thee more, and Siloa's brook that flowed Fast by the oracle of God. . . .	Ou si la colline de Sion, le ruisseau de Siloé, qui couloit *rapidement* près de l'oracle de Dieu, te plaisent davan- tage . . .

Milton's "fast" here is no more to be translated "rapidement" than "hard" in the same context could be translated "durement"; it means, of course, "close," or "near." Less understandable, in the light of Chateaubriand's indignation with translators who irresponsibly convert singulars to plurals and vice versa, is his rendering of "above th'Aonian mount" as "au dessus des monts d'Aonie." Surely Milton had only Helicon in mind, as even the verse-translating Abbés understood, though naturally they had to fancify what Milton said about it

Chateaubriand's toleration of Milton's vagaries is not altogether unlimited, however; and on occasion theological odium rears its ugly head. Sin and Death, building a bridge across Chaos, are assimilated to the Pope in one outrageous word by Milton the punster:

> Now had they brought the work by wondrous art
> Pontifical. . .
>
> (X, 312).

Here Chateaubriand simply omits: Sin and Death work "par un art merveilleux," and never mind the "Pontifical." He also declines, for reasons of tonal dignity, to render the pun which animates Satan's easy leap over Eden-wall:

> and in contempt
> At one slight bound high overleapt all bound . . .
> (IV, 181).

par mépris [Chateaubriand translates], d'un seul bond léger il franchit tout l'enceinte. . . .

Other difficulties beset Chateaubriand in passages where Milton's loose grammar or his reliance on subsurface Latinate constructions allow him to play tricks with wide, vague suggestion which a translator cannot, or can hardly, follow. Two passages of contrasting tendency make the point:

> Since this day's death denounced, if aught I see,
> Will prove no sudden, but a slow-pac'd evil,
> A long day's dying, to augment our pain . . .
> (X, 962–4).

And, from an earlier line in Book X (828):

> Him after all disputes
> Forced I absolve.

In the first passage, the English expression "this day's death denounced" works about equally well as "the death we were told about today" or as "the death we were told would come someday." Syntactically speaking, Milton didn't have to decide whether "denounced" modified "day" or "death"; Chateaubriand is obliged by the nature of French to make up his mind. When he decides on "denoncée" (to agree with "la mort"), he automatically erects a barrier against the word applying to "jour"; and that barrier corresponds to nothing in Milton. As for "a long day's dying," he seems to have it quite wrong as "comme un jour qui meurt longuement."

The metaphor isn't where he places it—"like a long afternoon," but rather "a long period of dying, a long succession of days on each of which we will die a little." It was perhaps the looseness and ambiguity of the syntax that misled Chateaubriand—that looseness and ambiguity of which he complained, with some asperity, in the "Remarques." * In the second passage, on the other hand, "him" is so strongly defined in English as the objective form of the pronoun that it can be hung out at a considerable distance (just as in Latin) from the predicate controlling it. Milton is fond of this trick (see Book I, lines 44 ff.: "Him the Almighty Power / Hurled headlong flaming from the ethereal sky"), but French cannot follow, except at a distance: "Lui, aprés tous ces débats, je suis forcé de l'absoudre" (or, in the other passage, "Le Souverain Pouvoir le jeta flamboyant"). Milton's sentence gets much of its power from its bold displacements; "Him" is far out of its expected position, "Forced" crowds its way into the sentence before we even know what it is going to modify, while we are still in search of a subject and verb to control "him." Latin could play these games of word order without effort; English does so with a great flexing of muscles; and French cannot follow at all.

Generally, it is in this matter of Miltonic suspensions and inversions (the product of hard-working, remote-control verbs) that Chateaubriand's translation comes off least well. This is surprising because his own style is so richly sustained and periodic. For example, in Book IV Milton is describing Paradise in terms of all the gardens of antiquity that it excelled:

> Not that fair field
> Of Enna, where Proserpine gathering flowers,
> Herself a fairer flower, by gloomy Dis
> Was gather'd, which cost Ceres all that pain
> To seek her through the world . . .
>
> (IV, 268–72).

Ni la charmante campagne d'Enna, où Proserpine cueillant des fleurs, elle-même fleur plus belle, fut cueillie par le sombre Pluton (Cérès, dans sa peine, la chercha par toute la terre). . . .

Something is lost in the patterning when "by gloomy Dis / Was gather'd" turns into "fut cueillie par le sombre Pluton"; Milton wants the material modifying "Proserpine" to begin with "gathering" and end with "gathered" (it is a way of gathering the whole story into a single tight knot). But then, using one of those "pronoms sans relatifs" which Chateaubriand so deplored, he gestures away with a loose "which" and an even looser "all that

---

* "De là ces phrases inachevées, ces sens incomplets, ces verbes sans régimes, ces noms et ces pronoms sans relatifs dont l'ouvrage fourmille. Le poëte commence une phrase au *singulier* et l'achève au *pluriel;* inadvertance qu'il n'aurait jamais commise s'il avait pu voir les epreuves," etc.

pain" at an endlessness of suffering and loss that we are supposed to re-member from the story or imagine for ourselves. Chateaubriand cannot en-dure these perilous bridges, flung up with only one abutment to stand on; his parenthesis cuts off Milton's loosely extended sentence, and creates a tight little island of syntactical completeness.

A last passage from near the end of the poem:

> So spake our mother Eve, and Adam heard
> Well pleased, but answered not: for now, too nigh
> The archangel stood; and from the other hill
> To their fix'd station, all in bright array
> The cherubim descended; on the ground
> Gliding meteorous, as evening-mist
> Risen from a river o'er the marish glides,
> And gathers ground fast at the labourer's heel
> Homeward returning. High in front advanced,
> The brandish'd sword of God before them blazed,
> Fierce as a comet; which with torrid heat
> And vapour as the Libyan air adust,
> Began to parch that temperate clime: whereat
> In either hand the hastening angel caught
> Our lingering parents, and to the eastern gate
> Led them direct, and down the cliff as fast
> To the subjected plain; then disappeared.
>
> (XII, 624–640).

Ainsi parle Eve, notre mère, et Adam l'entendit charmé, mais ne repondit point; l'archange étoit trip près, et de l'autre colline à leur poste assigné, tous dans un ordre brillant les chérubins descendoient: ils glissoient, mé-téores sur la terre, ainsi qu'un brouillard du soir élevé d'un fleuve glisse sur un marais et envahit rapidement le sol sur les talons du laboureur qui re-tourne à sa chaumière. De front, ils s'avançoient; devant eux, le glaive bran-dissant du Seigneur flamboyait furieux comme un comète: la chaleur torride de ce glaive et sa vapeur, telle que l'air brûlé de la Libye, commen-çoient à dessécher le climat tempéré du Paradis, quand l'Ange hâtant nos languissants parents, les prit par la main, les conduisit droit à la porte orientale; de là aussi vite jusqu'au bas du rocher, dans la plaine inférieure, et disparut.

There is a gross mistranslation here, in "De front, ils s'avançoient." Milton's "advanced" is in fact a passive participle modifying "sword"; "high in front advanced" means simply "held high before them." But Chateaubriand was misled in this matter only because he was trying, throughout the passage, to get his grammatical feet under him. Milton's verses slither forward with a terrible indirect swiftness, from one subordinate clause to another; lines 5–9 of the quotations are almost invertebrate in their lack of independent verbs. Chateaubriand slips in verbs of his own where he can—no fewer than three new independent ones "ils glissaient," "qui retourne," and "ils s'avan-çoient"). Besides, he reinforces other connectives by repetition, as in "la chaleur torride *de ce glaive";* and he substitutes, as the subject of "com-mençoient," "chaleur . . . et vapeur," replacing Milton's much more in-definite "which"—a doubly indefinite pronoun, which could refer to "the sword of God" as well as the "comet" to explain the scorching of Paradise. But in all these transactions, the effect of the translation is, in one way or another, to diminish the reach and elasticity of Milton's poem.

All of this bears directly on the quantity and quality of elevation in Chateaubriand's version and Milton's original, and on the greater importance of the quality. It is true that the French version does not "plane," does not give the effect of being liberated from its grammatical supports. However hard to describe, this is a quality of *Paradise Lost* to which many readers have borne witness—as if, somehow, there were two tracks for Miltonic verse, one associative, patterned, imagistic, musical; the other a minimal un-derpinning of syntax. Surely it's not an infrequent experience to read a Mil-tonic passage of dazzling energy and total unity, and then turn back to parse out painfully subject, verb, object, and modifiers under the shell of irridescent imagery. By strengthening the sometimes overburdened syntax, Chateaubri-and inevitably modifies the independence of the free imagery. His close trans-lation tends to level down and consolidate the cloud-peaks of Milton's poem, while shortening its seven-league strides; and, as we have seen, he makes no effort to get the rhetorical formalities of French "high style" into his ver-sion. Precisely for that reason, though, because he had an ear tuned to Milton's free-soaring rhythms, he did bring to the French reader an irregular and Biblical kind of "sublime" which feels Miltonic if only because it is not traditionally French. In short, by *not* doing what it is sometimes said a trans-lator ought to do (adopt the idioms of one language to those of another), he has come far closer to the real Miltonic texture and pattern of feeling than any previous translator. At the root of this success is, no doubt, the fact that Milton did not write, in English itself, a smooth, correct, translucent style; his verse feels, by contrast with other English verse, gigantic, turbid, sculptural. For those qualities there are no practical "equivalents," there are only the qualities themselves; and no method comes so close to true eleva-tion as that which disregards it altogether.

Compressing *Paradise Lost* into French is a task to the difficulty of which Chateaubriand in his testy "Remarques" did ample justice; we have noted above some of his complaints about the imprecisions, allusions, and dic-tional hazards of the English text, and there can be no doubt that these ob-stacles loomed formidably before the translators. Apart from reproducing an effect they thought they felt, conventional elevation saved the transla-tors from confronting many stylistic Gorgons, and evidently encouraged that lofty laziness and imprecision of which we're aware in too many of the versions. On the other hand, none of the translators failed to recognize the sublimity of the original—at worst, they merely took that sublimity as an occasion for the laxities of the conventional "sublime." They may even have felt that they were saving Milton from himself—doing for him what, if his eyes had been open (culturally as well as physically), he would surely have done for himself. The rough, commercial milieu of the theater, on the other hand, dealt far more crudely with the style and structure of Racine's *Phèdre,* when it was turned into English. In *Phaedra and Hippolytus* (1709), one Edmund Smith produced what he thought the theme of incest demanded, a vociferous, fustian melodrama which had good reason to conceal, as much as possible, its dependence on a French original. After this artless travesty, the next English version did not appear till 1776, when *Phèdre* was translated into English prose, and the slumber was prolonged until about mid-nineteenth century, when a version by R. B. Boswell of Racine's entire *Dramatic Works* started appearing. Boswell was being reprinted as the standard version as late as the 1930's; and indeed, as we see, he did not have much competition. Among the curiosities we note a "Bernhardt" edition (bilingual, and obviously for the use of the semi-Frenched at performances by the actress). But one cannot find more than sporadic, isolated ventures at translation of *Phèdre* much before so-called "modern times." Since the 1930's, however, no fewer than nine new versions have appeared: by Robert Henderson (n.d., starts turning up in anthologies in the thirties), P. Landis (1931), A. Tobin (1958), Lacy Lockert (1958), O. Pucciani (1959), M. Rawlings (1961), Robert Lowell (1961), Kenneth Muir (1962), and John Cairncross (1963). Evidently the great age of French curiosity about Milton began about two hundred years ago, the great age of English curiosity about Racine some forty years ago. There are probably social and cultural morals to be drawn from these comparative timetables, but no need to make them explicit. For the moment, it's enough to note that the Racine problem looks like the exact obverse of the Milton problem: it is not the Gothic sublime of a craggy exterior that's to be rendered, but a polished and formal surface that, though chilly and correct, must be kept from seeming *merely* chilly and correct.

The first Englishman to lay hands on Racine's play went at his work in a roistering, freebooting mood, which sacrifices Racine's polished surfaces at once, with the joyous clatter of a rock going through plate glass. It is a gaudy pattern of shards that results. The later nineteenth-century version of Boswell which held the field as standard for so long looks more like a translation, but has a cornucopia of different disastrous features, perhaps the first of which is its essential unspeakability. Miss Margaret Rawlings points out, with a working actress's cruelly accurate ear, what technological change has done to the lines in which Theramenes remonstrates with Hippolytus:

> You have been seldom seen with wild delight
> Urging the rapid car along the strand. . . .

. . . where what's meant is driving a chariot along a beach, and what's conveyed is racing an Aston-Martin down a major traffic artery in London.* Writing before the internal-combustion engine, Boswell was simply unfortunate here; but it's a misfortune to which his high-flown literary style is particularly prone. Homonyms like sighs/size, mien/mean, and so on, which are automatic for an eye-writer to distinguish, can easily baffle and mislead when delivered from the stage. Even the manipulation of a queen's costume, when it gets too involved, can become confusing to an audience which has to pick up and adjust a number of perhaps metaphorical details on the fly, as it were. When fretful Phaedra first appears, Boswell has her say,

> Ah, how these cumbrous gauds,
> These veils oppress me! What officious hand
> Has tied these knots, and gather'd o'er my brow
> These clustering coils? How all conspires to add
> To my distress!

The passage he is rendering reads:

> Que ces vains ornements, que ces voiles me pèsent!
> Quelle importune main, en formant tous ces noeuds,
> A pris soin sur mon front d'assembler mes cheveux?
> Tout m'afflige, et me nuit, et conspire à me nuire.

The "cumbrous gauds" are hard to hear, in the first place; they suggest barbaric, gaudy pieces of jewelry, where Racine's "vains ornements," being lighter, can more easily be identified with the veils themselves. The English involves us in a metaphorical tangle of veils, knots, and clustering coils from which we do not easily break loose; Racine liberates us in time with the simple, literal word, "cheveux." And, most painfully, Racine's last line, with the infinite art of its sigh, its repetition, its inner rhyme, and its broken languor, disappears completely from the translation as a poetic line to be felt.

Phèdre is querulous but queenly; Oenone is an exasperated maidservant, and talks like one. "Comme on voit tous ses voeux l'un l'autre se détruire," is her response to the royal complaints above—it is half an aside, as her

---

* Automobiles and other modern inventions, because their terminology is often borrowed metaphorically from previous usage, are likely to play havoc with older texts. In a famous passage of denunciation, the prophet Isaiah threatens the wanton daughters of Zion not only with disagreeable scabs and infections, but with loss of all their gaudy adornments; and the motorcar has done strange things to the King James version of their disgrace:

> In that day the Lord will take away the bravery of their tinkling ornaments
> about their feet, and their cauls, and their round tires like the moon,
> The chains, and the bracelets, and the mufflers. . . .

(Isaiah iii, 18–19)

Without tires, chains or mufflers, one sees the poor girls immobilized in their Mercedes-Benzes.

third-person locutions imply. But Boswell translates into a jargon of impersonalities that no maidservant would ever speak and no audience could conceivably understand:

> What is one moment wish'd,
> The next is irksome.

"She doesn't know what she wants, from one minute to the next"—that or something like it is the sentiment in its natural, maidservantly dimension; but the form it takes under Boswell's pen needs translation almost as much as the original. When they are inflated, simple sentiments seem inevitably to get confused as well. Phèdre could scarcely summarize in plainer language the effect of her program to alienate Hippolytus by being mean to him: "Tu me haïssois plus, je ne t'aimois pas moins"—"You hated me worse, I loved you no less." But the translator manages to stumble over even this simplicity, bringing it out as: "Hating me more I loved you none the less." It will certainly be heard, as it ought, grammatically, to read, "I hated myself worse without loving you any less"—and that's not Racine at all.

Where the text is simple, anyone can see that it's bad translation to fail of an equivalent simplicity; but Racine is not always simple, and when he seems gratuitously entangled, it is not always the fault of his translators. In the course of his long, strained declaration of affection for Aricie, Hippolytus tells the young lady that he cannot get her out of his mind, and thus (according to Boswell)

> For fruit
> Of all my bootless sighs, I fail to find
> My former self.

It is a passage likely to evoke a bootless sigh or two from a reader, as well; and it is not much improved by going back to Racine:

> Moi-même, pour tout fruit de mes soins superflus,
> Maintenant je me cherche, et ne me trouve plus.

The idea underneath this ingenuity is not really very complicated; I think he is just saying that since he gave up his former pursuits because of his new attachment, he now doesn't have them to fall back upon. The problem with the original is that it sounds self-conscious and frigid; obviously, that problem is not solved by turning the passage into equivalent English frigidities. If the conceits were simply isolated and occasional, one might contemplate short-circuiting them, reducing them to something direct and simple. But they are built into the very structure of the verse; the crucial difficulty of the Racine translator comes with an absolutely characteristic line like that from Phèdre's last speech,

> Le ciel mit dans mon coeur une flamme funeste.

What does a translator do with a line like that? If he does not try to change the whole level of the poet's dialect, he is likely to come up with something not far removed from Boswell's

> Heav'n in my bosom kindled baleful fire.

This isn't a translational disaster, by any means: even modern versions are not likely to come out much better. Miss Rawlings, who has as sharp an ear as one could want for a speakable line, gives us:

> Heaven in my heart kindled the fatal flame.

Robert Henderson, Lacy Lockert, John Cairncross, and Robert Lowell come up with, respectively:

> The gods had lit a baleful fire in me;
>
> Heaven lit a fatal flame within my breast;
>
> Heaven in my heart lit an ill-omened fire;
>
> The flames of Aphrodite maddened me.

But none of these translators can make Racine's line into a convincing line of English poetry, because, try as they will, none of them altogether overcome the roadblock metaphors of the line, "Heaven" and "flame." These words are at once too abstract (too conventional) a form of diction, and too concrete (too untransparent and resistant) to convey the sense of a real psychological fact. They sound both grandiloquent and empty as a way of saying that A has a yen for B. Modern English simply won't sustain itself on metaphors of this quality; yet they are the very substance of the French line, and one can't diminish the metaphorical stiltedness without dissolving the poise and luxurious resentment of the statement. Mr. Pucciani, who feels a necessity of doing something more with the line than it does for itself, gives it texture indeed, but scarcely of a Racinian sort:

> It was I when I first set eyes on your son
> Who burst into flames like a torch of sea-rotten wood,
> The Gods lit the torch, Theseus, but I was the one to burn.

He is absolutely right in trying to express the slow, smoky, smothered heat of an inner fire; even the overtones of resentment against the gods and personal helplessness are really present in Racine's line; the extrapolations are in genuine sympathy with the spirit of the text. But tonally, they are all off key. Phèdre as she approaches her death is not making picturesque literary comparisons or fine lines; she compresses her rhetoric, as she limits her gestures, to an imperious, queenly shorthand.

To see the problem in its full dimensions—the austere rhythms to be imitated, the passionate feelings to be suggested, the narrow range of linguistic devices with which to gain one's effects—a final example may be found in one of Phèdre's great speeches to Hippolytus. She is saying that he instead of Theseus should have come to Crete, so that she instead of Ariadne could have guided him through the labyrinth:

> C'est moi, Prince, c'est moi, dont l'utile secours
> Vous eût du labyrinthe enseigné les détours.
> Que de soins m'eût coûté cette tête charmante!
> Un fil n'eût point assez rassuré votre amante.
> Compagne du péril qu'il vous falloit chercher,
> Moi-même devant vous j'aurois voulu marcher;
> Et Phèdre, au labyrinthe avec vous descendue,
> Se seroit avec vous retrouvée ou perdue.*

There is not one of these resonant, majestic Alexandrines that runs in what we would think of as "natural" word order. Each is impeded on its march to the inevitable rhyme by an inversion or parenthesis, and by an act of overcome resistance emphasizes its own ineluctable, foreseen termination. Though it affirms an act of passionate individual choice and desire, the passage reaches its shuddering climax in a deliberate shift to the perspective of a third-person locution—as if, standing at a distance, Phèdre were watching herself and Hippolytus disappearing—absorbed, together, indifferent—into the gates of hell. We can't fail to notice the tremendous power of the word "descendue," in which the labyrinth is subtly, irresistibly identified with the nether regions, the hell of Phaedra's anticipation. There is majesty in the speech, there is artifice, there is control; and my eighteenth-century editor cannot let the lines pass without a footnote bearing witness to his response: "Voilà sans doute le dernier degré où la passion puisse être portée au théâtre." From a modern perspective we are doubtless tempted to smile at this conception of ultimate passion; but the deep current of intense feeling in the narrow channel of formal expression is nothing less than Racine himself. For an English translator it is not just a matter of compressing King Lear feelings into "Rape-of-the-Lock" versification; the reader must somehow be made to feel that the stylistic limitations have a reason, an inevitability, that in fact the English stage never gave them, and is disposed to give them now less than ever before.

---

* John Cairncross, making use of the freedoms of blank verse, gets the passage into smooth English—almost too smooth, perhaps, since it's only a short step from smooth to flat:

> I, only I, would have revealed to you
> The subtle windings of the labyrinth.
> What care I would have lavished on your head!
> A thread would not have reassured my fears.
> Affronting danger side by side with you,
> I would myself have wished to lead the way,
> And Phaedra, with you in the labyrinth,
> Would have returned with you or met her doom.

The problem is thus one of depth. When one can take a convention for granted, it is relatively easy to get an audience to see an individual passion behind it; when both the screen and the action behind-screen are being actuated at the same moment, they tend inevitably to attenuate, if not to undermine, one another. The English translator of Racine is condemned by social circumstance to gun his rhetorical motor as he applies his brakes; and that's not good for even the best machines. It's certainly not much like Racine. The French translators of Milton had, by contrast, a far easier job: to do one thing with your basic language is bound to be easier than doing two, especially when they are self-opposing.

CHAPTER VIII

Ipso-Translators (Mostly Joyce)

When an author turns to translating his own work (either by himself or in collaboration), most of the problems he faces are identical with those of a regular translator. In one respect only he has a special, and perhaps troublesome, advantage: he has privileged access to the "true intention" of the original text, the full process of thought and feeling that brought it into existence. How he chooses to use that privileged information, and in what way, will determine very largely the interest of his translation. He can be, by choice or by circumstance, either a generous or a stingy translator.

As late as the seventeenth century, it was frequent enough for men to write their poetry twice over, once in the vernacular, once in the classical language; to do so was a kind of academic exercise. Thus Richard Crashaw published his *Epigrammata Sacra* in 1634 and reproduced a number of them in English, in 1646, under the title *Divine Epigrams*. Despite the dates, it's not altogether a foregone conclusion that every one of the epigrams was written first in Latin, then translated into English; some of them may have undergone the contrary process. But in fact, there is not generally much to be learned by reading one group against the other. Crashaw did not exercise any difficult options in one tongue that he avoided in the other, did not add or diminish in any significant way between the two versions. He simply transcribed in one tongue what he had done in the other; and because he was deft in both, the results are often equivalent or nearly so. His extraordinary skills, combined with his limited intent, made him a stingy, an unrevealing translator. But his contemporary Marvell, when he wrote "Hortus" as a partial version in Latin of his English poem "The Garden," gave away more. In writing Latin verses, he was just as skilful as Crashaw; but I think his translation reveals that it was done under different circumstances and for different purposes. Unless I misread the two versions radically, Marvell began the poem in Latin and wrote the first four stanzas in that tongue. He then translated what he had done into English, eliminating the clumsier strokes of wit and reinforcing the fine ones, and continued in English through the "Christian" stanzas of the poem (V–VIII). Satisfied with these in English, he never translated them back into Latin; but the last stanza of the poem (IX), which was originally written in English, he did translate back into Latin. One way we can be confident of this is that a pun occurs which can only be felt in the Latin though it could only be conceived in English:

And, as it works, th'industrious Bee
Computes its time as well as we.

Sedula quin et apis, mellito intenta labori,
Horologo sua pensa thymo signare videtur.

The "horologo thymo" or thyme-clock is witty only if one has an English pun in mind, yet in the English poem it isn't a pun at all. For what reason we can hardly imagine, Marvell evidently back-translated the stanza, to give the impression that there had once been a complete Latin version—as it seems very dubious that there ever was. He thus revealed, with perhaps unintentional generosity, more about the growth and structure of this much-discussed poem than one could ever discover from either version in isolation.

Among modern writers, T. S. Eliot can be taken as a type of the stingy ipso-translator. His concern with French literature was deep and of long standing, his command of French idiom excellent; so one might expect interesting things of M. Jean de Menasce's first version in French of "The Waste Land" * when one learns that it was "revue et corrigée par l'auteur." The title is particularly provocative. "La terre mise à nu" carries all sorts of confessional and romantic overtones from Baudelaire's "Mon coeur mis à nu." But in fact nothing is further from the intent of the French version than to set anything à nu. It is, on the whole, a wooden and literal translation. Many of the nuances in the English original Eliot either allowed, or was forced to allow, M. de Menasce to sacrifice without a trace. For instance, the distorted half-quotations from Milton (line 98) and Marvell (line 196) disappear completely, and trifles like Eliot's delicate play on the word "antique" also get lost.** Trifling as they seem, these losses and

---

* It appeared in *Esprit*, May 1926, pp. 174–94.
** We have the authority (for what it's worth) of Eliot's own notes in supposing that Milton is being alluded to in the line "As though a window gave upon the sylvan scene," and Marvell in the line, "But at my back from time to time I hear." But the allusion depends so heavily on catching the exact turn of a few words from a well-known phrase, it's so engrained in a particular complex of words and feelings, as to be almost unreproducible; at least, none of the

others like them diminish sharply the depth and complexity of the entire poem.

Another problem raised by the French translation has to do with the inability of that language to follow easy, agile, indeterminate English verbs. A main effect of the following passage is the detachment of the verbs from their subjects, the sense one has of their acting almost spontaneously; the form taken by the French translation is to the right:

In vials of ivory and coloured glass	
Unstoppered, *lurked* her strange synthetic perfumes,	sommeillaient
Unguent, powdered, or liquid— *troubled, confused*	troublaient, confondaient
And *drowned* the sense in odours; stirred by the air	noyaient
That freshened from the window, these *ascended*	montaient
In *fattening* the prolonged candle-flames,	alourdissaient
Flung their smoke into the laquearia,	projetaient
Stirring the pattern on the coffered ceiling.	emouvant

The vague, drifting syntax of the English, with all those indeterminate, free-floating verbs, is clearly deliberate; it suggests the shapeless drift of air currents, shade, and smoke through the darkened room. To be sure, French doesn't have a beautifully ambiguous form like English "troubled," which (as used here) can be first, second, or third person active imperfect, singular or plural, or else a past passive participle. So literal translation was out of the question. But to settle for so many heavy-footed verbs in a row was to confess oneself an unambitious or unimaginative translator. In another passage, a genuinely strained and intricate verb of Eliot's is rendered, after a fashion, but by means which amount to the translator's throwing up his hands:

> Under the firelight, under the brush, her hair
> Spread out in fiery points
> Glowed into words, then would be savagely still.
>
> Sous la lumière du feu, sous la brosse, ses cheveux
> Dressées en pointes de feu
> Luisaient à devenir des mots, puis, sauvagement immobiles.

translations of "The Waste Land" that I have seen (including Professor Curtius into German and Professor Praz into Italian) have made any effort to capture such nuances. As for "antique," it's applied to Lil in the vulgar sense—"You ought to be ashamed, I said, to look so antique" (line 156)—not far from its appearance in the customary polite sense, "Above the antique mantel was displayed" (line 97).

"Spread" offers us the familiar verb-participle dilemma, "still" an un-translatable pun on the concepts "silent" and "motionless"; but the "would be still" is an extraordinarily rich construction. It could parse out as "used to be still" and "tried to be still," the latter with a kind of buried imperative, as in *"Will* you be still!" M. de Menasce's solution, which was simply to omit the verb altogether, doubtless came at the end of a long series of experiments; it's the kind of negative accomplishment one would think an author would be primarily concerned to prevent, where the translator comes off gracefully at the expense of his original.

James Joyce, on the other hand, was a remarkably generous translator of his own work, not only in the sense of putting a lot of time into the task, but in trying hard to define the exact nuances of his meaning. Joyce was such a remarkable linguist in his own right, and worked so closely with the French and German translators of *Ulysses* (especially those turning it into French) that these versions often give us special light into the original. *Ulysses* in English presents so many departures from standard speech, in the form of slang, sound effects, multilingual puns, musical imitations, fragmented thoughts, and private allusions, that translations can hardly fail to help out now and then.* One passage where a great many of these problems occur is the end of the section known as "Oxen of the Sun." After a series of parodies which trace the history of the English language from Anglo-Saxon through the nineteenth century, the diction of the chapter breaks down into an extraordinary mixture of slangs, pidgin, and general gibberish. The dramatic pretext for this disintegration can be found in the fact that the hour is late and the speakers are drunk, confused, and tired; on a more symbolic level, the chapter has traced the development of English from conception to viable foetus, and birth must now be followed by afterbirth. Thus the English original is a messy and frequently obscure muddle of twisted allusions, which the French version very often does a good deal to clarify. On the left, we print Joyce's original text, to the right phrases of the French translation that seem particularly illuminating:

All off for a buster, armstrong, hollering down the street. Bonafides. Where you slep las nigh? Timothy of the battered naggin. Like ole Billyo. Any ₅ brollies or gumboots in the fambly? Where the Henry Nevil's sawbones and ole clo? Sorra one o me knows. Hurrah there, Dix! Forward the ribbon counter. Where's Punch? All serene. Jay, look at	1. bras dessus bras dessous 4. A la tant que ça peut 8. Voyez rubans!

* French version by Auguste Morel, Stuart Gilbert, Valery Larbaud, and "l'auteur" (Paris, A. Monnier, 1930); Italian version by Gulio de Angelis (Milano, Mondadori, 1960); first German version by Georg Goyert (Basel, 1927), third corrected edition (Zurich, Rhein, 194–?).

10 the drunken minister coming out of the
maternity hospital! *Benedicat vos omni-*
potens Deus, Pater et Filius. A make,
mister. The Denzille lane boys. Hell,
blast ye! Scoot. **Righto, Isaacs,** shove
15 em out of the bleeding limelight. Yous
join uz, dear sir? No hentrusion in life.
Lou heap good man. Allee samee this
bunch. *En avant, mes enfants!* Fire
away number one on the gun. Burke's!
20 Thence they advanced five parasangs.
Slattery's mounted foot where's that
bleeding awfur? Parson Steve, apos-
tates' creed! No, no. Mulligan! Abaft
there! Shove ahead. Keep a watch on
25 the clock. Chuckingout time. Mullee!
What's on you? *Ma mère m'a mariée.*
British Beatitudes! *Retamplan Digidi*
Boum Boum. Ayes have it. To be
printed and bound at the Druiddrum
30 press **by two designing females.** Calf
covers of pissedon green. Last word in
art shades. Most beautiful book come
out of Ireland my time. *Silentium!* Get
a spurt on. Tention. Proceed to nearest
35 canteen and there annex liquor stores.
March! **Tramp, tramp the boys are**
(**attitudes!**) **parching.** Beer, beef business, bibles, bulldogs, battleships, bug-
gery and bishops. Whether on the
40 scaffold high. Beerbeef trample the
bibles. When for Irelandear. **Trample**
the trampellers. Thunderation! Keep
the durned millingtary step. We fall.
Bishops' boosebox. Halt! Heave to.
45 Rugger. Scrum in. No touch kicking.
Wow, my tootsies! You hurt? Most
amazingly sorry!
Query. Who's astanding this here do?
Proud possessor of damnall. Declare
50 **misery. Bet to the ropes. Me nantee**
saltee. Not a red at me this week gone.
Yours? Mead of our fathers for the
Ubermensch. Dittoh. **Five number ones.**
You, sir? Ginger cordial. **Chase me, the**
55 **cabby's caudle.** Stimulate the caloric.
Winding of his ticker. Stopped short

12–13. Un petit sou, m'sieur

14. Ca colle, Anatole

21–2. L'air est pur la route est large,
où est ce bougre d'officemar?

26. Qu'est-ce que tu prends?

30. par deux femelles pleines d'astuce

36–7. Marchons, marchons, qu'un vin
impure (à droite, alignement!)
abreuve nos gaviots.

41–2. Marchant sur les marchands

44. Le bistrot des Bichots

49–51. Orgueilleux possesseur de peau
de balle. Je passe la main. Dans
les cordes. Ye n'ai pas oune
rotin.

53. Cinq Bass extra

54–5. Pige-moi ça, de la tisane de col-
lignon.

never to go again when the old. Absinthe
for me, savvy? *Caramba!* Have an egg-
nog or a prairie oyster. Enemy? Avun-
60 cular's got my timepiece. Ten to. Obligated awful. Don't mention it. Got a
pectoral trauma, eh, Dix? Pos fact. Got
bet be a boomblebee whenever he was
settin sleepin in hes bit garten. Digs up
65 near the Mater. **Buckled he is. Know
his dona? Yup, sartin, I do. Full of a
dure.** See her in her dishybilly. **Peels
off a credit.** Lovely lovekin. None of
your lean kine, not much. Pull down
70 the blind, love. **Two Ardilauns.** Same
here. Look slippery. If you fall don't
wait to get up. Five, seven, nine. Fine!
**Got a prime pair of mincepies, no kid.
And her take me to rests and her anker
75 of rum.** Must be seen to be believed.
**Your starving eyes and allbeplastered
neck you stole my heart, O gluepot.**
Sir? Spud again the rheumatiz? All
poppycock, you'll scuse me saying. For
80 the hoi polloi. I vear thee beest a gert
vool. Well, doc? **Back fro Lapland?
Your corporosity sagaciating O K?**
How's the squaws and papooses? **Wo-
manbody after going on the straw?**
85 Stand and deliver. Password. **There's
hair.** Ours the white death and ruddy
birth. Hi! Spit in your own eye, boss.
Mummer's wire. Cribbed out of Mere-
dith. **Jesified orchidised polycimical
90 jesuit!** Aunty mine's writing Pa Kinch.
Baddybad Stephen lead astray goody-
good Malachi.

59–60. Combien de plombes? Mon oig-
non est chez Ma Tante.

65–7. Est de la Confrérie de St Pris.
Tu connais sa gonzesse? Gy.
J't'écoute. Passe pas par la
porte.

67–8. Un déballage je ne te dis que
ça.

70. Deux Guinness

73–5. Elle vous a une de ces paires de
mirettes, blague dans le coin.
Elle d'offrir ses trains antéropostérieurs.

76–7. Vos yeux désastres et votre cou
albaplâtré m'ont ravi le coeur, ô
mon petit Dardant.

81–2. Retour de Lapevinie? Votre flairosité merdicale à la hauteur?

84. Y en a-t-il une en train de
mômir?

85–6. Ça gaze.

89–90. Jesufiant testicouillard polypuci-
que jésuite

Among the riches here spread out for observation, we note that "arm-
strong," instead of being a possible associate of our noisy roisterers, describes a method of walking, with arms linked. "Full of a dure" is a way
of emphasizing a lady's embonpoint; "attitudes!" is an order to dress right,
and "what's on you?" is a way of asking a man what he'll have to drink.
The question "Enemy?" means "What time is it?", while "starving eyes
and allbeplastered neck" are evidently degradations of "starry eyes and
alabaster neck," but why the creature thus happily endowed should be
called a "gluepot" in English is not rendered much plainer by her title in

French, "mon petit Dardant." There are enough other unanswered questions to make the whole comparison of versions chancy; not every reader will find an "officemar" clearer than an "awfur" (line 22); "Voyez rubans" doesn't convey very much of the self-mockery of "Forward the ribbon counter" (line 8); and something has clearly been lost in the solemn translation, "deux femelles pleines d'astuce" for "two designing females" (line 30). (The reference is to Yeats's sisters, who did the artwork for The Dun Emer, later the Cuala Press, at Dundrum.) Though French argot is often more accessible than the equivalent Dublin slang, some of the occasions where it isn't simply confirm that language is being used to baffle or blur the mind, as in the "flairosité merdicale" of line 81. An earnest, eager symbol-seeker might be tempted to look for some significance in the conjunction of "ole Billyo" in line 4 with "Henry Nevil" in line 6, perhaps some diabolic allusion; but the translation, by rendering the first phrase mildly and the second with obscene energy, "Ous qu'est foutu le calouquet," etc., closes off that possibility. A reader unacquainted with Cockney rhyming slang might not twig to "her take me to rests and her anker of rum" (breasts and bum: lines 45–46), but "ses trains antéropostérieurs," without being in itself much more explicit, makes unmistakably clear what is being talked about. There are plenty of passages where the translation merely replaces an Irish puzzle with a French one, on the familiar principle of getting one equivalent texture for another; thus the reference to "Slattery's Mounted Foot" in line 21 is not in any way clarified by the translation "l'air est pure, la route est large"—they are both refrains of songs, but that is as far as it goes, and the reader who cares will simply have to find for himself the Dublin street ballad about Slattery and his thirsty heroes. Still, there are a surprising number of instances where acquaintance with the translation gives a lead toward an understanding of the original.

Sometimes this happens when the translators felt an allusion was too abrupt or local for someone outside the immediate Dublin milieu to grasp; for instance, as Mr. Bloom sits with Richie Goulding in the dining room of the Ormond, the thought occurs that Goulding is a musician and singer himself: "Sings too. *Down among the dead men.* Appropriate. Kidney pie. Sweets to the. Not making much hand of it. Best value in. Characteristic of him. Power. Particular about his drink" (p. 268). The translation can follow most of this rather macabre train of thought without much trouble (Bloom thinks it appropriate that Goulding, who is dying of Bright's disease, should be eating kidney pie); but the single word "Power" is too abrupt to be clear, even though there's a context for it; the French translation softens and explains by translating it "Du whisky Power." Occasionally a name is translated in order to retain a symbolic or representative quality which it wouldn't have in the To-language if simply transcribed. Richie Goulding talks to Bloom about that wonderful tenor Joe Maas, who happens to be an historical figure, a former lead singer in the Carl Rosa Opera Company; but the account culminates in a pun: "Choirboy style. Maas was the boy. Massboy" (p. 268). The translators found the pun more important than the historical figure, and transformed Joe Maas to Joe Coeur, so that the account could culminate: "Style d'enfant de choeur. Mais Coeur c'était l'as. L'as de coeur" (p. 308). The ace of hearts, with an untranslatable pun on coeur/choeur represents a pretty successful rendering of the original; and it's fair to assume that it clarifies Joyce's intention in evoking the memory of this long-dead tenor. Elsewhere, Wisdom Hely converts, in the French version, to Lesage Hély, Alexander Keyes to Alexandre Cleys (with a pun, of course, on French "clef" = key), and an usher at Trinity College, Hornblower, becomes Corcorne. Not even the circumstance that these were real biographical Dubliners prevented Joyce from translating their names, with the implication that the theme was more important to him than the "factual" authenticity. On the other hand, it is not at all clear why a very minor, almost imperceptible name like Maurice Butterly should be twice translated as Maurice Lamèrement—it clearly aims at being a pun on "bitterly," but the overtone adds nothing whatever to the two widely separated passages in which the name occurs (*Ulysses* 18, 477; French translation 17, 547).

One of the book's famous puzzles is the anonymous postcard that Mr. Denis Breen is carrying around, with the words "U.P. up" written on it. Everyone, including demented Mr. Breen, has sensed that this cryptic comment implies an insult. Mr. Breen is in search of a lawyer to institute suit against the unknown sender. But there has been some doubt as to the exact significance of the expression, and the reason why it is so disturbing. The ordinary English slang meaning of the phrase is "finished," or "done for." But the French translation by its rendering "Fou Tu" suggests that the basic insult is sexual, with an added implication of *non compos mentis* ("fou" = crazy, "foutu" = screwed). The German translator gave, as his attempt at an equivalent, "P.L.E.M. plem", which has no meaning beyond simple "crazy." The French version is rich in this instance. But mysterious MacIntosh is just as enigmatic in French as in the original, the shaggy-dog riddle that Stephen poses to his students at Mr. Deasy's academy is just as pointless, and a phrase like "Agenbite of Inwit" translates, very literally indeed, into "morsure de l'ensoi," without any of the medieval overtones it carries in English.

A special, if not particularly profound, problem for the translator is posed by Joyce's generous representation in *Ulysses* of the world of unverbalized sound. Squeaks and hisses and slops and bumps and swirls are lavishly scattered through the novel, and a translator who undertakes to render them generally has to make use of equivalents wholly different from those of English. Mr. John Ferris has noted (*Saturday Review*, Jan. 23, 1965, p. 6) that when Simon Dedalus has finished his rendition of

"M'appari" in the Ormond bar, the applause of his listeners is recorded in the English novel just as we are accustomed to seeing it:

—Bravo! Clapclap. Goodman, Simon. Clappyclapclap, Encore! Clapclipclap. Sound as a bell. Bravo, Simon! Clapclopclap. Encore, enclap, said, cried, clapped all. . . .

(*Ulysses*, p. 271)

But in Italian, to Mr. Ferris's distress, the sound of applause is represented quite differently:

Bravo! Ciac. Ottimo. Simon. Ciacciacciac. Bis! Ciaccicciac. Come una campana.
Bravo, Simon! Ciacciocciac. Bis, bisciac dicevano, urlavano, applaudivano tutti . . .

(Italian, p. 372)

If it offers any comfort, a glance at other versions will show that there too the sound of hand meeting hand is represented still differently:

Bravo! Clacclac. Soua-soua, Simon! Claqueclacclac. Bis! Clacclicclac. Quel coffre.
Bravo, Simon! Clacclocclac. Bis, un ban, disent, crient, claquent tous . . .
(French, p. 313)

Bravo! Klatschklatsch. Herrlich, Simon. Klatschklatsch. Encore. Klatschklatsch.
Encore klatschen, sprachen, riefen, klatschten alle . . .

(German 3rd ed., I, p. 449)

The blind stripling who passes through the "Sirens" chapter rapping with his stick goes "Tap Tap Tap" in English and German, but "Tic Tic Tic" in Italian and "Toc Toc Toc" in French; only Bloom's cat remains constant in all languages, saying, with increasing emphasis, "Mkgnao, Mrkgnao, and Mrkrgnao," whatever the tongue being spoken around her. Cats, of course, are far superior to linguistic conventions; but the point of the other passages is that people are not, and most representations of wordless noises are purely conventional. Joyce, who heard all the sounds the same way, represented them differently as he translated *Ulysses* into different tongues, or supervised other men's translations. Tic, Toc, and Tap are different conventional representations of the same sound. When Bloom imagines table talk among the gross eaters at the Burton restaurant, the English is pretty well deformed by food in the mouth:

I munched hum un thu Unchster bunk un Munchday. Ha? Did you, faith?
(*Ulysses*, p. 167)

but the translators have no particular trouble in providing equivalent distortions for their own idioms:

Chlé henchonthré lunchdi tans L'Unchster Bunck. Ah? Pas possible?
(French, p. 191)

Am Chmondag chtraf chíhn chin der Unchster-Bunck. So? Wirklich?
(German, 3rd. ed., I, 275)

Joyce took particular care with this German rendering, correcting it from an inferior brand of garble in the first, hastily prepared edition; it wasn't just any mumble that would satisfy him.

As Bloom enters Nighttown, he sees an incoherent idiot being teased by children; they call at him "Kithogue! Salute!" to which he answers, "Grhahute!" Then they ask him, "Where's the great light?" and get the (apparently satisfactory) reply, "Ghaghahest." These exchanges are represented in the French and German versions as:

"Gaucher! Salut!" "Kralut!" "Où est la grande lumière?" "Ghaghahouast."
(French, p. 487)

"Linkshänder! Tag!" "Trrag!" "Wo ist das grosse Licht?" "Ghaghahest."
(German, 3rd ed., II, p. 82)

"Kithogue" clearly means "left-hander" in Gaelic; the question about the great light may concern the sun, and the idiot's answer may be "In the west," but there clearly is an occult point involved, and such a point translations do little or nothing to clarify.

A final instance puts us in that twilight zone, beloved of Joyce, where immense nonsense words are constructed out of distorted and perhaps only half-formed particles of other words which may or may not have a relic of decipherable meaning. Bloom as he stands in the brothel has a vision of Blazes and Molly vigorously fornicating in his shamefaced presence; and their cries of animal pleasure, which are largely incoherent as they appear in English, take on extra meaning when seen in the relief afforded by translation. Boylan's cries are those on the left, Molly's those on the right; the To-languages are French and German.

E   Ah! Gooblazeqrukbrukarchkrasht!   O! Weeshwashtkissmapooisthnapoohuck!

F   Hah! Bondacheerokbrutarchkrachtt!   Hoh!   Ouissouassbizimapoothnapoojoui!

G   Ah! Gublasruckbrukrachkrasch!   Oh! Wiwawuschküssichbiarisnaarfuck!

It helps in explicating the English to see that "goo" must mean "good" since it translates as "bon" and "gu" = gut; "blaze" is definitely Boylan's own nickname, since it translates as "Dache" in the French version. Molly's "kissmapoo" is evidently a unit, translated "bizimapoo" in French; as a female, we might be disposed to think her associated with water and rivers, hence "weeshwash" (cf. *FW*, 199.17); but the French opts to begin and end her word with a "oui." Doubtless this is a back-formation from

Molly's repeated "Yes-Oui" at the end of the book, since there is no equivalent "yes" in the English word. A dubious "translation" therefore— perhaps too creative to be a translation at all. Yet it may answer in the end to some element of Joycean intent; her English word does, indeed, begin with the word for "Yes" in modern French, and end with the word for "Yes" in Provençal ("uck" = oc).

Brushing these cobwebs aside (they are doubtless more of a nuisance than an advantage), we may take note of the extraordinary, and perhaps excessive, *depth* of these translations of *Ulysses*. This brings up a paradox: the more creative and imaginative they are, the more pleasure they give in their own right, the farther they sometimes take us from the original. "Buckled he is," someone says about Bloom in the "Oxen of the Sun" passage; it is a way of saying he is married. "Est de la Confrérie de St Pris" says basically the same thing in *argot*, but says something more and different as well. Joyce himself worked the language in depth, and the more he worked at it, the more he distorted (effectually, translated) it into an idiom of his own devising. The process of reading *Finnegans Wake* is a great deal more than an act of translating it out of Wakespeech into ordinary English, but an element of this activity enters into the reading of the book, as an element of translation from ordinary English into Wakespeech went into its composition. Joyce's first drafts are often in the form of relatively straightforward English sentences, which he thereupon tortured into inconceivable complications of dialect, imagery, punnery, and allusion. It's foolish to strip them down to their bare sense—as foolish, Joyce says in the book itself, as it would be to disrobe mentally a lady to whom one had just been introduced (*FW*, p. 109). But there is no need to get so uppity that we pretend to be beyond all occasion for a trot. Joyce himself expended a great deal of time and effort to make the text as intricate as we find it, and following him through the process of translating his thought into Wakespeech is sometimes of considerable help in enabling us to translate it out again. A passage occurring relatively late in the printed *Wake* (p. 611) was one of the first written; it can be compared in early, middle, and late stages, as follows:

> The archdruid then explained the illusion of the colourful world, its furniture, animal, vegetable and mineral, appearing to fallen men under but one reflection of the several iridal gradations of solar light, that one which it had been unable to absorb while for the seer beholding reality, the thing as in itself it is, all objects showed themselves in their true colours, resplendent with the sextuple glory of the light actually retained within them.

> Bymby topside joss pidgin fella Berkeley, archdruid of Irish chinchinjoss, in the his heptachromatic sevenhued septicoloured roranyellgreeblindigan mantle finish he show along the his mister guest Patrick with alb belonga

him the whose throat he fast all time what tune all him monkafellas with
Patrick he drink up words all too much illusiones of hueful panepiphanal
world of lord Joss the of which zoantholithic furniture from mineral through
vegetal to animal not appear to full up together fallen man than under but one
photoreflection of the several iridals gradationes of solar light that one which
that part of it (furnit of huepanepi world) had shown itself (part of fur
of huepamvor) unable to absorbere whereas for numpa one seer in seventh degree of wisdom of Entis-Onton he savvy inside true inwardness of
reality, that Ding hvad in idself id ist, all objects (of panepiwor) alloside
showed themselves in trues coloribus resplendent with sextuple gloria
of light actually retained inside them (obs of epiwo).

Tunc. Bymeby, bullocky vampas tappany bobs topside joss pidgin fella
Balkelly, archdruid of islish chinchinjoss in the his heptachromatic seven-
hued septicoloured roranyellgreenlindigan mantle finish he show along the
his mister guest Patholic with alb belongahim the whose throat hum with
of sametime all the his cassock groaner fellas of greysfriaryfamily he fast
all time what time all him monkafellas with Same Patholic, quoniam,
speeching, yeh not speeching noh man liberty is, he drink up words,
scilicet, tomorrow till recover will not, all too many much illusiones through
photoprismic velamina of hueful panepiphanal world spectacurum of Lord
Joss, the of which zoantholitic furniture, from mineral through vegetal to
animal, not appear to full up together fallen man than under but one photoreflection of the several iridals gradationes of solar light, that one which
that part of it (furnit of heupanepi world) had shown itself (part of fur
of huepanwor) unable to absorbere, whereas for numpa one puraduxed
seer in seventh degree of wisdom of Entis-Onton he savvy inside true
inwardness of reality, the Ding hvad in idself id est, all objects (of panepiwor) allside ashowed themselves in trues coloribus resplendent with
sextuple gloria of light actually retained, untisintus, inside them (obs of
epiwo).*

The "archdruid" expanded, as the passage grew, to become "topside joss
pidgin fella Berkeley," that is, "big-man-in-the-god-business" Berkeley and
then to be "bullocky vampas tappany bobs topside joss pidgin fella Balkelly"
—from which, with a good deal less certainty, we can extract the following
cognates: "bullocks-and-wampum, Tammany-boss, big-man-in-the-God-
business Berkeley-Bulkley-Kelly's City." The trouble with a reading like
this is that "bullocks-and-wampum" is a pretty wild guess as "bullocky
vampas"; as a reading it's possible, but it feels more like an overtone than
a central significance. At a little further distance, one could get "ballocky
vampire" out of the words, or "bullock-covered pampas." To find out, by
comparison with earlier versions, that it's not integral to the syntax of the
passage—that in fact it was only added at the last stages of the text—is at

---

* The first two versions of the passage are taken from A. W. Litz, *The Art of James Joyce* (N.Y., Oxford U. Press, 1961), pp. 78–79; the final version appears in the *Wake*, p. 611.

least to put our difficulties in perspective. A parallel is the help one gets with an overqualified sentence by the simple process of stripping off the subordinate clauses, for a moment only, in order to put them back again when one has the structure clear.

Seeing the *Wake,* at least in selected passages, under the aspect of a development, yields advantages, pleasures, and perspectives quite apart from simplified understanding. Puns like those in "Patholic" and "islish" are better appreciated as growths (from "Patrick" and "Irish") than as terminals —the strength of the original meaning has been buried under that of the afterthought, and needs resurrection. Words like "puraduxed" and "untisintus," when we see that they are relatively late arrivals, can be taken as problem centers, toward the understanding of which we particularly invite the neighboring words to cooperate. It is not hard to see that "puraduxed" involves the words "paradox," "pure," Latin "dux" = leader, and probably "paradise"; "untisintus" includes Latin "intus" = within, plus an anagram or reverse of it, "untis," which (though meaningless in itself) suggests an outside, hence inside-outside; plus Latin "tinctus" = dyed or "untinctus," and perhaps French "tisane" = infusion. But the words are slow to reveal their full treasure, and if we know they are on the top rather than the bottom of Joyce's verbal structure, we shall probably treat them differently. One could even get some awareness, by such a process of depth-reading, of the degree to which typographical errors disfigure the text. For example, in the passages cited, "roranyellgreenlindigan" must necessarily read "roranyellgreeblindigan" (otherwise the color "blue" is not properly represented in the spectrum), "huepamvor" is patently "huepanwor" ("hueful panepiphanal world" abbreviated), "heupanepi" should be "huepanepi" (for the same reason), "zoantholitic" should be "zoanthrolithic" (to get in minerals, animals, and humans), and perhaps "he fast all time what time" should be "he fast all time what tune." I am not very confident of this latter emendation (the others seem much more secure), but put it forward in evidence of the fact that once we start to regard the w's, m's, n's, i's, and u's of this text with the suspicion that seems to be called for, there are not very many distinct limits to the interpretive possibilities we have to consider. In any event, and whatever the difficulties involved, it is clear that to read the *Wake* is in some measure to translate it; perhaps not to translate into ordinary discursive English every word and buried concept, but to let the language-effects of the text run through one's mind in loose tandem with what one knows (or discovers, or guesses) is the minimal plain sense.*

Some special conditions of studying works of art are that, for the most

---

* As for the incredible task of actually translating *Finnegans Wake,* with its hundred linguistic layers, into other tongues, it has been attempted, at least in sample form, and quite remarkably carried out. But as the problem is somewhat special, discussion of it may be relegated to an appendix of this chapter.

part, they are unique, atemporal, and noncomparable, and control the reader's approach to them in ways both subtle and obvious. These various characteristics have one important effect in common: every reader is to some degree an unprepared reader, in the sense that he does not know, as he reads, exactly what he is looking for. (By contrast a scientist, looking at the results of an experiment, has some limitations on what he's looking for. He may be wrong in his anticipations, but he looks at his results—such as they are—with an eye informed by the hypothesis on which the experiment was set up.) The literary reader, by the very nature of what he is reading, cannot form such a focus, or if he does can be pretty sure he has been allowed it only so that he may be rendered less suspicious in a more important direction.

At various times, this unsullied innocence of the reader has been quite vigorously defended as not only a Good Thing in itself but one which must be, even artificially, fostered and preserved. We have been told that it is wrong to "take advantage" of outside information because it might contaminate our responses to the work of art; on these grounds, various sorts of biographical and historical information have been ruled irrelevant. But when we study two versions of the same work by the same author, and allow one version gently to interrogate the other, then indeed we may become aware of how little innocent eyes see after all. At a rough estimate, ninety percent of our reading is the act of recognizing something familiar —and how easy it is, when we have accepted something familiar, to overlook the possibility that there is an unfamiliar dimension to what we have seen. A single trifle, from *Ulysses,* can stand for the general rule. Joyce uses the word "atone" in a special, literal, and philologically accurate sense—not at all in the primary dictionary sense of "make amends or reparations." When one reads the first unit of *Ulysses,* "Telemachus," one finds the Englishman Haines reflecting on the Hamlet story:

> —I read a theological interpretation of it somewhere, he said bemused. The Father and the Son idea. The Son striving to be atoned with the Father (p. 20).

The French translation makes perfectly clear the latent meaning of the verb, to be *at one* with: "Le Fils s'efforçant de s'identifier au Père." In any large sense, the difference between one reading and another is not overwhelming; but the instance is deliberately slight. If the careful comparison of two versions by the same author can give rise, from time to time, to even modest illuminations of this nature, then—quite apart from our advantage in possibly understanding the work more fully—we shall be training our eyes, and sensibilities, to question in specially fruitful ways the old, familiar texts that we have seen so often we no longer see them at all.

Appendix to Chapter VIII

Translating into different "languages" *Finnegans Wake,* which is itself such a mouthful of linguistic tutti-frutti, was bound to be a somewhat rarefied experience. Only little, special bits of the immense task were ever actually completed, and usually they depended on the help of the omnilingual (Panglossic?) author. An Italian version, by Nino Frank (though officially, for political reasons, it had to be attributed to Ettore Settanni) appeared in Curzio Malaparte's Roman magazine *Prospettive* (IV, 2, February 15, 1940; and IV, 11–12, December 15, 1940); a German version by Georg Goyert, though completed as early as 1929, did not appear until after the war (*Die Fahre,* I, 6, June, 1946). But Joyce seems to have been most interested in the French version, which was worked on by a cenacle of devoted acolytes, after the leisurely fashion of a chess society working out collectively a specially intricate problem. In a prefatory note introducing the finished sample (*Nouvelle Revue Française,* May 1, 1931, XXXVI, 633 ff.), Philippe Soupault described the congenial proceedings. A first version had been made by one S. Beckett—"irlandais, lecteur à l'Ecole Normale"—with the help of Alfred Perron. This venture was then given a first revision by Paul Léon, Eugène Jolas, and Ivan Goll, with the occasional help of the author; that product was then subjected to a second revision at the hands of Soupault, Léon, and Joyce himself—and this second revision was very thorough indeed. The translators met religiously once a week (Tuesdays at two-thirty in Léon's apartment); they worked slowly through the translation and the original, a phrase at a time, groping after exactly the right rhythm and tone, as well as the various laminations of meaning. Fifteen sessions of three hours each enabled them to complete (with some few omissions) a translation of pages 196–201 and 215–16 of the *Wake.* In all, that is about seven pages out of 628, but by no means a contemptible accomplishment, given the nature of the task, and the way the friends went at it. When they had finished, they sent copies of their work to Jolas and to Adrienne Monnier, and devoted two more meetings to discussing the criticisms received from these ultimate reviewers.

As to the enchantments of the translation that resulted from all this care and concern, it is hard to speak highly enough; one need only compare a passage at the top of page 197 with the French rendition of it—which, for ease of comparison, can be printed interlinear:

> Reeve Gootch was right and Reeve Drughad was sinistrous! And the cut
> Sbire Kauche était droit mais Sbire Troyt senestre.   Et son chic!

of him! And the strut of him! How he used to hold his head as high
  Et ses tics!   Et son bec haut en pic

as a howeth, the famous eld duke alien, with a hump of grandeur on him
de crête de monts, le vieux deuc alien célèbre, avec sa bosse de follyo

like a walking wiesel rat.   And his derry's own drawl
grandeur tel sieur rat qui sort de sa tourte. Et sa voix qu'il traîne

and his corksown blather
derryère chaque phrase de sa bouche onflée de mots corquets et tous ses

and his doubling stutter   and his gullaway swank.
bégaiments à doublintente, le farceur qu'il est sans égalouégauax.

The original has perhaps an extra river here and there—the Wiese, for
example, in "wiesel rat," and a geographical feature like the Hill of Howth.
But the "Deucalion" pun persists, "rive gauche" and "rive droite" are suit-
ably transformed, and "follyo" with its overtones of grandeur ("folio") and
idiocy is a useful addition to the image of Humphrey. The various verbal
devices by which Derry, Cork, Dublin, and Galway have been shoehorned
into one French sentence must surely stir amazement, if nothing else. Where
they could not get an equivalent quality, the translators have sometimes
been content with an equivalent quantity—with the curious effect, in several
instances, of softening the French more than the English version. ALP
speaks in her prayer of "my old Dane hodder dodderer," getting into
one phrase a reference to HCE's trade (he carried a hod), his marital
condition (he's a cuckold, i.e., hoddy doddy), his age (he's a dodderer), his
speech (he's a stutterer), plus a reference to the useful little creek which
passes through Dublin, the Dodder. The French "mon vieux Danois
d'addodérateur" adds the strong overtone of "adorateur," preserves the
stutter, but sinks the hod and the Dodder far beneath the surface. Or again,
"Poor deef old deary" (200.15) translates beautifully into "Dear dur
d'untendre!"

As this last example suggests, when several languages are at work in a
passage simultaneously, a translator can exercise the unusual option of
translating any of the languages he finds convenient; since the basic effect
of the passage is spotted and macaronic, one doesn't have to reproduce the
exact combination of elements to get the dappled impression. Generally,
the less elaborate puns and allusions convert better to another tongue than
the big ones; "our staly bred" (198.6) comes out, wittily, "notre pain
crotidien" ("quotidien" = daily, plus "croûte" = crust); and "With neu-
phraties and sault from his maggias" (199.14) emerges as "Avec des
pommes d'Oder nouvelles et du sèle de ses fennys"—where Irish praties
become "pommes de terre" as the Euphrates becomes the Oder. In the last
part of the sentence we cannot feel so confident; does Joyce mean "zèle" =

zeal to be felt as contaminating "sel" = salt; if his English "maggias" suggests "maggies," where is the equivalence if French "fennys" suggest the *phénix?* There is in the French translation a good deal of this sort of substitution of one confusion for another. On one occasion, the four policemen or readers (who may also be the four gospellers and the Four Masters of Irish history) are asked to bear witness as to what was HCE's original name:

> Ask Lictor Hackett or Lector Reade or Garda Growley or the Boy with the Billyclub. How elster is he called at all?
>
> (197.6)

The French rendering hardly helps us at all here:

> Demande à Lictor Huckett ou à Lector Noiret ou à Gardar de Norval ou au Boy dit Browning. Comment le préenomme-t-on encore?

I think I see in the third policeman shadows of the Gare du Nord and Gérard de Nerval; but why Reade turned into Noiret and what the Browning Boy is doing in there remain, after more reflection than the passage is probably worth, impenetrably dark.

A special problem of manageable dimensions and some interest involves the various songs mentioned in the sections of "Anna Livia Plurabelle" and the level at which their titles are translated. There is, for instance, a mention of "The Heart Bowed Down" (*FW* 199.27); it is a major aria from Balfe's best-known opera *The Bohemian Girl;* when translated into French, it comes out as a melancholy title, "Je n'ai gardé dans mon malheur," but with no immediate reference to Balfe or to any other familiar composition. "The Rakes of Mallow" (*FW* 199.28) is a rowdy Irish folk song, celebrating eighteenth-century roisterers; the translation, by equating it with a French nursery rhyme, "Cadet Roussel a trois cheveux," makes it seem a little more infantile than the original English—there may be a satiric slant here, or else Joyce wanted to suggest the recurrence of the English song, its round-and-round shape. "Chelli Michele's *La Calumnia è un Vermicelli*" (*FW* 199.28) is a reference to the famous aria in Rossini's *Barbiere di Seviglia,* "la calunnia è un venticello"—attributed to Michael Kelly, a famous Irish singer and composer who had an extensive and very successful career on the Continent in the early nineteenth century. There is no translation at all into French; Joyce evidently thought the joke made itself about as well in the original form as it needed to. "A balfy bit ov *old Jo Robidson*" (*FW* 199.29) does not answer to anything immediately visible in Balfe's rather voluminous record; the French translation, "un morceau bien charpenté du 'Gouronnement de la Buse' " may keep us from looking too hard through the Balfiana. Apparently in the translation "Charpentier" was thought to serve quite as well as "Balfe," and the French title could imply either "the crowning of the blockhead" or "the crowning of the liquor = booze." If we take the former, we may think it was influenced by the overtones of "balfy" = balmy. Two other English titles are translated more or less straight: "Phoebe, dearest, tell, O tell me" (*FW* 200.10) becomes "J'ai tout quitté pour l'inchaste Sylvie," and "I loved you better nor you knew" (*FW* 200.11) turns into, "Je crains que t'avoir trop aimée." The first is an identifiable English song, the second isn't; neither of the two French titles rings a bell. But at least we can tell from the translation that the thing Joyce thought most important to imitate was the general tone of the title. The last title from this group is the most puzzling; it is one of the "warbly sangs from over holmen" with which ALP soothes her restless husband: "High hellskirt saw ladies hensmoker lily-hung pigger" (*FW* 200.12). As it comes from overseas, we can perhaps guess that its original tongue is Dansk or Norsk; if this were the case, the first words might be a crude distortion of the Danish for "I love you," "Jeg elska." Some part of this guess is confirmed by the French translation, "Ya elle square sot ladys insmoking lill et un piqué"—we can at least guess that there's an original in some other tongue that both these garbled passages are imitating, after the fashion of that great line in the colloquy of Mutt and Jute ("Come on, fool porterfull, hosiered women blown monk sewer?" = "Comment vous portez-vous aujourd'hui, mon blond monsieur?" *FW* 16.4). What exactly ALP's warbly sang was I cannot say for sure (it is *not* Hans Christian Andersen's "Hjertets Melodier," from which Grieg got the words for his "Jeg elska dig"); but at least one knows, with the help of the translation, where to look and what to look for.

Where a text contains so many ragged, only-half-soluble problems, it is a pleasure to be able to clear one up entirely, however small it may be. At the very beginning of the ALP section, the sentence occurs (196.7): "Wash quit and don't be dabbling." It translates: "Lave tranquillement ton linge et ne patauge pas tant." "Tranquillement," of course; the original should read "quiet." And in how many other passages of the *Wake* would a missing letter or a corrected spelling make the difference between intelligent comprehension and the blank endurance of inexplicable oddity!

CHAPTER IX

Some Limits of the Possible

Generally when we think of translation in the abstract, we have at the back of our minds a relatively simple model of the process; and with such a model in mind, the problems don't seem particularly complex or pressing. A bit of ingenuity, a trick or two of style, and a dictionary, we tend to feel, will solve most of those problems that need a solution. We accept, without looking at them too closely, the discount areas, where we don't need equivalents, and those where we can't have equivalents, however much we need them. But as long as the model in the back of our minds is simply the matter of getting one piece of relatively plain French prose into equivalent English, we are unlikely to disturb our own complacency very radically. When we start at the other end of the stick, by trying to define what sorts of things cannot be translated—because the linguistic gap is too wide, or too narrow, or complicated by conventions that are not linguistic at all, the real complications of the task, and the real difficulties of generalizing about it, will start pressing in on us.

Basically, there is not much to say about the disparity between concepts that in one language can be concentrated into a single word but in another language must be diffused through several different words. It's nothing more than a matter of incompatible packaging, and it happens all the time. We need simply point to examples like "Geist" and "Verstand" in German, "machismo" in Spanish, "Logos" in Greek, or "virtù" in Italian to see that they cover a spectrum of meanings that English cannot possibly match with equivalent economy. Why does a Yiddish word like "chutzpah" spread into the vocabulary of people who know no other Yiddish, if not because it defines a quality for which other languages have no handy equivalent? Translating these words into English is often a problem less pressing than it might be, because over the years English has been so receptive about adopting this sort of word into itself. Yet for the translator, especially where space is at a premium, this matter of packaging is not negligible. He may be forced to say more than his original, or less, or something different, or to say it in a different way (with adverbs, not verbal inflections, in several successive units rather than at a single stroke), because the proper equivalent is not in his chosen To-language. In itself, the packaging problem is hardly an impossible one; between paraphrase and amplification and explication and exemplification and qualification and redefinition, an adjustment can generally be made. But can a meaning thus laboriously constructed ever be the same as one struck off at a resonant blow? The price to be paid, in ungainliness and complexity, becomes higher as the demands of tone or structure are considered more urgent; and when laborious ingenuity becomes self-defeating, we may well conclude that supreme difficulty has faded into downright impossibility.

In a much less portentous dimension, there are problems of intimacy as well as of distance and remoteness, and they may be even harder of solution. What, for example, would one do about translating Hemingway's novel *For Whom the Bell Tolls* into Spanish? The reader will recall that much of the original dialogue is in English-strongly-flavored-with-Spanish, English through which the peculiar idioms of Spanish make themselves vigorously felt. Obviously, it would be relatively simple to turn such prose into plain Spanish prose, which it half-is anyway. But how to convey to the Spanish reader that the original is a rather exotic variety of English? The tu/te locution, which is perfectly natural to Spanish, carries a wholly different flavor, a rather ecclesiastical and sacramental mood, when transformed into English thee/thou; and this exotic flavor necessarily disappears when the novel is returned to Spanish. It can't help being a flatter, a less mannered performance than it is in English. The problem of rendering an equivalence is essentially that of seeing through green-tinted glasses a rather delicate shade of green; and there seems no reason to postpone the conclusion that it's insoluble. The same issue would come up, less massively perhaps, if one were translating into French a play or novel (*Lolita,* perhaps), containing a character who spoke English with a strong French accent or quoted a lot of French; he would have to be given some other sort of accent, or made to quote from some other tongue, if the exotic quality of his speech were to be preserved.* A cognate problem arises when translating into

---

* In fact Eric Kahane, who did *Lolita* into French for the Livre de Poche series (1959), elected to do nothing at all, i.e., he reproduced the French phrases of the original unchanged in the translation, setting them off by italic type and a following asterisk—with consequences noted below.

English Pirandello's *Sei personaggi in cerca d'autore:* in this drama, Madama Pace is supposed to speak Italian (the native idiom of the play) with a strong Spanish accent. The two languages are close enough so that this is very possible; a bastard jargon of Spanish and Italian is perfectly conceivable, though grotesquely uncouth and ugly to Italian ears. So what is to be done when the basic language of the translation becomes English? Giving the lady simply a vulgar accent, as of a slum, won't suffice and won't equate; she wouldn't be running a fancy dress-shop if she had a merely vulgar accent, yet she has to be almost incomprehensible in the distortion of her diction. Adding to the complication is the fact that, though the play is being translated into English (by the terms of the problem), there is no way of pretending it isn't an Italian play under the skin. For a basically English play, a strong German accent might be the closest thing linguistically to what a Spanish accent is for an Italian play. But when we translate this play, it becomes *both* English and Italian as far as the audience is concerned; and an option appropriate to one of its existences will probably be grotesquely incongruous with the other. So once again there is no clearcut solution to the problem, just a helpless compromise. A vaguely "foreign" accent, a neutral-odd accent, can perhaps be devised, that won't commit Madama Pace either to Spain or to Germany or to any other particular country, but that will sound as strange as she is supposed to sound.

The more deeply an idiom is involved in peculiar institutions, the harder it may be to reproduce under circumstances where those institutions don't exist or can't be taken for granted. A contemporary Arab novelist who wants to represent a boy and girl boy-and-girling it in a rustic scene, cannot, without shocking his audience out of their wits, make his characters speak the sort of Arabic that everyone knows boys and girls speak in actual Arab villages. Because they are characters in a novel, a work of literary art, they must speak literary Arabic of a sort that, even if they knew it (most improbable!), they would never conceivably use under these circumstances. Literary Arabic is not the same as popular Arabic—as literary Greek is far removed from popular Greek.* Shall we then translate a novel written in such a literary idiom into an equivalently flowery and artificial English,

---

* There are, to be sure, writings in many different popular dialects of Arabic; but they are exceptions that prove the rule. They are the lowest and most vulgar form of subliterature, printed in the cheapest possible format, and until quite recently never printed at all. Regardless of their (probably hypothetical) merits, they are never mentioned in literary discussions, because they are not considered real literature. Yet the literary language is not, and cannot be, spoken; a novelist who writes polite literature in the polite idiom cannot discuss it, except in the vulgar dialect. And if he is employed writing for television or the movies, he must use the vulgar tongue there, even though as a "serious" novelist he is so disdainful of popular idiom that he refers to it as a "linguistic disease." For information on these matters I am much indebted to Mr. Mattityahu Peled, whose unpublished dissertation on the novelist Najib Mahfuz will not, I hope, remain long unpublished.

which would have no roots whatever in English usage, fictional or otherwise? Obviously not. But then what? Shall we make the young people sound like Thomas Hardy yeomen, or Faulkner crackers, or Lawrence gamekeepers, or anybody's peasants? Conceivable alternatives, all of them, and none necessarily viable; some of our decision depends on the audience we want to appeal to, some on the tone of the novel we are dealing with. But that tone won't be determined by the level of diction; apparently literary Arabic is inevitable, so long as one is writing a work of art. Thus, to put the matter in the most general terms, different cultures have different conceptions of literary decorum, and different stylistic options within that decorum. And there may not be any option in one culture that quite corresponds with a mode of feeling that is instantly felt to be natural and familiar in another.

We have only to look at ourselves, in this matter of literary dialect, to be aware of anomalies that, for an outside culture, would require considerable explanation and thus complicate enormously the matter of translation. When an American novel is set in Brooklyn, for example, or a British novel in Cheapside or Limehouse, the characters are usually made to speak the dialect typical of those districts, or popularly accepted as such. It is important that they do so; we shouldn't feel that we were getting the proper measure of local color if there weren't certain distortions in the spoken language. But to the hero and heroine of our romance, this rule generally does not apply; though born in exactly the same milieu as their accented contemporaries and raised there, they commonly speak much more correct English. Dickens' subordinate characters may gape, gargle, and distort the English tongue most extravagantly, but Master Pip and Master Oliver speak from the book. And if they had to play a scene of high passion in nonstandard English, we readers, enlightened as we are, would find about it something distressing, something distracting. By convention, a strong Brooklyn or a strong Cockney accent is not appropriate for the expression of serious sentiments or "deep" passions. Similar conventions apply to Shakespearean plays, where the noble characters talk dignified blank verse, the low characters prose. And if one were translating a Dickens novel or a Shakespeare play into the language of people who knew no class distinctions (Martians, perhaps?), it would be necessary either to explain elaborately why they spoke such different language, or to stuff them into a single speech pattern, on the score that what they say is only obscured by a set of incomprehensible and inconsistent conventions regarding the speech in which they cast it.

Regional dialects are notoriously inseparable from the character of the regions and social circumstances in which they grow up. Not long ago an adventurous translator tried to render into American slang some of the sonnets of G. G. Belli, the nineteenth-century Italian poet who wrote his greatest work in the popular dialect of a lower-class district of Rome, the

Trastevere.* An ingenious effort it was, indeed the only effort so far to get a sampling of Belli's glorious achievement into English. But it was only a limited success, because the idioms in question are not really congruent. Belli in *romanesco* is a wit, with a carefully thought-out anti-poetic: he is concerned to present, not popular poetry, but popular speech fallen, as if by accident, into his own quite elegant and artful poetic form. In American slang he becomes a deliberate and rather clumsy vulgarian. What is more, incongruities between the new dialect and some of the concepts indigenous to the old dialect are inevitable:

> If ya wanna be funny, it's enough to be
> A gentleman. . . .

The phrase grates on our ear, because a man who is represented as saying "ya wanna be" simply doesn't use the word "gentleman" straight.** "Per èsse bbuffo abbasta èsse siggnore," says Belli ("L'Usanze Buffe," Sonnet 1431 of the big Mondadori edition); it couldn't come out more simply and inevitably. But what to do about equivalents in a culture where the distinction between "signori" and other folk doesn't exist is a problem that the use of a "low," realistic dialect simply exaggerates. "Giuveddí Santo" ("Holy Thursday," Sonnet 932) is a characteristic Belli piece, a little dramatic vignette involving a vigorously coupling couple who pause for a moment to receive, by remote control, a papal benediction. (They hear the cannon shot that heralds the pope's appearance at his balcony.) There is a fine balance in the sonnet between natural impulses, religious awe, and a kind of solemn, meticulous legalism—this is one of those special days when the

---

° G. G. Belli, *The Roman Sonnets*, tr. Harold Norse, pref. by W. C. Williams, intro. by Alberto Moravia (Highlands, N.C., J. Williams, 1960).

°° As a matter of brute phonetic fact, most of us when we speak this phrase rapidly and casually probably say something much closer to "ya wanna be" than to "you want to be." Most dialect is only a stylizing and exaggeration of phonetic distinctions too subtle to be represented in the relatively crude notations of the regular alphabet. That is why sustained passages of dialect quickly become wearisome. If Mr. Norse had translated more than a handful of Belli's 2279 sonnets, he would quickly have wearied of American slang as a medium for representing them. (For the same reason, Mr. William Weaver elected to forego dialect altogether when Englishing C. E. Gadda's novel in *romanesco, Quer pasticciaccio brutto de via Merulana.*)

Another difficulty with finding an equivalent for Roman dialect is that *romanesco* is not ordinary Italian pronounced badly (which is what phonetic representations of American slang often amount to), but the everyday speech of a population. What is more, this dialect, like dialect generally, has a different standing in Italian than it does in English. "Standard Italian" is a much-disputed topic; it developed late, sank few roots, is hard to define. Urban variants on it (Venetian, Florentine, Genoese, Neapolitan) are many and established; they involve differences of vocabulary as well as of pronunciation. In America, urban dialects are few (Brooklyn and Boston), they involve minor differences of pronounciation (Boston "yahd" or "fahm," Brooklyn "boid"—which is actually something like "beuihd"), and they are tied up with quite special feelings. By tradition, Brooklynese is comic, Bostonian aristocratic; there is nothing in American slang really to correspond with Roman irony and anger, the "tristiloquio" that so fascinated Belli.

pope's blessing is valid even on the other side of the river. There is no reason why such a scene couldn't be made comprehensible in any dialect the translator wanted to use, but no organic reason why he should use a dialect at all. The scene, the event, the habit of mind, are just as exotic to Weehawken or the Bronx as to places where perfectly standard English is spoken, perhaps more so.

The more remote languages are from one another and the more different syntactically, the harder it must obviously be to express the same concepts and feelings in both. One does not need more than a peripheral awareness of Japanese (which, as a problem for translators, can stand for an immense number of non-European tongues) to sense the complications of translation from one set of syntactic structures to another. To pick a rudimentary example, the single English pronoun "I" can have a whole spectrum of Japanese equivalents, each carrying a distinct and specific overtone that the English original knows not of, none neutral and all-purpose as the English pronoun is. Hence the hard question for a translator into Japanese is not simply of catching all that his original (English or European of whatever nationality) says in its fullness, but of being able to say as *little* as his original requires. An English "I" does not define the social circumstances under which it is used; a Japanese "I" not only does, it must. Indifference to social circumstances and unawareness of them are bound to be even harder to render than positive meaning, simply because there is no process of linguistic subtraction or erasure equivalent to those of addition. A writer is the victim, many times, of what his language requires him to say. We note above (pp. 134–146) how men like Eliot and Joyce, when put to translating their own works, were sometimes forced to forego suspensions and duplicities very natural in English in order to have grammatical French. Thus the author's preferred intent was gratifyingly revealed. But the case is altered when the author is not involved in the translation. Then the translator on his own responsibility may be required to make up his author's mind on points that he never so much as contemplated. There are some long passages of intimate, agonized dialogue in *The Sound and the Fury,* where a reader cannot be sure whether Caddy or Quentin Compson is speaking; that confusion (sometimes momentary, sometimes extended, occasionally permanent) is part of the author's main intent. But Japanese, by requiring that male and female speakers use quite different inflectional forms, forces the narrative voice to commit itself unequivocally, publicly, in advance.

In theory, there is no reason why one couldn't translate language that is violent or impressionistic in the original into a second language which should be equally strained and elliptical; but a glance at English translations of Pindar or Mallarmé will suggest some of the practical difficulties involved in rendering very textured or very allusive diction. The connections between symbol and symbol must commonly be made, in such language, by following out the overtones and implications of each image—the words are used for their resonance quite as much as for their meaning. Occasionally and by accident, some form in the To-language may have usable overtones and implications equal to those in the From-language, but one can't expect such good fortune as a regular thing. If they aren't to be found in the linguistic substructure, the connectives which distance as they unite symbols have to be explicitly constructed or left blank—and neither alternative corresponds to the original. Above all, it is difficult to deform usage in a second tongue to correspond with deformations in a first tongue, without giving the impression of intolerable artifice. We may very well appreciate the energies of thought and feeling that distort and compress an original; a translation can scarcely avoid appearing a more deliberate, secondhand undertaking, and when it turns out choked and knotty, we attribute its resistant character to the translator and his deliberate option. Browning, for example, took for granted that the Greek reader of the fifth century B.C. found Aeschylus so supremely difficult that he had to struggle for the basic sense of almost every line in the *Agammemnon;* hence, his own version must offer equivalent resistance to an English reader. Perhaps so: but there is a difference, hard as it is to define, between struggling through Aeschylus to get at Aeschylus and struggling through Browning to get at Aeschylus. Reading the Browning version, one cannot be unconscious for a minute of Robert Browning, breathing heavily in the foreground. *He* is the one responsible for lines like those in the Watchman's opening soliloquy, describing a watchman's assignment:

> And now on ward I wait the torch's token,
> The glow of fire, shall bring from Troia message
> And word of capture: so prevails audacious
> The man's-way-planning hoping heart of woman.

The words "prevail" and "audacious" in the third line, combined with the vagueness of "so," seem more likely to apply to the enterprise of capturing Troy than to a monarch's decision to keep a lookout—it is the way the English sentence is put together that misleads us, it is the English with which we have to struggle. As for "the man's-way-planning hoping heart of woman," to feel that this represents the difficulty of Aeschylus' thought, we have to fight our way through a wall of English words deliberately assembled, it would seem, to keep the mind at a distance from the meaning. Mr. Richmond Lattimore gives us, not an abjectly easy rendering of the same passage, but one where the difficulties seem to belong more to Aeschylus than to the translator:

> I wait; to read the meaning in that beacon light,
> A blaze of fire to carry out of Troy the rumor

> And outcry of its capture; to such end a lady's
> male strength of heart in its high confidence ordains.

Partly the good work seems to be done by keeping the English syntax straight, the agglomerations moderate, and the contortions of usage as slight as may be, while retaining strong metaphors and bold diction. I think we instinctively, and without making any conscious division out of it, attribute word order and syntax to the translator's choice, though in the basic metaphorical stuff and assertive substance of his poem, he is bound to an original. Thus we can hardly help feeling Browning's presence as gratuitous and intrusive when he perpetrates lines like

> Well, may it hap that, as he comes, the hand
> O'the household's lord, I may sustain with this hand!

As a matter of hard textual fact, Browning is following his original in repeating the word "hand" at the end of two successive lines; but that odd iteration may strike the ear less harshly in Greek, which doesn't rhyme, than in English, where it sounds like a flat rhyme or failed rhyme. In any case, the word order in English feels more distorted than in Greek because any language that inflects its forms can move them around more freely than one that does not. We know immediately we see Aeschylus' first "$\chi\acute{\epsilon}\rho\alpha$" = hand, that it is in the accusative form, therefore we can confidently anticipate a subjective form with an operative predicate nearby. Browning's first "hand" looks like a subject because of its position, and we feel a violent wrench take place when it is converted to an object by means of syntax overcoming word order in the second line.) And when we see normal English word order being twisted violently in order to *achieve* what English verse generally goes out of its way to *avoid*, the same word at the end of successive lines, we can hardly help feeling that Browning has made himself responsible for a special layer of perverse difficulty that blocks our access to Aeschylus' own proper difficulties. Even if the translator has a warrant in the Greek for everything he does in English, it isn't necessarily the same thing when it's done in English, and by a translator, as it is when done in the Greek and by Aeschylus. For the sake of comparison, I reproduce Lattimore's rendering of these same lines:

> May it only happen. May my king come home, and I
> take up within this hand the hand I love.

In this whole matter of translating a contorted and violent style (Persius, for example, or Gongora, or Gerard Manley Hopkins, to pick deliberately disparate instances), the translator is caught amid riptides of conflicting demands. The underlying connectives may be only implied, not expressed, so that one must overstate them to bring them out. Then the difficulties and resistance of the original have to be brought out too, but in such a way as to make clear that the original, not the translator, is responsible. So in effect one must illuminate the dark parts, soften the resistant parts, and yet not diminish the relief or underplay the texture of the original.

Finally, even though the translator virtuously declines all those obvious temptations to "improve on" or "enliven" his original, it is not only legitimate but inevitable that he will select those qualities for emphasis which appeal to his own taste and the taste of his readers, while minimizing those which make the original seem (let us say) ludicrous or contemptible. Yet at the same time he is drawn to "fidelity"; and between these two qualities of a translation, being acceptable and being accurate, there may well be grave contrasts. As Charles Perrault said nastily, à propos of the manners that Theocritus assigned to shepherds:

> Ils devraient, ces auteurs, demeurer dans leur grec,
> Et se contenter du respect
> De la gent qui porte férule.
> D'un savant traducteur on a beau faire choix;
> C'est les traduire en ridicule
> Que de les traduire en françois.*

Shallow rascal that he was, Perrault has just enough of a point here to give us pause. As manners, morals, and styles vary across the oceans and through the centuries, plenty of works become classics in one culture which one couldn't transate literally into another without translating them into ridicule. Translators of such work exercise tact and a bit of cross-cultural ingenuity, readers exercise imagination and a bit of indulgence; between them, they conspire to soften points that otherwise would create what (begging the question) we call a "wrong impression." There is nothing in this process to be ashamed of. Pope was trying to mute and suppress such inconvenient overtones when he circumlocuted out of existence Homer's comparison of Ajax to an ass; Graves did the same thing with the unfortunate prose style of Apuleius; when we have different productions of the same play, or different "readings" of the same poetic passage, an equivalent adjustment of values is often at work. And yet, depending on how much transformation is needed to avoid, let us say, grotesque and irrelevant responses, and how much accuracy in translation is required, we may be in a way of making a "fair" translation either very difficult or impossible.

---

* The occasion of Perrault's epigram was the great quarrel over ancients and moderns which he sustained against Boileau. We might translate his sarcasm:

> In Greek these authors had better remain,
> Since there they can safely maintain
> Their place by the pedagogue's stool.
> To pick a proper translator is vain,
> Since you turn them to ridicule
> When you turn them to anything plain.

At the root of all translational difficulties, it goes without saying, always lies a failed or inadequate equivalency. This may spring from simple linguistic difference, as English has no intimate pronoun equal to French or Spanish "tu," no word with the full richness of German "Geist," no idiom comparable to literary Latin with the special overtones it confers on an occasional word from vulgar Latin, few variations of pitch such as are frequent and significant in Chinese, no such power as Hebrew possesses to differentiate verbs according to the sex of the agent, no such gift as Aztec enjoys for varying the verb according to the character, animate or inanimate, of the object.* Or again disparity may arise from simple differences of experience, as English social life has no exact parallel for the office of a French prefect, nothing very much like a Spanish paseo, no real equivalent that can be simply and casually expressed for a Japanese tatami-mat, or the everyday honorific enclitic, -san. And these differences (variously, partially superable) shade off into tonal variations and idioms such as each tongue manufactures for itself—a rotten movie being a "turkey" in English while in French it's a "turnip," "un navet," and a watch at the pawnbroker's being with "uncle" in English, while in French it's at my "aunt's," "chez ma tante." These differing idioms we think of as the translator's natural, easy milieu, and so they are, while problems present themselves single file. But when we get two linguistic layers interreacting with one another (as above, in the matter of *Lolita,* where a character in an English novel affects a great many French phrases, and the novel then comes to be translated into French) the texture of feeling is so tied up with the specific tongues that there are no conceivable equivalents. Without changing Humbert Humbert's whole background, he can hardly dapple the plum pudding of his style with anything but French—even though French, in the translation, is the natural milieu of everyone's conversation, and it becomes absurd for Lolita to say, in elaborate French, that Humbert shouldn't speak so much French. "Mais est-ce que ça te dérangerait beaucoup de laisser tomber toutes ces tirades en français. Ca ennuie tout le monde" (*Lolita,* tr. E. Kahane, p. 384). An original may thus be too intimate with the tongue into which it is being translated as well as too remote from it; and the same thing happens in a larger dimension (ungrateful though it seems to remark on it) when a translator carries fidelity itself to an excess which we might name "mimicry." An instance is the Latin "Lycidas" done in the mid nineteenth century by the great Oxford amateur of academic light verse, Charles Stuart Calverley. During the seventeenth and eighteenth centuries, translating popular vernacular poems into Latin was a frequent and thoroughly serious undertaking. English was supposed to be

---

* Some of my examples here are taken from Margaret Schlauch's *The Gift of Languages* (N.Y., Dover, 1955), formerly (and better) titled *The Gift of Tongues,* Chapter 6.

an upstart language, too local, too vulgar, and too friable to give an author who wrote in it any hope of wide diffusion, distinguished readership, or long life. *Paradise Lost* was turned into Latin by one Gulielmus Hogaeus (*vulgo*, William Hogg) in 1690, nearly forty years before the first version appeared in French. But Calverley bears witness to a basic change; for him, English is the serious language, and Latin is a kind of joke that he enjoys handling with dexterity and turning to unexpected uses. The haziest and least defined of Tennyson's poems, "Tears, Idle Tears," was the one he worked most diligently into Latin; a song in Scots dialect by Robert Burns, "Ca' the Ewes," he turned into Latin Sapphics; and "John Anderson, My Jo, John" he converted to Greek. In something of this same spirit, of strenuous and slightly perverse levity, he translated "Lycidas" into Latin hexameters, in such a way as to catch not only the meaning, but the very turn and rhythm and inflection of the English verse:

Bitter constraint, and sad occasion dear,	Causa gravis, pia causa, subest, et amara deûm lex;
Compels me to disturb your season due:	Nec jam sponte mea vobis rata tempora turbo.
For Lycidas is dead, dead ere his prime,	Nam periit Lycidas, periit superante juventa
Young Lycidas, and hath not left his peer:	Imberbis Lycidas, nec par manet illius alter.
Who would not sing for Lycidas? he knew	Quis cantare super Lycida neget? Ipse quoque artem
Himself to sing, and built the lofty rhyme.	Nôrat Apollineam, versumque imponere versu.
He must not float upon his watery bier	Non nullo vitreum fas innatet ille feretrum
Unwept, and welter to the parching wind,	Flente, voluteturque arentes corpus ad auras,
Without the meed of some melodious tear.	Indotatum adeo et lacrymae vocalis egenum.

In lines 3 and 4, the interwoven repetitions of "dead" and "Lycidas" are exactly reproduced; "watery bier," not overlooked or shirked, becomes "vitreum feretrum"; and the "melodious tear" converts neatly to a "lacrymae vocalis." Even the precise placement of a word like "unwept" is not neglected, the Latin making use of its inflections to suspend "nullo" far at the beginning of the previous line so that there's an almost audible click as "flente" falls in with it. "Parching wind" is an extraordinarily bold expression in English; we scarcely think of a drowned body in the ocean as suffering from "parching" winds; but Calverley follows the trail like a fox hunter, and gives us the exact word in Latin, "arentes auras." Indeed, he is so resourceful and relentless that for all his celebrated lightness of touch and delicacy of tone, we are apt to feel that he is out to debauch and exploit, rather than to recreate his original. We feel, for example, the rhythm of the English line asserting itself through the Latin words, using the Latin, imposing itself on the Latin. Would we have this feeling about it if the original were not so powerfully established in our minds? Probably not; yet between translation and mimicry there is a basic distinction. The former aims to substitute for an original, the latter to stir admiration or amusement by the closeness with which it follows its original. So the fact that Calverley chose a famous original, and imitated it in a way that continually brings the exact texture of the English words before us, becomes a kind of distraction from the translation proper—like an actor who impersonates the mannerisms of a great historical figure so "successfully" that we feel ourselves in the presence, not of a spirit or a person, but of a performance.

Still another variety of translational impossibility is suggested by the old adage about a silk purse and a sow's ear. Converting one into the other may be very much a translator's ordinary business. Inevitably and despite himself, he creates so many sow's ears out of silk purses that we can scarcely grudge him the right to indulge in the contrary process whenever the opportunity presents itself. He is only restoring to his original a little of what he has been forced to take away; and so long as it is not radically out of key with the true tone, a touch of literary glitter or imaginative insight is always welcome. But a translator may rashly refine, and set out to demonstrate, certain qualities of his original, which his version then fails to sustain. A famous instance of such a fiasco is provided by the versions in French of Edgar Allan Poe's poetry.

It is a matter of long record and some curiosity that both Baudelaire and Mallarmé had a far higher opinion of Poe the poet than any English or American reader. Their comments abound in metaphors drawn from precious stones—"comme un bijou de cristal" (Baudelaire), "pur comme un diamant" (Mallarmé). Baudelaire was cautious enough to translate only four of Poe's poems, two because they were inseparable from the stories that were his primary concern—the other two were "The Raven" and Poe's sonnet to his mother-in-law, which served as a dedicatory sonnet for the whole of the *Histoires extraordinaires*. And in his handling of Poe's poetry, such as it was, Baudelaire exercised great caution and considerable conservatism. Using unrhymed, loosely rhythmic French prose as his vehicle, he declined all temptations to enrich Poe's sometimes flat and scanty lines. The third stanza of "The Conqueror Worm" may fairly represent his dealings:

That motley drama—oh, be sure
  It shall not be forgot!
With its Phantom chased for evermore,
  By a Crowd that seize it not,

Ce drame bigarré! oh! à coup sûr
  Il ne sera pas oublié,
Avec son Fantôme éternellement pour-
    chassé

Through a circle that ever returneth in
To the self-same spot,
And much of Madness, and more of Sin,
And Horror, the soul of the plot.

Par une foule qui ne peut pas le saisir,
A travers un siècle qui toujours retourne
Sur lui-même, exactement au même point!
Et beaucoup de Folie, et encore plus de Péché
Et d'Horreur font l'âme de l'intrigue.

Did Baudelaire mean his "siècle" (line 5) to translate or to comment on Poe's "circle"? Whatever his intent (from which linguistic accident is by no means excluded), the translation imposes a narrower meaning than the original possesses; and in general, it is a plodding, distinctly unluminous Poe that emerges. Would Baudelaire ever have dreamed of publishing, as his own, verses like

A travers un siècle qui toujours retourne
Sur lui-même, exactement au même point?

Wherever he could, and even at the cost of pedestrianism, Baudelaire simplified syntax and cut down on the overtones of Poe's verse. A line like "But see, amid the mimic rout" becomes "Mais voyez! à travers la cohue des mimes" because Baudelaire has accepted "mimic" at precisely its most literal level (a rout of mimes, to the exclusion of the meaning, an imitation rout, a mock rout). From his own professions we know at least what the translator was aiming at. Did he actually see these crystalline qualities in Poe and fail to render them? Or did he strongly imagine he saw them, and come up against unacceptable reality only in the actual moment of translation? Thoroughly ungrateful alternatives—from which we turn to Mallarmé's performance with the body of Poe's poetry (*corpus delicti*?) only to experience an even greater sense of collapse.

For the fact is that Mallarmé's translations of Poe (done, like Baudelaire's, into rhythmic, unrhymed French prose and much worked over in the years between 1862 and 1888) are of an ineptitude that is hard to credit. In translating "Israfel," for example, our hermeticist was faced with lines that read:

Therefore thou art not wrong,
Israfeli, who despisest
An unimpassioned song . . .

He evidently looked up "unimpassioned" in the dictionary, and got, as a not inconceivable French equivalent, "impassible." But somewhere in the process of transcription, the "a" changed to an "o," and Mallarmé's command of the general sense of the passage didn't allow him to feel uneasy about where he had come out. so his final reading is "Voilà pourquoi tu n'as pas tort, Israfel, que ne satisfait pas un chant impossible." *Chant impossible,* indeed! Not much harder to understand is the process by which, in the same poem, the lines

> And the shadow of thy perfect bliss
> Is the sunshine of ours,

came to be translated, "et l'ombre de ta félicité parfaite est le sommeil de la nôtre." Plainly, Mallarmé slipped from "soleil" to "sommeil" as in a daze or a doze. Generally, the translator seems to have little respect for English pronouns or possessive adjectives, and substitutes one for another with remarkable liberality. Thus when Poe, addressing the Coliseum, says,

> I feel ye in your strength,

Mallarmé translates, inconceivably, "Je vous sens dans ma force." Or again, in "The Raven," we find

> Nothing further then he uttered—not a feather then he fluttered,

which Mallarmé translates: "Je ne proférai donc rien de plus; il n'agita donc pas de plume." Baudelaire had at least got it straight: "Il ne prononça rien de plus; il ne remua pas une plume."

Crude as the point seems, it really is not to be overlooked as a condition making translation impossible that the translator may wholly have misunderstood the nature of his original. Mallarmé, to be sure, might have understood English a great deal better than he did, and yet not have created a more diamondlike version of Poe's poems than the one currently standing, with downcast eyes and shuffling feet, in the *Oeuvres complètes.* But there's always the possibility that if he had read Poe more clearly and objectively, he wouldn't have tried to make a diamond out of him in the first place. In a word, Poe's poems as they actually are can be translated, and by an honest craftsman like Eugène Lefébure as well as by anyone else; but they cannot be transfigured, not even by Baudelaire and Mallarmé.

Having faced some of the disasters and impossibilities of poetic translation, the reader deserves a cheerful counterbalance. A poetic reproduction does sometimes manage to be better than its original. Now and then a certain sort of translator is born to fill out a lean original or sleek down a plump one. When we see what Picasso could do in the way of variations on a fine painting by Delacroix, or what Beethoven could make out of Diabelli's *Schusterfleck,* we shouldn't be surprised if a confident imitator/translator now and then improves on his model. Clearly, the job is harder to do, the more seriously one takes the injunction of fidelity. Yet it does not necessarily follow that sweeping changes, even in mediocre poems, make great improvements. A tasteful, dexterous translator, by the accumulation of little connectives and delicate economies, can sometimes work an uncouth poem into an elegant one without destroying the character of the original. A fine instance of this process is provided by Richard Crashaw's translation of Book I of Giambattisto Marino's *Strage degli innocenti*.

Nobody is going to make much of either poem who does not have a fairly strong relish of the baroque in poetry (and already that precondition may limit the interest of the discussion to an occasional eccentric), but the merits of Crashaw's translation and the defects of Marino's original do complement one another strikingly. The first thing to note is that Crashaw's is a remarkably faithful translation—faithful by the standards of our own day, as well as by the somewhat looser standards of the seventeenth century. The translation never fails to parallel the original, stanza for stanza; it's frequently line for line, and on occasion word for word. Furthermore, Crashaw's English stanza, like Marino's Italian one, alternates three A-rhymes with three B-rhymes, topping them off with a couplet; the greater paucity of rhyme words in English makes this more of a triumph than it seems. Stanza 5, in both versions, introduces us to a rather horrid Satan:

Sotto gli abissi, in mezo al cor del
    mondo,
Nel punto universal de l'universo,
Dentro la bolgia del piú cupo fondo
Stassi l'antico spirito perverso;
Con mordaci ritorte in un groppo im-
    mondo
Lo stringe di cento aspidi a traverso;
Da tai legami in sempiterno il cinse
Il gran campion che'n Paradiso il vinse.

Below the Botome of the great Abysse,
There where one Center reconciles all
    things;
The worlds profound Heart pants;
    There placed is
Mischifes old Master, close about him
    clings
A curl'd knot of embracing Snakes,
    that kisse
His correspondent cheekes: these loath-
    some strings
    Hold the perverse Prince in eternall
    Ties
    Fast bound, since first he forfeited
    the skies.

Getting "the world's profound heart" out of a subordinate clause, and giving it a verb of its own, especially a strong one, does wonders for the opening of Crashaw's stanza. Marino's first periodic sentence, with its four preliminary clauses, hangs on the relatively weak and inactive verb "stassi"—stood, was placed. Moreover, Marino's third line is something of a filler, and Crashaw has helped his own version along by picking it for omission. When we have already been placed below the abyss, at the very heart of the world and its central point, to say that we are in a pit and that it is very dark there seems superfluous. On the other hand, Crashaw has added the notion of the serpents kissing Satan as they hold him fast; it's part of his method to make language work hard, and the image of erotic snakes twining about Satan, kissing his cheeks and finding them somehow "correspondent" to their own seems poetically very rich indeed. Satan is a serpent from way back; he is cold-blooded, hypocritical, erotically aggressive, insinuating, and self-involved. "Mordaci ritorte" carries some of these connotations, to be sure; but Crashaw gets more erotic revulsion into the scene, and lets it make its effect thoroughly before he comments on it; he will not use a distancing, judging adjective like "immondo," for instance (his equivalent for it is "loathsome"), till all the cumulative sexual suggestion of "curl'd," "embraces," "kisses," and "cheeks" has been worked out. And finally (for it is only one stanza, and one out of 66), by excluding from the final couplet "Il gran campion che'n Paradiso il vinse," Crashaw holds the focus of his reader's attention on Satan and avoids a mention of God in unwelcome contexts—it is Satan's defeat, not God's victory, that is most present to our mind as we are introduced to "Mischife's old Master."

Teasing and untwisting the strands of a stanza after this fashion may seem like a special and not particularly exhilarating activity, but it reveals in brief something of the texture which gives to a poem its characteristic coloring. And it puts in evidence an aspect of translation not very often considered, where the translator may stand in a position of advantage over his original. He has a set of suggestions before him to choose among, to work from, to carry further as he chooses. Especially in translating a highly ornamented and linguistically busy work, he can atone for inevitable losses with equivalent developments. Crashaw is particularly good at warming and animating images of Marino which in the original seem cold and nerveless because they don't have strong verbs or because the adjectives used have a distancing, a commentator's effect. (English critical vocabulary fails me here, but the effect under consideration is easily illustrated in a line of Milton: "With adamantine chains and penal fire"—where the second adjective, far from making one feel the heat or see the color of the fire, asks one to stand at a distance and consider its function in terms of the large structure of God's purposes.)

A last quality of the style is its extraordinary assurance in manipulating rhythmic syncopation—a quality nowhere better evidenced than in the last two stanzas of Crashaw's translation:

Di che paventi, Erode? e quale acceso
Hai di sangue nel cor fero desire?
Umana forma il re de' regi ha preso
Non per signoreggiar, ma per servire.
Non a furarti il regno in terra è sceso,
Ma te de' regni suoi brama arricchire.

Why art thou troubled *Herod?* what
    vaine feare
Thy blood-revolving Brest to rage doth
    move?
Heavens King, who doffs himselfe
    weake flesh to weare,

Vano e folle timor, ch'abbia colui
Che'l suo nome ne dona, ad usurpar
   l'altrui!

Comes not to rule in wrath, but serve
   in love.
Nor would he this thy fear'd Crown
   from thee Teare,
But give thee a better with himselfe
   above.
Poore jealousie! why should he wish
   to prey
Upon thy Crowne, who gives his owne
   away?

Già per regnar, per guerrigiar non
   nasce
Fanciullo ignudo e poverel negletto,
Cui donna imbelle ancor di latte pasce,
In breve culla in pochi panni stretto.
I guerrier son pastor, l'armi son fasce,
Il palagio real rustico tetto,
Pianti le trombe, i suoi destrier son
   due
Pigri animali: un asinello, un bue.

Make to thy reason, man; and mocke
   thy doubts,
Looke how below thy feares their
   causes are;
Thou art a Souldier, *Herod;* send thy
   Scouts,
See how he's furnish't for so fear'd a
   warre.
What armour does he weare? A few
   thin clouts.
His Trumpets? Tender cryes. His men
   to dare
So much? Rude Shepheards. What his
   steeds? Alas,
Poore Beasts! a slow Oxe, and a sim-
   ple Asse.

The direct address to Herod, for which Marino's first stanza (or 65th) provided hints, blossoms in Crashaw's second (or 66th) into a set of rich dramatic persuasives—as if Crashaw were for the moment appealing directly
to Herod's conscience. It may be possible to hear in the verse echoes of
George Herbert's homely style—a kind of pressing, urgent, simple speech of
immense directness. The pressure of his queries builds with great art, especially in the abrupt, stichomythic, verbless exchanges of the last stanza.
We note that line 5 of that stanza consists of two complete syntactical units,
line 6 of three, line 7 of no fewer than four (and it's only a pentameter
line!); after all that squeezing and crowding, the last line, with its relaxed,
pathetic motion, makes a gesture of special humility to which the new adjectives (slow, simple) specially contribute. It's not precisely a literary
effect of Crashaw's translation, but it is a direct consequence of his style
that one finds his stanzas much fuller and more crowded than those of
Marino. In this final stanza, when he devotes the first three lines (out of
eight) to rhetoric of his own, we look to see what major element of Marino
has been omitted—and are struck to find that it contains, not only a great

deal of Crashaw, but all of Marino too. Trained on bilingual epigrams, Crashaw was an expert at getting *multum in parvo.*

For poetic translators, the power of compression is greater than that of inflation; one is more likely to improve on an original by cutting off its excess than by filling it out to new dimensions. When Rainer Maria Rilke undertook to persuade Mrs. Browning's *Sonnets from the Portuguese* into German, it was essentially a matter of slimming, trimming, and cutting down; one has to have pretty firm prepossessions in favor of overstuffed verse not to feel the result as an improvement. At least by modern standards, Mrs. Browning cultivated an adjectival melancholy vein which can only be improved by being stripped down; it was Rilke's achievement when he turned the poems into German to retain their emotional softness while getting rid of their adjectival luxuriance and rhetorical drag:

I thought once how Theocritus had sung
Of the sweet years, the dear and wished for years,
Who each one in a gracious hand appears
To bear a gift for mortals, old or young:
And as I mused it in his antique tongue,
I saw, in gradual vision through my tears,
The sweet, sad years, the melancholy years,
Those of my own life, who by turns had flung
A shadow across me. Straightway I was 'ware,
So weeping, how a mystic Shape did move
Behind me, and drew me backward by the hair,
And a voice said in mastery while I strove . . .
"Guess now who holds thee?"—
"Death," I said. But there
The silver answer rang . . . "Not Death, but Love."

Und es geschah mir einst, an Theokrit zu denken, der von jenen süssen Jahren gesungen hat und wie sie gütig waren und gebend und geneigt bei jedem Schritt:

un wei ich sass, antikischem Gedicht nachsinnend, sah ich durch mein Weinen leise
die süssen Jahre, wie sie sich im Kreise aufstellten, traurig, diese von Verzicht

lichtlosen Jahre: meine Jahre. Da stand plötzlich jemand hinter mir und riss
aus diesem Weinen mich an meinem Haar.

Und eine Stimme rief, die furchtbar war:
,Rate, wer hält dich so?'—,Der Tod gewiss.'
—,Die Liebe'— klang es wieder, sanft und nah.

The decisive excisions here are in Mrs. Browning's second and seventh lines, where the years accumulate a truly burdensome string of adjectives—

"sweet, dear, wished for, sweet, sad, melancholy." The divergence of the adjectives is supposed, evidently, to set up a contrast between time as Theocritus accepted it, gladly, and time as the poet reviews it, wearily; but the adjectives are burdensome, and are properly cut. "Durch mein Weinen leise" still preserves a blend of gratification and melancholy, but "Verzicht" = renunciation gives a reason, at once vague and sufficient, for the melancholy mood. Finally, the confusions of the third and fourth English lines is cleared up. Mrs. Browning doesn't tell us in whose hand the years appear (it's even possible that the "in" of line 3 should be a "with"); Rilke not only clears up this blur, but with "bei jedem Schritt" gets in an elegant double reference both to passages of Theocritus and to the passage of time. What is going on here before our eyes is simply an intelligent and tasteful bit of cutting. Doubtless for reasons of national prejudice, we're not likely to think that an English lyric transformed into German could achieve a slimmer and more graceful figure than the original; in fact, Rilke has taken something like fifteen crucially misplaced pounds off Mrs. Browning, and she looks all the better for it.

Generally speaking, then, a translator is not helpless before problems of obsolete style and differing taste; without wholly betraying his original, he can soften asperities, animate frigidities, and (easiest of all) lop excesses. The important insoluble problems come when the sense of the original is entangled in several levels of social circumstance or verbal texture—when one has not only simultaneous objects to imitate, but a complicated relation between them, as with Madama Pace's Spanish Italian, or Humbert Humbert's French tags in an English context. Verbal knots and difficulties in an original represent a problem of the middle order: they can perhaps be translated, but only if the translator can somehow make clear that responsibility for them belongs to the original.

A final consideration involves differences about which nobody can express an assured, unprejudiced opinion—yet which everyone can observe for himself. Languages differ among themselves in their readiness to render up meaning to, or to absorb meaning from, another tongue. This isn't just a matter of primitive languages lagging behind sophisticated ones; it has to do with factors like rigidity of syntax, richness of idiom and metaphor, and some quality, however vague, that we can only call "plasticity." Quite apart from the matter of cultural distance, these inherent qualities of a language seem to work in quite specific ways, about which the only confident thing to be said is that we don't properly understand them. Why is it, for instance, that German is relatively easy to translate into, and very difficult to translate out of? Why are German versions of Shakespeare consistently so much better than English versions of Goethe? Naturally, style is a complicating factor here; one wouldn't be surprised to find Swift translating into French more gracefully than Spenser, and it's clear that the sort of German written by Kafka and Thomas Mann translates more easily (into English, at any rate) than that of Schiller and Hölderlin. Still, there's an order of difficulty in the To- and From-languages themselves, as well as in the relation between them; and in these matters, as in so many others, even the best translator is in some measure the plaything of chance and circumstance.

CHAPTER X

Attempt at an Attitude

An ancient jape about America has it that ours is the only country in history which went from barbarism to decadence without a period of civilization in between. Setting this canard aside with dignity, it *can* be said, and seriously, that America is practically the only country in history which has had to feel, almost simultaneously, that its language is a mere backwoods dialect and that it is an imperial idiom. Each of these feelings, by itself, can have interesting implications; taken in conjunction, they invite us to become as conscious as we possibly can of our linguistic situation. As we become more aware of that peculiar situation, it is almost inevitable that our concern with the process of translation, and our suspicion of the many elements involved in it, will radically increase.

Culturally speaking, America is in effect a big island off a little one. We are the cultural offspring of an island culture, given a continent of our own to play with, and encouraged thereby to think that if any featherless biped on the planet does not understand a plain English sentence, the solution is to repeat it in a louder tone of voice. If our linguistic history had begun in 1776 and were limited to the continental United States, that might be one thing. But our language has been widened by the entire history of the British Empire, considered as an extension in time and space. Our native Doric gives us access to conquered continents, monuments of thought and discovery, a thousand years of rich and various literary history. It enables us to walk with some confidence into Goomalling, Australia (where we can order steak-and-eggs for breakfast), to carry out a business transaction in Bulawayo by the banks of the Limpopo, or to read Locke's *Essay Concerning the Human Understanding*. The idiom which is every urchin's birthright in Coldwater, Kansas gives him almost automatic access to DeQuincey and Malory, to C. W. Doughty, Shelley, and the Dictionary of National Biography, whichever he has a mind to. His chance to stand outside this idiom, to become conscious of what it does to and for his mind, is about as great as the chance of a Grand Banks halibut to become critically aware of the Atlantic Ocean.

A good deal of current thinking about languages, as about societies, is predicated on the notion that they are most usefully regarded as units, self-contained structures, to be looked at only from within. There are many reasons for the prevalence of this attitude, including an altogether healthy reaction against earlier and more naïve provincialisms. It used to be possible to classify societies on the complacent premise that they were more "advanced" as they displayed more of the features of a western democracy. *Per contra,* they were "primitive" (with a double implication of "savage" and "infantile") the fewer such features they showed. And languages too were all supposed to be aspiring toward the state of English, French, or German—those tongues which served the "civilized" countries so well, and were understood to be a condition if not a cause of their civilization. From this essentially barbaric complacency about the peculiar virtue of our special habits, we have undoubtedly done well to escape. Institutions (political as well as linguistic) must be judged, not as they approximate one chosen model or another, but as they function in the context of the operative society. All right: the point is conceded. Yet it seems idle to deny the tangible evidence of history, that one language may be very different from another, and in a cosmopolitan world is likely to be *experienced* very differently.

To be born into a secure and widely rooted linguistic tradition is obviously an experience very different from being born into one of a dozen struggling dialects, with few or no literary precedents. A language about which there's simply no major question is different from a language that represents a perhaps painful individual option. There are dozens of tongues in use today (throughout the subcontinent of India, for example) which carry with them the moral assurance that they are wholly useless more than a hundred miles away from one's home. A man who writes in such a language can count on a certain sort of intimacy with his readers—chances are he can know personally, and without any special effort, most of the people who will read his books. (In the Swiss valleys there are languages spoken by fewer than a thousand people, within which wholly competent novelists yet flourish.) But the very intimacy of such readers may render their influence oppressive; and a small number of relatively homogeneous speakers can hardly develop a language's verbal resources very largely. Any little language enclave suffers competition from its neighbors, and if the neighbor has a flourishing literary culture, it may simply overshadow development of the smaller and weaker tongue. From a severely practical point of view, authorship is a far more dubious undertaking when one's potential readers are a thousand than when they are a million. The existence of a literary tradition, with a rich variety of accepted forms and themes, stimulates imitation, competition, rejection, counterassertion; or, to put it in the negative, a language without literary models and traditions lacks a texture of overlaid and comparative experience, a kind of patina, that authors in richer languages not only enjoy but can turn to the account of their own work. It was not very long ago that Henry James was making precisely this plangent complaint about the raw culture and crude language of his native land; without altogether solving this problem, we seem to have acquired another one, not so often discussed, that of inheriting a late-imperial idiom.

What are the qualities of an imperial dialect? In the first place, an extraordinary richness of heterogeneous linguistic materials. The incredible resources of contemporary English can be suggested by a simple, unstrenuous riffle through a good unabridged dictionary. Such a survey will reveal in an instant thousands of borrowings and adaptations, some so deeply buried that in ordinary speech we never appreciate their exotic origins—words like "thug," "boomerang," "kaleidoscope," "denouement," with all their multitudinous metaphorical applications. Add to these elementary building blocks the rich orchestral effects that one can get by quoting or adroitly misquoting from the rich literary heritage which is itself a composite of borrowings from the "classics." Then there are the resources of dialect and slang, foreign idioms adopted for their special appropriateness (after all, given a certain sort of person, *nouveau riche* is the only *mot juste*); there is a panorama of ethnic expressions, picturesque, explicit, vigorous, and various. Less to be celebrated than this Edenic opulence of linguistic growth, perhaps, are the badlands and bald spots of our imperial language. Nothing is more apparent than the fact that certain English words have by now been exhausted, drained of their content by overuse, deprived of all meaning and significance. "Love" is perhaps the most obvious of these—the bleating, mooing monosyllable, as someone has called it. I think it was an Oxford undergraduate who reported that the word's chief impact for him was of a display of rubber goods in a drugstore window. "Sincere" is another word that can hardly be pronounced without a jeer; and then there is "beautiful," which has had to shift completely out of its former meaning, and include the meaning formerly occupied by "ugly," so that it can take on fresh meaning as the opposite of "plastic." (A really hideous Victorian house will be "beautiful" to the young, while a Denny's Restaurant, whatever its actual esthetic qualities, will be dismissed with contempt as "plastic.") "Romantic," "ideal," "heroic," "dream"—the list of "nothing-words" (so baptized by my witty colleague Professor Pasinetti) could be extended almost indefinitely. Each reader will have his favorites. And nothing-words are only indices to nothing-attitudes.*

Not only particular words, but a whole language can be completely worn out for certain purposes. There are a couple of striking scenes in *Sons and Lovers* (Chapters 7 and 9), where Paul Morel, feeling rather confined by the earnest, intent cultural aspirations of Miriam Lievers, finds relief in a nuzzle with old Jimmy, a pit-pony, or a tussle with Bill, a bullterrier; and when he communes with these homely, loving creatures, it is not the language of Milton, Ruskin, or Matthew Arnold that he uses—rather he falls, almost unconsciously, into broad Lancashire. That he can find this resource within the wide boundaries of English is, of course, one of its marvelous latitudes. In the mansion of the English language are many rooms, and lucky the man who has a background of Gaelic or Welsh or even, at a pinch, broad Lancs to fall back on. But the need to fall back simply proves that the imperial tongue, for purposes of expressing intimacy with pit-horses, bullterriers, or other creaturely creatures, is no good at all. If we accept the idea that language, as long as it is vital, is in perpetual flux, it follows that every living language stands at different times in different relations to particular themes and structural possibilities. For language "A," theme "X" may be a lode of untapped possibilities, while for language "B" it is something so old and hackneyed as hardly to be worth considering. One doesn't have to endorse the notion that a language is progressing for some mystic reason *toward* some particular goal, to sense that all have a particular dynamic *away* from the past, a dynamic provided simply by the boredom of writers. New generations of writers do not want to repeat over and over what has already been done; they are tired of old formulas. That is why languages develop bald spots, from overuse, overwear. That is why writers are bound to "experiment," because the opposite of "experiment" is "formula." But simply to push off from the last previous

---

* One of the deeply influential and only half-perceived conditions of English culture is the fact that it has cultivated to such a remarkable degree the arts of biography and autobiography. In many other cultures, a man may be enormously powerful and popular, yet remain almost anonymous; even after his death, not a thing will be known, not a word will be published, about his private life. We can know so much about so many people, it is so hard not to feel that all the available attitudes have been exhausted.

So too, and perhaps even more strikingly, in the matter of literary response. The deep-ranked volumes of critical materials that stand in the student's way when he tries to say what he feels in the presence of a play by Shakespeare or a poem by Milton are often utterly intimidating. A very bright undergraduate girl once said to me in passing a great deal about American liberal education, when I asked her how she liked a certain advanced "honors" seminar. "Oh, it's all right," she said without enthusiasm. "We get together around this table twice a week and pretend to be individuals." Poets have been urged to seek their individual "voice," painters and musicians a style uniquely their own; it's hard to imagine this explosion of individualities continuing indefinitely without enormous pressures building up on the limited resources of the artistic vocabulary.

novelty-seeker is to condemn oneself to the modish and voguish, tomorrow's gimmick that will be forgotten day after tomorrow. Translation, properly pursued and studied, can make us conscious not only of the idiosyncrasies and limitations of our native tongue, but of wider definitions of "modernity," and more various ways of achieving it, than we would otherwise possess.

At this stage in the development of English, it is surely necessary that language no longer be used with the nineteenth century's full faith in its facade-effects. Probably authors must somehow make known the anxiety they so generally feel over the bad faith implicit in the artistic process. And this will doubtless lead to the disintegration of certain familiar literary forms, their reconstitution and recombination in patterns which can't at present be clearly foreseen. In itself, this unclarity need not particularly disturb us. There have been similar stages of radical, confused transformation before in the history of the language, stages when it was necessary that extravagant books like Lyly's *Euphues* or Blackmore's *Prince Arthur* should be written, so that larger developments or more viable compromises might be undertaken. But while we are pushing forward to whatever lies ahead for the English language, it is folly to lose sight of what is being done in other languages, whose "modernism" may no longer—or not yet—be possible for us.

As long ago as the eighteenth century, we got rid of the naïve notion that the arts are bound to make, or are capable of making, linear progress. Yet the delusion still lingers that we can derive one stage of literary "development" from its predecessor, that because Joyce wrote very great fiction in the first half of the twentieth century, the second half must therefore be recognizably "post-Joycean." So it may be, in fact. But among the great post-Joyceans, it must be recognized that Jorge Luis Borges owes an extraordinary debt to H. G. Wells, Vladimir Nabokov is similarly engaged with Gogol, and Carlo Emilio Gadda draws heavily on a predecessor as remote as Alessandro Manzoni. These post-Joyceans have not absorbed Joyce mechanically but combined him with some specially vital element in their own backgrounds and cultures. The characteristic gait of literary "progress" may well be the proverbial three steps forward and two steps back—even, on occasion, two steps forward and three steps back. By seeing, through the active agency of translation and comparison, what happens to the influence of Joyce when it is brought up against other traditions, other tongues, other conceptions of modernity, we may become more aware of the state of our own language, while widening our awareness of alternatives that for us are, or perhaps only seem to be, closed.

A quick for-instance: it needs no more than a glance at a selection of modern Spanish and Latin-American poetry to become aware of lyric simplicity and directness, an unashamed assertion of unadorned personal emotion, such as English poetry can no longer even contemplate. It isn't

simply that "love" as a subject is more directly confronted, more unhesitatingly asserted—so that words like "amor" and "felicidad" and "querida"
and "tristeza" are used, not only without irony, but climactically, as the high
point of the poems in which they occur. Even in severely controlled verse,
such as an elegy, we find a kind of direct statement that English is hard
pressed to imitate—for example, in Federico García Lorca's noble "Lament
for Ignacio Sánchez Mejían," which we excerpt, with a literal English
translation alongside:

No hubo principe en Sevilla	There was no prince in Seville
que comparársele pueda,	could compare with him,
ní espada como su espada	nor sword like his sword
ni corazón tan de veras.	nor heart so true.
Como un río de leones	Like a river of lions
su maravillosa fuerza,	his marvellous strength,
y como un torso de mármol	and like a torso of marble
su dibujada prudencia.	his sketched prudence.
Aire de Roma andaluza	Air of Andalusian Rome
le doraba la cabeza	gilded his head
donde su risa era un nardo	where his smile was an ointment
de sal y de inteligencia.	of wit and intelligence.

How can we in English walk up to a heart full of truth, a quality described
as "sketched" or "depicted" or "delineated" prudence, or a smile which
is a nard of salt (wit) and intelligence? English cannot manage such blunt-
ness and simplicity, abstractions combined so unselfconsciously with violent
images. Either we do something to complicate the Spanish directness with
English cleverness, or we turn it into a kind of lame, flat speech that no
modern poet would think of writing on his own. The simpler (and more
Spanish) Spanish poetry becomes, the harder it is to translate. Among his
Elemental Odes Pablo Neruda has a sly and delightfully naïve celebration
of the cat, the beginning of which is here printed, with an English translation by Ben Belitt:

Los animales fueron	The animal kingdom came
imperfectos,	faultily:
largos de cola, tristes	too wide in the rump or too
de cabeza.	sad-headed.
Poco a poco se fueron	Little by little they disposed
componiendo,	their proportions,
haciéndose paisaje,	invented their landscape,
adquiriendo lunares, gracia, vuelo.	collected their graces and satellites,
	and took to the air.
El gato,	Only the cat
sólo el gato	issued
apareció completo	wholly a cat,
y orgulloso:	

nació completamente terminado,   intact and vainglorious:
camina solo y sabe lo que quiere.   he came forth a consummate identity,
                                         knew what he wanted, and walked
                                         tall.

Unless my modest Spanish misleads me, the translation of "lunares" as "satellites" is Mr. Belitt's major, and perhaps indefensible, liberty; I cannot find any meaning for it other than "spots" or "flaws." But the chief change he has imposed on Neruda is in animating and energizing and exaggerating the tone of the original. Translated simply and literally, Neruda's last two lines say, "he was born completely finished, / walked alone and knew what he wanted." That's pretty flat going for English verse, and Mr. Belitt felt the necessity of making the language do more, work at higher tension. The whole level of his translation is pitched one step above Neruda's original; the verb "to be" becomes something more active, the polysyllables are sesquipedalian, not down to earth. This point appears vividly in another line from the same poem, illustrating the theme that all creatures except the cat are dissatisfied with their condition:

> La mosca estudia para golondrina.

Mr. Belitt renders it as "flies ponder the swallow's prerogative"; but what it says, simply and abruptly, is merely, "the fly studies for swallow"—as if that were a degree one could earn by accumulating credits—"his doctorate," "his swallow's diploma." The more we work at it, the less we get.

What Spanish-language poetry finds easy, English finds hard; what our tongue and our culture manipulate naturally and freely (for example, ironic mingling of speech levels, Yeatsian combinations of conversational speech with a high mantic mood), other tongues and cultures either cannot manage or don't care to attempt. We know this sort of thing in a general way; it is the merest commonplace of cultural relativism. But to find what it really means, to get a glimpse of ourselves as specimens, not just theoretical observers, there is nothing like working with the fabric and texture of two languages in intimate association—that is, translation. Either as a translator oneself (and that's the better alternative), or as a conscious student of translations, one gets to know verbal resources and limitations, cultural equivalents and disparities, as in no other way. It is the difference between attending an illustrated lecture on swimming and getting wet.

The experience I'm talking about is a little different from just knowing several languages, however well. That is an admirable thing in itself, which needs no particular advocacy under these circumstances. But many people who have foreign languages keep them in separate compartments, and never bring them (as a translator is bound to do) into point-for-point confrontation. Actually, one can get the translation-experience without knowing, or at

any rate using, more languages than one. Putting some Chaucer or the tale
of "Sir Gawain and the Green Knight" into modern English verse may not
yield any immortal masterpiece of poetry, but it can scarcely fail to bring
about, as a side effect, a deepened awareness of the qualities of fourteenth-
century English, contemporary English, and radical differences between
them. Indeed, it is no very startling discovery to announce that back-and-
forth translation from tongue to tongue is the best, and very likely the only
proper, school of stylistics. For many years into-and-out-of translation was
the core of all humane academic training. Conceded that we no longer
think seriously of its having value as "discipline" or want it as an initiation
rite, the translation game may yet have suggestive value. Particularly now,
when so many streams of traditional English seem to be running dry, and
we see men casting about for ways to use the language in intimate combination with other tongues, or in ways first indicated by them, the more
we know about equivalents, verbal weights and balances, tones, levels—the
wider our range of options is likely to appear.

The least one can hope to acquire from a study of translation is the loss
of some potentially troublesome innocence. Belief that the world's literature
can be adequately known through the use of English and translations into
English is not likely to flourish vigorously after a study of what translators
do to get their equivalents. Even when they improve, they convert; it is
inseparable from the function. Obviously their doings have to be looked
on with the very gravest suspicion, with eyes alerted imaginatively to the
dangers, if not linguistically to the very misdeeds themselves. There are,
of course, differences to be noted and evaluated, both in the quality of the
original and in the translator's definition of his task. Machiavelli's *Prince*
can be translated more completely, and to a higher standard of accuracy,
than Baudelaire's "Voyage à Cythère." (A good question to ask anyone
proposing a course in "World Literature" is "Whose translation of Baudelaire are you going to use?") A translator who tells one bluntly what qualities he has tried to get in his translation, and what he has sacrificed to get
them, may sometimes be trusted. The bravest translator is perhaps he who
prints the original across-page, where it can stare at his version with re-
proachful or defiant eyes. Publishers may not think well of this fellow, on
the grounds that those who can read the original won't like the translation,
and those who need the translation won't profit by the original. But it's
probably fair to say that any two versions of an original are better than
any one version; and that no man, unless he's ignorant of the script and
alphabet of the original tongue, can fail to profit from having it to compare with the translation. There are, I think, more of us semi-languaged
readers than publishers are ready to admit; and bilingual versions, which
are flourishing already, should flourish even more in the years to come. Yet
the main thrust of the bilingual version is to bolster and fortify our suspicion

of the translation—to deny its value as a façade and enable us to look around or through it. At a minimum, we can hear an echo of the melody from the original, and work out a bit of the syntax; at best, we can abandon the translation altogether (no doubt to the translator's secret delight), coming back to it only when we get into trouble.

That, after all, is the point: translation, which can be an exhilaration for the translator, and an amusement for the critical student, is a snare and a delusion for the man who takes it at face value. Though convenient and sometimes indispensable as a crutch, it is grossly inadequate as a wooden leg. Because it is always a compromise, and great art is rarely a compromise, the odds are always against it.

If a formula for literature is a contradiction in terms, so (doubly) is the idea of a ratio for the success of literary translation. At best, translation is a set of desperate gambles, and like all gambles recommended only for those who have secure investments elsewhere. So long as one doesn't rely on them for one's daily bread (literal or figurative), there's a great area for translations to delight, inform, and tantalize us. Almost always, those people enjoy translations most who need them least; this is a regrettable instance of the old rule governing literary interpretation, that whosoever hath, to him shall be given. It is sad but true that reading a translation by itself is like looking at a landscape with one eye and it half-shut—one doesn't easily get a sense of depth without the stereoscopic advantage of two fixes.

Yet the decline of England as an imperial power has inevitably been paralleled by the decline of English as an independent and self-sufficient area of study; and the long road from Beowulf to Thomas Hardy no longer seems to debouch anywhere near that strange corner of the forest where (if we know anything) we know ourselves to be. We are but monocular if one tongue, one culture, one tradition—that native to us—is all we know. True enough that we cannot know another culture properly through translations alone—imagine trying to construct an image of Racine from the several perfectly worthy translations in print! But translations may be a stage on the road to knowing more than they alone can teach, even about our own indigenous culture. It is a familiar notion that we don't know how to read *Paradise Lost* properly till we have done some reading in the Renaissance epic and the hexameral tradition; for the sorts of things we want to know about this perspective, translations may well provide adequate access to the forest without danger of losing us amid the trees. And in the other direction, it's quite conceivable that if we have some sense of how Bodmer's translation of Milton's poem worked on the mind of young Klopstock, we'll appreciate better the presence of certain elements in Milton's original. Literature is not, perhaps, a wholly seamless web, but it is woven of long strands, deviously connected and reaching in many directions; a work reveals itself in its various contacts as well as, and sometimes better than, in its text. An agreeable essay could be written on the response of Giambattista Vico to the influence of James Joyce.

If everything we did were the only thing we did, translation would have no place; but there are for all of us things we must do, and want to do, but don't want to do too well. We have to eat, and it's nice to eat well; but to make it the central business of life is obscene. Colleges and universities must be administered, and who would speak against the job being done well? But if nobody thinks of anything else, we shall have a set of impeccably administered mental vacuums. So, there are books we must read, and want to read, but cannot afford to read as well as we are maximally able, that is, if we start with the alphabet and grammar and work our way up through the years. Some books we want to read, not for their own sake, but for some reason more important to us; and here, lacking the elevator of the original tongue, we may well throw up the ladder of translation for the advancement of our second-story work. If it does not reach, we can always clamber down and try some other, less makeshift, mode of elevation.

"Poetry," says some magisterial, cynical definer, "is the thing that, when a poem is translated, gets left out." Nothing easier, if that were the case, than to use translations as sieves, for separating the chaff from the grain. But it isn't always the case. If one sort of poetry gets left out, another is sometimes added; and occasionally it seems to be true that what a translation adds to its original is, precisely, poetry. So Shakespeare in managing his borrowed Plutarchan descriptions; so Ben Jonson, shuffling bits of that shallow rhetorician Philostratus into new patterns and coming up with "Drink to me only with thine eyes." Far from being reducible to formulas and glib sayings, the relation between original and translation provides a challenge for judgment, an open problematic. When the work is done sloppily or ignorantly, it goes without saying that howlers result; but it may also be true that what we denounce as a howler is the result of our own rigidity and imperception, our assumption that there's only one thing to imitate in a text. There is no privileged position; the chief reward of studying translations lies in an augmented sense of suspicion, including suspicion of one's own assumption and responses. How much of our mind is made up about a text before ever we approach it! How blithely we slide past doors that would swing open if we pushed them ever so slightly! If only because it slows down our pace, and forces us to question some of those headlong assumptions that make our reading semi-automatic, the careful study of translations can be sound and rewarding discipline.

Somebody has pointed out the tendency of scholarship and criticism to cluster around familiar, nodal difficulties in poems. Because there are already seventy-seven inadequate, unnecessary explanations of the two-handed-engine passage in "Lycidas" it is like death and taxes that we shall have within the year a seventy-eighth, a seventy-ninth, *und so weiter* to no fixed term. Apart from the sheeply character of scholars, there's a natural reason for this: every angler is drawn to fish where the big one seems to be lurking. But after a while the crowd gathers whether the big one is there or not—drawn by one another, not by the fish. Translation, by making us question our texts, not where habit invites, but where linguistic and literary problems make them difficult to render, gives us a chance to find virgin or at least relatively uncrowded waters. It is like a literary conversation with a fresh reader, whose point of view is just odd enough to deepen a running dialogue now and then toward the possibility of fresh vision.

Reading a translation as running commentary works, to be sure, at cross-purposes with the translator himself, whose aim is to hypnotize his reader, to make his façade suspicion-proof; but it's pretty much the way a reader schooled in the critical ideas of Kenneth Burke is bound to treat any literary facade. What does Mr. Burke's spokesman do in that magnificent skit "Antony in Behalf of the Play," but give away systematically the whole game? If the facade couldn't be reconstituted by an instant act of the mind after its dismantling, one might have some sense that the technique reduced literature to a mere jumble of rhetorical tricks. But that's no necessary consequence; we are only victimized by a critical approach if we let ourselves be. Indeed, it's a peculiar quality of the translator that though he exposes the stratagems of the original, it isn't out of any invidious or reductive impulse—quite the contrary. He's quite the most useful translator who sheers as close to the original as he can, and does what he does to isolate the untranslatable by involuntary, perhaps compelled, divergences.

A good deal of modern criticism, when we think of it, takes the form of paraphrase, which is intralingual translation of a special sort. To think that the essence of a poem can be captured in a prose paraphrase is doubtless heresy, and it is foolish as well. But a critical paraphrase or explication doesn't aim to capture any essences; if done with minimal discretion, its aim is more modest—to make apparent specific connections which seem operative, even though obscure, in the original. We tease out three or four different translations from the tightly knotted texture of the original, test them against one another, cast aside what we can't use, and incorporate what we can in an enriched awareness of the structure. Provisional and temporary paraphrase-translations of this summary nature we probably make whenever we reflect upon literature; they are formulas that enable us to think and talk of *Paradise Lost* without having every word of it immediately present to our memory. Though more and less inadequate as among one another, they are all inadequate to the original; and when they have served their limited function they are all, quite properly, dismissed. So with translations as means of access to an original—they are better and worse instances of a secondhand experience.

In all this discussion of translation, paraphrase, and imitation, we take happily for granted the uncontaminated neatness of our schematic triangle:

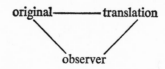

But in fact we know that the observer is himself a composite of paraphrases and translations—the very texture of what he sees is a composite of what he has been taught to want to see and to be afraid of seeing. Our culture is a copy and we copy copies within it. We style ourselves on literary models, sympathetic and antipathetic, control our motions by sidelong glances at our elected rivals/authorities within the herd (not too far ahead, not too far behind, always more and better pasture but not so much more that you invite gang-attack); and so pretend with one side of our minds to pass independent judgment on that which has, under one slight disguise or another, acted to constitute the judgment itself. Life the Hack in Swift's *Tale of a Tub*, we undertake to pronounce pompous Panegyrics on the World as if we were no part of it, as if we could disavow at will what we are committed to by the simple position of our feet, or our posteriors. All this is to say that no man stands clear of the multiply contaminated stream of literary history; the risk of self-deception in trying to do so is out of all proportion to the (presumed) rewards of succeeding. The logic is despairing, but the practical conclusions simple; if we can't escape the current of distorting, contaminating opinion, we'll have to navigate within it, and guide ourselves (like prudent Mr. Lintott in the epigraph) between the contrasted errors of the translators and the correctors. When the blind lead the blind, there's a very good chance they will both fall into the ditch; but when the ditches are full of vocal unfortunates, a man may very well guide himself a little way onward through the darkness by the noise of their clamor.

List of Books

❧

There are numerous bibliographies of translations, generally covering limited periods of time and concerned with translation into or out of one particular language. There are also more manageable bibliographies of books and articles about translation; a useful one on which to build is found in Reuben Brower's anthology, *On Translation*. (As of this writing, *Delos*, a magazine devoted to discussion of translation and experiments in translation, is no longer afloat; in its day, it provided a valuable forum for discussion of translation problems and a survey of current developments in the field.) But what I have assembled here is not a bibliography in any form, or an attempt at one. It is simply at list of the books cited in the course of this discussion. It is not a guide to anything; it aspires simply to direct the interested reader to a book in which he can either verify my quotation or extend his own reading. By summarizing this unsightly though doubtless necessary information in the back of the book, I've tried to keep it from cluttering my pages: hence the "list of books."

Baudelaire, tr., Poe, *Histoires extraordinaires* in *Oeuvres complètes,* ed. Crépet (Paris, L. Conard, 1923) Vols. VI–X.

Baudelaire, *Les fleurs du mal in Oeuvres complètes,* edd. LaDantec and Pichois (Paris, Bib. de la Pléiade, 1961).

Beckett, Samuel, *Fin de partie* (Paris, ed. de Minuit, 1957) tr. as *Endgame* (N.Y., Grove, 1958).

Belitt, Ben, tr., Neruda, *Selected Poems* (N.Y., Grove, 1961).

Belli, G. G., *I sonetti,* ed. Vigolo (Milano, Mondadori, 1963).

Belloc, Hilaire, *On Translation* (Oxford, Clarendon, 1931).

Blaydes, W., tr., Flaubert, *Madame Bovary* (New York, Collier, 1902).

Boileau, *Oeuvres* (Paris, Garnier frères, 1873).

Boswell, R. B., tr., *Dramatic Works of Jean Racine* (London, Bell, 1889–90).

Brower, Reuben, *On Translation* (Cambridge, Harvard, 1959).

Browning, E. B., *Poems* (New York, Crowell, 1887).

Browning, Robert, tr., Aeschylus, *Agamemnon* in *Works of R.B.* (London, Centenary ed., E. Benn, 1966), Vol. VIII.

Browning, Robert, "Balaustion's Adventure," in *Works* (London, E. Benn, 1966), Vol. VII.

Buckley, T. A., tr., *Prometheus Bound* in *The Tragedies of Aeschylus Literally Translated* (New York, Harper, 1893).

184 LIST OF BOOKS

Butcher and Lang, tr., Homer, *The Odyssey* (New York, Macmillan, 1893).

Butler, Samuel, tr., Homer in *Works of Samuel Butler* (London, Shrewsbury ed., Cape, 1923–26), *Iliad*, Vol. XIII, *Odyssey* Vol. XV.

Cairncross, John, tr., Racine, *Phaedra and Other Plays* (Baltimore, Penguin, 1963).

Calverley, C. S., *Verses and Translations* (Cambridge, Deighton, 1877).

Catulli Carmina (Boston, Heath, 1924).

Chapman, George, tr., Homer, *The Odyssey* in *Works of G.C.* (London, Chatto and Windus, 1874–5), III.

Chateaubriand, tr., Milton, *Paradise Lost* in *Oeuvres complètes* (Paris, P. H. Krabbe, 1855), XVI.

Chaucer, *Troilus and Criseyde* in *Works* (London, Macmillan, Globe ed., 1928).

Chicago Bible, i.e., *The Bible an American Translation* (O.T. ed. J. M. P. Smith, N.T. by E. J. Goodspeed (Chicago, U. of Chicago Press, 1940).

Coindreau, Maurice, tr., Faulkner, *The Sound and the Fury* as *Le bruit et la fureur* (Paris, Gallimard, Livre de Poche, n.d.).

Crashaw, Richard, tr., Marino, "La strage degli innocenti," in *Poetical Works of R.C.*, ed. L. C. Martin (Oxford, Clarendon, 1957).

Curtius, E., tr., Eliot, "The Waste Land" in *Die Neue Rundschau*, LXI (1950), 327–345.

DeAngelis, Giulio, tr., Joyce, *Ulysses* (Milano, Mondadori, 1960).

DeLille, Abbé Jacques, tr., Milton, *Paradise Lost* (Paris, Giguet et Michaud, 1805).

DeLille, Abbé Jacques, tr., Vergil, *Eclogues*, as *Les Bucoliques de Virgile* (Paris, Giguet et Michaud, 1806).

DeMan, Paul, tr., Flaubert, *Madame Bovary* (New York, Norton, 1965), a substantially new translation based on the Marx-Aveling version.

Deutsch, Babette, tr., Rilke, *Poems from the Book of Hours* (Norfolk, New Directions, 1941).

Donne, *Poetical Works*, ed. Grierson (Oxford, Clarendon, 1951).

Dryden, tr., Juvenal, "Satire 10," *Poetical Works* (Boston, Houghton, Student's Cambridge ed., by G. R. Noyes, 1909).

Dupré de St. Maur, tr., Milton, *Paradise Lost* (Amsterdam, Pierre Mortier, 1729).

Edmonds, Rosemary, tr., Tolstoy, *Anna Karenin* (Baltimore, Penguin, 1954).

Faulkner, William, *The Sound and the Fury* (New York, Modern Library, 1946).

Frank, Nino, tr., Joyce, *Finnegans Wake* in *Prospettive* (15 Feb. and 15 Dec., 1940).

Fitzgerald, Robert, tr., Homer, *The Odyssey* (London, Heinemann, 1962).

García Lorca, Federico, *Obras completas* (Buenos Aires, Losada, 1938).

Garstang, Walter, tr., "The Song of Songs," as *The Sacred Eclogue* (Blackburn, Douglas, 1882).

Geneva Bible, facsimile of 1560 ed. (Madison, U. of Wisc. Press, 1969).

Gide, André, tr., Shakespeare, *Hamlet*, ed. bilingue (New York, Pantheon, 1945).

Good, John Mason, tr., "Song of Songs" (London, Kearsley, 1803).

Goyert, Georg, tr., Joyce, *Finnegans Wake, Die Fähre* (June, 1946).

Goyert, Georg, tr., Joyce, *Ulysses*, third ed. (Zurich, Rhein, 194?).

Graves, Robert, tr., Apuleius, *The Golden Ass* (New York, Pocket Library, 1955).

Hamilton, Edith, tr., Aeschylus, *Prometheus Bound* in *Three Greek Plays* (New York, Norton, 1937).

Hopkins, Gerard, tr., Flaubert, *Madame Bovary* (London, Hamilton, 1949).

Horatii Opera, cum notis Josephi Jvvencii (Romae, 1829).

Johnson, Samuel, *Poems* in *Works* (New Haven, Yale ed., 1958–   ), IV.

Jonson, Ben, "Discoveries" in *Works,* edd. Herford and Simpson (Oxford, Clarendon, 1954), VIII.

Joyce, *Finnegans Wake* (New York, Compass Books, 1965).

Joyce, *Ulysses* (New York, Vintage, n.d. but actually 1972).

Juvenal in Loeb Classical Library, ed. G. G. Ramsay (London, Heinemann, 1920).

Kahane, Eric, tr., Nabokov, *Lolita* (Paris, Gallimard, Livre de Poche, 1959).

King James Bible

Lang, Leaf, and Myers, tr., Homer, *The Iliad* (London, Macmillan, 1911).

Lattimore, Richmond, tr., Aeschylus, *Agamemnon* in *Greek Tragedies,* Vol. I (Chicago, Phoenix Books, 1961).

Lattimore, Richmond, tr., Homer, *The Iliad* (Chicago, Phoenix Books, 1961).

Lattimore, Richmond, tr., *The Odes of Pindar* (Chicago, U. of Chicago Press, 1947).

Leishman, J. B., tr., Rilke, *Poems* (London, Hogarth, 1934).

LeRoy, Abbé, tr., Milton, *Paradise Lost* (Rouen, E. V. Machuel, 1775).

Letourneur, Pierre, tr., *Oeuvres complètes de Shakspeare* (Paris, Ladvocat, 1821).

Lewis, C. Day, tr., Vergil, *Aeneid* (New York, Anchor Books, 1953).

Litz, A. W., *The Art of James Joyce* (New York, Oxford, 1961).

Lowe-Porter, H. T., tr., Mann, *Der Zauberberg* (New York, Modern Library, 1932).

Lowell, Robert, *Imitations* (New York, Noonday, 1961).

Lowell, Robert, *Near the Ocean* (New York, Farrar, 1967).

Mallarmé, tr., Poe, *Poems* in *Oeuvres complètes,* ed. Mondor and Jean-Aubry (Paris, Bib. de la Pléiade, 1956).

Marino, Giambattista, *Dicerie sacre* (Torino, Einaudi, 1960).

Marvell, Andrew, *Poems,* ed., MacDonald (Cambridge, Harvard, 1952).

Marx-Aveling, Eleanor, tr., Flaubert, *Madame Bovary* (New York, Rinehart, 1948), originally pub. 1886.

May, J. L., tr., Flaubert, *Madame Bovary* (New York, Wiley, 1940).

Menasce, Jean de, tr., Eliot, "The Waste Land" in *Esprit,* May, 1926, pp. 174–94.

Morel, Auguste, *et al.,* tr., Joyce, *Ulysses* (Paris, A. Monnier, 1930).

Muir, Edwin, *An Autobiography* (London, Hogarth, 1954).

Neruda, Pablo, *Odas elementales* (Buenos Aires, Losada, 1954).

New English Bible (New York, Oxford and Cambridge, 1970).

Norse, Harold, tr. G. G. Belli, *The Roman Sonnets* (Highland, J. Williams, 1960).

Peck, A. L., tr., Rilke, *The Book of Hours* (London, Hogarth, 1961).

Petrarch, *Il canzoniere* (Milano, Rizzoli, 1954).

Poliziano, *Opere volgari* (Firenze, Sansoni, 1885).

Pope, Alexander, *Poems* (Twickenham ed., New Haven, Yale U. Press, 1939–1967).

Pope, Alexander, tr., Homer, *The Iliad* (Twickenham ed., Vols. VII, VIII, New Haven, Yale U. Press, 1939–1967).

Pound, Ezra, *Collected Shorter Poems* (London, Faber, 1952).

Praz, Mario, tr., Eliot, "The Waste Land," in *La Terra Desolata,* etc., (Torino, Giulio Einaudi, 1967).

Propertius, ed., H. E. Butler (Loeb Classical Library, London, Heinemann, 1962).

Revised Standard Bible (New York, Oxford, 1962).

Rieu, E. V., tr., Homer, *The Odyssey* (Baltimore, Penguin, 1967).

Rilke, R. M., tr., E. B. Browning, "Sonnets from the Portuguese" in *Gesammelte Werke* (Leipzig, Insel-verlag, 1927), VI.

Rilke, R. M., *Das Stunden-buch* (Leipzig, Insel-verlag, 1913).

Robert, Tournay, Feuillet, *Le cantique des cantiques* (Paris, Gabalda, 1963).

Ronsard, Pierre, *Oeuvres complètes,* ed. G. Cohen (Paris, Bib. de la Pléiade, NRE, 1950).

Rouse, W. H. D., tr., Homer, *The Iliad* and *The Odyssey* (New York, Mentor Books, 1953, 1956).

Saintsbury, George, *A History of English Prose Rhythm* (London, Macmillan, 1912).

Sandys, George, tr., "Song of Songs" in *Poetical Works,* ed. Hooper (London, J. R. Smith, 1872), II.

Schlauch, Margaret, *The Gift of Languages* (New York, Dover, 1955).

Scott-Moncrieff, C. K., tr., Proust as *Remembrance of Things Past* (New York, Random, 1932–34).

Scott-Moncrieff, C. K., tr., Stendhal as *The Red and the Black* (New York, Modern Library, 1953) and *The Charterhouse of Parma* (New York, Anchor, 1954).

Shakespeare, *Works,* ed. John Munro (New York, Simon and Schuster, The London Shakespeare, 1958).

Shaw, T. E., tr., Homer, *The Odyssey* (London, Oxford U. Press, 1935).

Smith, Edmund, tr., Racine as *Phaedra and Hippolytus* (London, 1709).

Soupalt, Philippe, *et al.,* tr. Joyce, *Finnegans Wake* in *Nouvelle Revue Francaise,* 1931.

Spenser, tr., DuBellay, "Antiquitez," in *Poetical Works of E. S.,* ed. De Selincourt (New York, Oxford Standard Authors, 1965).

Steegmuller, Francis, tr., Flaubert, *Madame Bovary* (New York, Modern Library, 1957).

Stendhal, *Le rouge et le noir,* ed. H. Martineau (Paris, Classiques Garnier, 1960).

Storrs, Sir Ronald, ed., *Ad Pyrrham* (London, Oxford U. Press, 1959).

Tasso, *Gerusalemme Liberata,* ed. Caretti (Bari, Laterza, n.d.).

Valéry, Paul, tr., Vergil, *Eclogues,* in *Oeuvres de P. V.,* ed. Hytier (Paris, Gallimard, Bib. de la Pléiade, 1957).

Vulgate Bible, i.e., *Biblia Sacra, vulgatae editionis* (Torino, 1965).

Index